POPULAR CULTURE AND CUSTOM IN
NINETEENTH-CENTURY ENGLAND

Popular Culture and Custom in Nineteenth-Century England

Edited by Robert D. Storch

CROOM HELM
London & Canberra

ST. MARTIN'S PRESS
New York

© 1982 Robert D. Storch
Croom Helm Ltd, 2-10 St John's Road, London SW11

British Library Cataloguing in Publication Data

Popular culture and custom in nineteenth-century
    England.
    1. England – Social life and customs – 19th century
    I. Storch, Robert D.
    942.081   DA533

    ISBN 0-7099-0453-3

First published in the United States of America in 1982
All rights reserved. For information write:
St. Martin's Press, Inc., 175 Fifth Avenue, New York, N.Y. 10010

Library of Congress Cataloging in Publication Data
Main entry under title:

Popular culture and custom in nineteenth-century
    England.

    Includes index.
    1. England–Social conditions.   2. England–Social
life and customs–19th century.   I. Storch, Robert D.,
1940-   .
HN398.E5P66   1982   306'.0942   82-3302
ISBN 0-312-63033-6   AACR2

Printed and bound in Great Britain

CONTENTS

ACKNOWLEDGEMENTS

The editor would like to thank the Controller of Her Majesty's Stationery Office for permission to use crown copyright material in the Public Record Office; Richard Price, Louise Tilly, Bernard Wong and Alfred Young for helpful comments and criticisms; Mrs Maureen Walker for typing; Mrs Anne Strong Storch for research assistance; and Kendall Storch for putting up with a study-bound father while this book was taking shape.

ABBREVIATIONS

ABG	*Aris's Birmingham Gazette*
AT	*Accrington Times*
BA	*Birmingham Advertiser*
BC	*Bolton Chronicle*
B.Chron.	*Birmingham Chronicle*
BDG	*Birmingham Daily Gazette*
B.D.Press	*Birmingham Daily Press*
BJ	*Birmingham Journal*
BRL	Birmingham Reference Library
CC	*Chelmsford Chronicle*
CEC	Children's Employment Commission
ECC	*Essex County Chronicle*
EFP	*Trewman's Exeter Flying Post*
LM	*Leeds Mercury*
LT	*Leeds Times*
Mail	*Birmingham Daily Mail*
M.Chron.	*Morning Chronicle*
OC	*Oldham Chronicle*
OS	*Oldham Standard*
Post	*Birmingham Daily Post*
PP	Parliamentary Papers
Procs.	Birmingham Council *Proceedings*
RO	*Rochdale Observer*
SA	*Sussex Advertiser*
SAE	*Sussex Agricultural Express (Sussex Express)*
SRA	*Surrey Advertiser*
STA	*Stockport Advertiser*
VCH	Victoria County History
WEPG	*Woolmer's Exeter and Plymouth Gazette*
WST	*West Surrey Times*
WT	*Western Times*

1 INTRODUCTION: PERSISTENCE AND CHANGE IN NINETEENTH-CENTURY POPULAR CULTURE

Robert D. Storch

Popular culture in the nineteenth century has its own particular interest, if for no other reason than that the contemporary rural and urban middle classes took it very seriously and were profoundly concerned with it.[1] By and large it was conceived as a set of lower-class beliefs and behaviours which were annoying, wasteful, immoral or even threatening and dangerous. Because many expressions of popular culture had, almost by definition, to be open and take place in public spaces, they frequently produced, as concomitants, crowds, noise, excessive drinking and, often, increased levels of violence:

> On Saturday night, if a foreigner had chanced to pass near the cattle market, he would have seen a sight after which all stories of English virtue and morality would have fallen upon his ears in vain. Crowds of men and women . . . drunk, surging up and down the streets, gurgling round the entrance of the . . . beer-shops; pickpockets . . . unfortunate women . . . children struggling through the crowded booths . . . witnesses of all the disgusting immorality, the ribald jesting, the cursing and profanity . . . and other nameless things in which these fairs and feasts abound.[2]

The annual scenes at Ilkley Feast in the 1870s could be truly frightening. Close to Leeds, Bradford and the populous villages on the railways which converged there, Ilkley was inundated each year. In 1870 'the scenes in the streets were simply disgraceful . . . owing to the number of disorderly, drunken people who were reeling about. The public houses were open from morning to night to 'visitors', many of whom [got drunk] on the Sabbath.[3]' The police were inadequate to keep order and few could be arrested because the town had no proper lock-up.

Most frightening of all were occasions such as Bradford New Year's mumming, when large numbers of men and boys with blackened faces and in bizarre disguises penetrated not only middle-class neighbourhoods but, occasionally, even the middle-class home. Importuning sometimes led to harsh words and violence when money or drink was refused — as in 1868, when a man and woman were assaulted and knocked down on their doorstep by a young man who had been refused.[4]

In the past, mumming had been 'used' to reaffirm the solidarity of local communities, a function which became less and less viable in the nineteenth century. Certainly by the 1860s the ritual meant something quite different both to those who mounted it and to the recipients of their attentions — although the outward *form* hardly changed at all. To the former it represented not only an opportunity to get drink and money from those who could well afford to give them (which was nothing new at all), but also a chance to extort, coerce and frighten — precisely to aggress. Mumming was, of course, a classical instance of a reversal ritual (and it survived in urban, industrial England long after some might have thought it would have vanished), but it could be used, like many other similar rituals, either to reaffirm or to attack the social order. The Victorian middle classes perceived it, quite rightly I think, as an attack. How could it have been otherwise? By the 1860s Bradford had long since ceased to be a locality in which old folk rituals could express communal solidarity, the mutual obligations of one social element to another, or even be used to recall those at the top of the local social order to their 'traditional' duties. No wonder such confrontations, when not directly prevented by the police, were suffused with mutual hostility and bad feeling.

The key event in the process of social and cultural rupture in this particular locality occurred long before — in the 1820s — when the old Bishop Blaize processions, previously participated in by both masters and men, foundered during the combers' strike of 1825 precisely on the rock of industrial and class conflict. No doubt 1825 was only the culmination of that process of rupture. Its origins could probably be traced back a number of decades. Looking back from the 1850s, a Bradford man wrote:

> Fifty or even Thirty years ago the connection between the employer and employed was quite different. It was then a matter of everyday occurrence for the master to mix socially with his workpeople, to enter into their pastimes with a healthy zest . . . But now . . . employers not only live apart from their operatives but are as socially separated as the Europeans at the Cape are from the Hottentots.[5]

The urban middle classes knew all about this rupture which, in addition to being social and cultural, was also political, and made strenuous (and sincere) efforts to recreate new patterns of deference and patronage either in the context of the workplace itself, or by reaching out into the working-class neighbourhood with conventicles of respectability and domestic missions. The object was to create a new kind of urban paternalism which would bypass, ignore and refuse to compromise with the old popular culture.

In some areas and to some limited extent this enterprise bore fruit. Joyce has clearly demonstrated the development of a new, paternalistic Lancashire factory culture. But here the masters occupied quite different places in the revised relations between the classes, remaining somewhat distant figures — symbolic clan heads, rarely met with in person, but like the Queen presiding from a distance over ceremonies and rites which often revolved around important events in their families.[6] Reaching out to the working-class neighbourhood was a very much less successful proposition for any number of reasons — one of them perhaps being that such enterprises took place at too many removes from the workplace itself.[7]

Popular culture was seen and redefined as a major problem by the dominant classes in the early nineteenth century. For any number of reasons the latter were considerably more anxious in the face of real differences in values, beliefs and behaviour within society than the components of previous English ruling classes had been in the recent past. The social world which they perceived between the 1790s and, say, 1860 seemed frighteningly lacking in normative regulation and moral authority. They believed strongly in the need to create some commonly affirmed array of values and 'morals' in society, thinking that this was the only solid and durable platform of social discipline and public order there could be. The reform of popular values and customs inevitably became intimately bound up with the nineteenth-century problems of public order and social and industrial discipline — and thus a matter of some importance. It may be that the more formal study of popular customs began in the late eighteenth and early nineteenth centuries, not only because they were thought to be disappearing and, like sperm whales, ought to be preserved (at least on paper), but also because popular values, rituals, customary practices, crowds (and also politics) were now reconstrued as problems. David Vincent illustrates the growing interest in popular traditions and customs within certain literary circles,[8] but these also became concerns of local elites, publicists, writers of letters to editors, writers on social questions and ideologists of the state. All were conscious of an immense cultural divide in contemporary society. This was perhaps new but, unlike the eighteenth-century gentry, they were neither complacent in the face of it nor indifferent to it.

The standard prescription was the clarification and broadcasting of new ethical and moral perspectives and norms – the hope of moralising the masses and remoulding the 'character' of the English worker. A major problem, however, was that, in the words of one education reformer, workers did 'not in the least comprehend that what is in the interest of society is their own also'. Neither simple restraint nor the discipline of mill or labour market alone seemed adequate to the task, for how could the magistrates or the police by themselves change men's characters and produce greater orderliness, less dangerous political ideas and social longings amongst those below? Thus within the numerous movements designed to alter, channel or restructure popular culture were contained (*au fond*) approaches to the solution of the important problem of reconstituting the lines of deference, patronage and moral authority in society. In the eighteenth century their proper functioning depended to a large extent on the degree to which they contacted (and accepted on their own terms) elements of popular culture at certain points. How to do it without such contact, or running the danger of creating something which could be perceived as ersatz was a problem in itself. Little could be done along these lines until the later nineteenth century in any case, for a necessary prerequisite was getting over the fear of popular public display and popular crowds in the first instance. Only then could intelligent techniques for the neutralisation and incorporation of, say, the old popular version of Guy Fawkes manifestations or the creation of new style 'consensual festivals'[9] be tried.

The later seventeenth and early eighteenth centuries, we are told, saw the efflorescence of a vigorous plebeian culture and a great bursting-out of wakes, feasts, communal rites and sports in a secularised form.[10] The extent to which this 'old'[11] popular culture flourished so freely was a result of both the fecundity of the people *and* the willingness of their rulers – either through active patronage or indifference – to allow it scope. E. P. Thompson has carefully outlined for us the extent and nature of the reciprocal dealings between England's eighteenth-century elites and popular custom, and shown us how the gentry were both able and willing to patronise or occasionally even manipulate it. What seems so remarkable to students of the nineteenth century is the degree to which England's rulers seemingly exempted from *their* musings about the disciplining and control of the poor, customs, values and practices which later would be redefined as intolerable and dangerous, and their sense of complacency in the face of immense differences of values within society. John Brewer has recently written about the beginning of the end of that particular line, demonstrating how, before a halt was called in the changed atmosphere of the French Wars, some of the greatest in the land lent their presence to the raucous mock elections at Garrat near London.

The complex of early-nineteenth-century attitudes towards popular culture which we have discussed above was a function of the process of class formation itself; but the withdrawal of the upper classes from participation in and patronage of popular culture had an important and closely related political dimension. The English upper classes as a whole became terrified by the 'French Revolution and the development of a domestic, natural-rights radical movement involving artisans and workingmen', and leery of 'all plebeian revel[s] that had political overtones'.[12]

The period of the French Wars and its immediate aftermath was crucial for our concerns in a number of respects. In the first place, a good deal of the support and patronage the 'old' popular culture had enjoyed was lost. In addition, this period saw a new concern about the underlying bases of social stability; the development of an independent radical politics; the appearance of a new rhetoric centring on doubts that workers could understand what was in the best interest of society and the imperative to moralise the masses and purvey new systems of moral authority; and the development of new techniques (and agencies) of policing and order keeping. But the period was crucial for one more reason.

Brewer reminds us that the Garrat mock elections were abandoned not only by their erstwhile patrons but by popular radicals as well. The latter now noticeably began to shun the old form of festival-cum-protest, rejected the patronage and upper-class manipulation which often accompanied it, and stressed sobriety, order, restraint, education and a new concept of worker self-respect. Popular radicalism began to develop its own new standards of personal conduct and repertoire of collective action which became standard components of working-class political rhetoric and practice by the 1850s. In Bradford, a woolcomber leader of a Non Electors Committee told a meeting after the 1837 election:

> You have . . . shown your more fortunate neighbours that . . . you are . . . their equals in knowing how to conduct yourselves with propriety . . . you have practically schooled them in the arts of civilised society. You have shown them that you can pursue an object publicly but yet peaceably . . . without breeding a riot in front of the Sun Inn . . . We challenge those who describe anarchy and con-

fusion and destruction of property as the results of entrusting us with the franchise, to say that we have been guilty of a single breach of the peace . . . Can they say as much for themselves?[13]

Later Chartists, trade unionists and self-improving workers of all varieties would set themselves firmly against older popular fêtes and forms of collective action which borrowed from them. Reid shows below how, by the 1870s, such elements refused to lift a finger to protect the old Birmingham wakes and fairs.[14] Hooting through the streets, excessive consumption of alcohol, disguising or masking, effigy burning and other types of folk violence had no attractions for the Vincents, Coopers and Applegarths − nor for their less-well-known local counterparts. In other words, by the 1840s at the latest the 'old' popular culture had not only been abandoned by the upper classes but had begun to fracture in many regions.

Before the nineteenth century popular fêtes contained within themselves a specific repertoire of beliefs, symbols and actions which, apart from periodically affirming local solidarities, had important uses in the statement of political and social demands. Public ceremonies were used to make protests and voice the complaints of communities and corporate groups; they employed raucous and vivid street theatre ('visual imagery, effigies, symbolic objects and other dramatic devices'); and frequently borrowed 'the authorities' normal forms of action'. In both 1830 and 1848, Charles Tilly writes, carnival and revolution could still 'link arms to dance in the streets' of France.[15] It would be useful to know more about how these linkages frayed and ruptured in England. It has been suggested that the appearance of 'modern' mass movements could have had rather sudden solvent effects on the older, explosive forms of collective action and festivity. Dorothy Thompson writes that Chartism

appears. . . to have reduced the violence in the community − the folk-violence of effigy burning and the direct action of the anti-poor law campaign gave way to the disciplined organisation of the Chartists in which thousands could gather . . . and yet remain completely peaceful.[16]

This seems quite sensible and correct but, useful as it is, it cannot be − nor does it pretend to be − an all-purpose explanation of nineteenth-century popular cultural change. Specific popular cultural items withered − or were incorporated into newer forms − for several reasons:

the withdrawal of social elements which had once played significant roles in their organisation or presentation; pressure by the state and its new, nineteenth-century agencies of discipline, regulation and repression; pressure on the uses of urban spaces; and the appearance of less *ad hoc,* more formalised and commercialised forms which attracted precisely because they never demanded complete sobriety, self-restraint or other personal virtues recommended by working-class political and trade-union leaders or the middle classes. In addition, there were regions – such as the small southern and south-western towns described by me in this volume – in which an older type of crowd and even, perhaps, an old style plebs remained in being, continuing to perpetuate many of the older forms until rather late in the century. Such areas *were,* incidentally, largely passed over by Chartism and lacked a strong trade-union movement.

We might further explore the crucial factor of the progressive withdrawal from the 'old' popular culture by social elements which had previously participated in some way. The context of this process was, of course, increasing differentials of wealth within localities and the process of class formation itself. Naturally these went hand in hand, resulting in altered 'styles of life' for some groups in the community. In the countryside the gentry had long since withdrawn from direct participation and, by the early nineteenth century, they had increasingly vanished as patrons as well.[17] Obelkevich helps us to see how this process unfolded in the microcosm of village England. He shows how the autonomy and self-sufficiency of communities diminished; how classes emerged and defined themselves; how first the gentry and then the farmers withdrew from the communal village culture; how all groups dealt with the irrefutable logic of altered community structure and class relations. The 'old' popular culture, which had rested on the social ties binding together different groups, was first left by default to the labourers – who were unable to relinquish their commitment to it as rapidly as others – and then unravelled as finally even they grasped the logic of an altered, local social world.[18]

I will argue in my own essay that a major factor in the disappearance, transformation or folklorisation of popular Guy Fawkes manifestations in the south was a deep rupture – both social and cultural – within southern small-town society. The withdrawal of local elites and the dissolution of a small-town plebeian culture put paid to the popular version of a celebration which had once functioned – and perhaps had been designed to function – as an annual reaffirmation of the solidarity of the whole community. Many popular manifestations were replaced by middle-class or officially sponsored demonstrations in the 1870s and 1880s. Ostensibly these were created to express similar solidarities in a more disciplined, orderly, 'tasteful' and harmless way; but in the process the whole context, the uses and internal meanings of the old celebrations, were subtly bypassed or, in some cases, obliterated.[19]

We might sum up by saying that two of the major handicaps of the 'old' popular culture in the nineteenth century were a decreased willingness by the state, upper classes and elites to either ignore or patronise it, and its abandonment by small, employing craftsmen and shopkeepers (who once appeared in eighteenth-century festive or protesting crowds and generally shared in the plebeian mental universe) and by the most articulate and politically conscious section of the working class. The loss of aristocratic or gentry patronage alone was itself far from fatal. More serious was the fragmentation and increasing cultural differentiation of elements of the old plebs. Having said this, however, we ought to remember that the nineteenth century saw the growth of a new, urban recreational nexus largely impervious to middle-class attempts to create an effective urban paternalism not based upon the workplace. Joyce has shown that a factory-based paternalist regime was created by mid-century in the Lancashire towns; but, by and large, the new recreational nexus, which centred upon developments of the old feasts, wakes and fairs, the music hall, the commercialised sporting ground, a bewilderingly vibrant public-house life and, ultimately, the seaside holiday, grew and developed quite freely – although within a new set of important and rather novel constraints.

Popular culture has never inhabited a hermetically sealed universe. Great and little traditions have always coexisted. Exponents of the former have sometimes participated in the latter; at others they have demanded or forced entry, sometimes with sermons, books or alternative views of how to understand and deal with the unseen world of spirits, demons or witches, sometimes with schools or domestic missions, sometimes with troops and truncheons. One of the great strengths of the eighteenth-century plebeian culture described by E.P. Thompson was its extraordinary degree of autonomy. Below the level of aristocracy and gentry it developed its own repertoire of collective action, folk wisdom, moral economy and so forth. Although it could not help but be sensitive to changes in political climate, law, urban development and the vagaries of ideological change in ruling groups and local elites, it entered the nineteenth century with some strengths. It certainly did not all go down like nine pins before the bowling of the post-Napoleonic War repression or the new institutions of urban industrial capitalism;

nor did it give up the ghost immediately it was bidden — whether in the countryside, the small town (where it persisted most strongly), or even, surprisingly, in industrial cities.

Hugh Cunningham has argued that 'old and "brutal" sports and customs had a remarkable ability to survive even after their demise had been celebrated', and continued to do quite well long after respectable patronage ceased.[20] Many did survive, following their own courses of evolution and mutation throughout the nineteenth century, although under new contraints and pressures. The essays in this volume by Douglas Reid and by John Walton and Robert Poole show that the Birmingham and Lancashire wakes and fairs are not to be understood as mere survivals, but persisted precisely because of their ability to adjust and adapt to an altered social world.[21] This was true as well of southern Fifth of November demonstrations which acquired new meanings and new uses in the very process of changing and adapting. A participant in, say, the 1850s or 1860s might have professed to a hypothetical folklorist (or to the magistrates and police authorities!) that things had been done in the current way from time out of mind — but he would have been quite wrong.

New Year's mumming persisted strongly in the north at least through the 1870s, although, as we have observed, its spirit and meaning changed in the context of nineteenth-century society. This writer knows that rough music was still everywhere to be seen in the industrial West Riding, again at least through the 1870s. In January 1866 a blackleg publican-cum-miner near Sheffield was serenaded with miscellaneous horns by union men when he went back to work before his mates. His pub and house suffered damage, and the home of some of his relatives was also besieged with horns, cries of 'Baa Baa', and renditions of the 'Union hymn about freedom'. In the same year the stang was ridden for the occupier of the Duke of Clarence beerhouse in York Street, Leeds, for marrying too soon after the death of his wife. The crowds, who also threatened an effigy burning, were composed largely of *mill-hands*. In June 1867 Kirkstall forgemen rallied before the house of a mate whose wife had just died to protest his abuse of her while she was alive. Here, too, an attempt was made to burn an effigy.[22]

We observed that a significant proportion of the articulate working-class leadership and certain other working-class groups did reject older forms of collective action, customs and sports, and developed a set of standards of personal behaviour which, to be sure, signalled a widening cultural gap within the working classes. But even here things can be more complex than they seem. The artisan values of independence and mutuality which underlay the nineteenth-century espousal of thrift, sobriety and orderliness were themselves not brand new. John Rule shows below that even when very large segments of working-class communities accepted ideologies seemingly in conflict with older patterns of behaviour and belief, there may well be another dimension to understand. Rule argues that Methodism was favourably received in Cornish mining villages because it was perceived as quite consonant with traditional local conceptions about the nature of the unseen world of devils and spirits as well as other elements of folk belief.[23] Peter Bailey, in a different context, argues that the nineteenth-century music hall — a new, highly commercialised, 'modern' entertainment medium — incorporated much older forms and built upon the emotional resonances they carried with them[24]

This writer discovered that in the West Riding police and magistrates made strenuous — and relatively successful — efforts to clear the countryside, highways and urban public spaces of all sorts of traditional sports: knur and spell, bizarre *ad hoc* contests of strength or endurance, horse- and foot-racing, as well as the gambling and disorder which usually accompanied them. But this sort of pressure and repression emphatically did not sweep away the old sports. By the 1860s publicans, usually operating under excise beer licences, created new commercial sporting grounds and welcomed the practice of all the old sports which the authorities were busy flushing out of the fields and highways. The landlord of one of them, the Green Stile Grounds near Huddersfield, even set up for pitch and toss — another major target of the police — providing gold, silver and copper rings to suit all pocketbooks.[25] Here, too, we observe the growth of another element in a distinctively new, specifically nineteenth-century, urban recreational nexus — more formalised, less *ad hoc*, highly commercialised — which helped to preserve and shelter an older popular sporting culture within a new setting.

Suspicion is often warranted of both contemporary assertions that given ceremonies, sports or customs had been practised in the same way from time immemorial, or else that they were rapidly dying away. Some nineteenth-century popular cultural items surely had histories which could be traced back centuries into the past. Although many were

indeed survivals from the past, they continue into the present, not because of inertia or of conservatism, but because they play important roles within . . . contemporary social settings. Indeed some . . . are revived from the past to serve in the same way. Others are of recent origin and yet others are being continuously created for new, or for old purposes.[26]

The lower classes persisted in creating and enacting evolving forms and versions of older customs, rites and ceremonies; sometimes meaning and uses changed, some items were abandoned under overt repression, yet others were abandoned in its absence. Historians who deal with popular culture must be sensitive to all of this, and attempt to understand it as much as possible in its own contemporary context and terms — which is to be aware of the often jerky or zig-zag trajectory of the process of popular cultural change.

Dealing adequately with the issue of the determinants of popular cultural change poses enormous problems. Not long ago a simple basis-superstructure model might have been employed as a major explanatory device. Surely popular culture and popular cultural change are intimately bound up with material life, property relations and forms of appropriation. E.P. Thompson has recently emphasised the 'simultaneity of expression of characteristic productive relations in *all* systems and areas of social life rather than any notion of the primacy (more 'real') of the 'economic', with the norms and culture seen as some secondary reflection of the primary'. William Reddy illustrates this point for France in his sensitive tracing-out of the complex transition from food riot to strike in Rouen. This process was not only complex but also prolonged, and to be understood not as a mere 'reflex response . . . to changes in the economy but rather a transformation of the labourers' own awareness that occurred in tandem with, but underneath, changes in the explicit ideologies of emerging organisations — whether of industry, of government, or of a revolutionary left.'[27]

It may be that in studying popular culture the basis-superstructure model may *sometimes* be useful the closer one's material is to the workplace and workplace culture. Reid, for example, was able to show how changes in the nature of work and industrial organisation in a particular set of industries can have major and rather prompt effects on certain components of a popular culture — reducing them fairly quickly to pointlessness and accounting quite successfully for their disappearance.[28] Similarly, in this volume Clive Behagg can show how changes in the organisation of the Birmingham industries led directly to the transformation of key elements of the local workplace culture.[29] But if we focus our enquiries on whole social classes or the level of the community, things become more difficult.

How can one fully account for the appearance of the great cultural divide within Cornish mining communities precipitated by the assimilation of Methodism in terms of a changing economic base alone? How can the late-nineteenth-century disappearance of the old popular version of the Fifth of November (or its denaturing or folklorisation) be understood without paying close attention to the changing ideologies and public-order strategies of local elites? My own feelings are that these outcomes can be best understood in terms of changing class alliances within small southern towns. But were these direct results of major changes in the economies of these towns? In some cases, perhaps, yes, but in others the pace of change in local economies was so leisurely that one is forced to consider a host of other factors. It is difficult to quarrel with the general statement that the rise of a specifically nineteenth-century form of capitalist society 'produced' far-reaching effects on popular culture, but it is still somewhat difficult to construct an adequate theory fully accounting for all the phenomena encountered by historians.

Hugh Cunningham recently reaffirmed that people are not passive or totally powerless before external agencies of change and are active in the making of their own history. The working classes in the nineteenth century, argues F.M.L. Thompson, were not 'perpetually on the receiving end of outside forces and influences', and not 'putty in the hands of a masterful and scheming bourgeoisie, a remote and powerful state, and a set of technological alternatives'.[30] This is quite sensible. The persistence and adaptation of many older cultural forms into the nineteenth century is, I suppose, one proof of it. So long as they continued to have point and function and serve concrete uses — the affirmation of local or class solidarities, the profession of loyalty or patriotism, the criticism or intimidation of bosses, local politicians or rulers, and so forth — people could (and did) defend them. But customs and practices themselves changed and mutated in the process of being defended, or when alternative and appropriate sources of amusement and entertainment, new ways of expressing criticism, loyalty or solidarity, were presented or devised. In these ways the lower classes certainly *did* make their own history and exercised initiative, choice and creativity in doing so.

It is a point which can be overstressed, however. History can rarely be made to any person's or group's measure. If it can be so made, it is usually more to the measure of ruling classes and elites than to anyone else's. Neither continuity nor change in popular culture can be understood without keeping in mind the sheer inequalities of power in nineteenth-century society, the existence of a ruling class which, on both national and local levels, was less indifferent to both popular culture and popular politics, the appearance of new conceptions of public order and social discipline, and the creation of new agencies of repression, regulation and constraint. It is still useful to remember that

> the initiatives and responses of the powerful ... helped suppress possible alternatives ... Some groups have more power to define the terms in which ... struggle occurs and through which they are experienced, and they do use this power. To concentrate on working-class response and resolution is like trying to understand a punch by looking at the bruise, not at the fist.[31]

Arguably the most remarkable achievement of the nineteenth-century ruling class (at least after the late 1840s) was to preside over as successful and stable a modern hegemony as has ever existed: the 'creation' of a social world in which turbulence, violence, crime and disorder declined to levels unimaginable before and, certainly, since.[32]

The Victorian urban working-class recreational nexus developed quite independently, free of evangelical meddling and middle-class disdain and suspicion. Yet one cannot escape the conclusion that nineteenth-century popular culture and working-class quotidian life unfolded in a context not so much of repression at every turn, as of a sometimes subtle proliferation of tightening constraints of all kinds. Even at its most creative and 'free', popular culture in the nineteenth century was primarily reactive and defensive. To appreciate this one must look beyond the individual histories of overt suppression and repression it is surely possible to write and take a more holistic and 'structural' view of nineteenth-century popular history. The period between 1850 and 1900 was one in which, perhaps, the outer limits of the possible were never clearer. If later nineteenth-century working-class culture was inward-looking, self-contained and defensive, perhaps defence was the only viable strategy at that moment. Certainly in cultural struggles, as in military and political ones, a defensive strategy is no bar to the winning of battles from time to time! Yet by this time there were all sorts of new and powerful constraints in place to buttress what E.P. Thompson has called the 'deafening propaganda of the status quo': new poor laws, new laws and regulations of *all* types, schools and policemen, as well as bosses and labour markets, which could not help but remind people every day of their limits. Much popular cultural change in the nineteenth-century was in the way of rolling with the punch. And necessarily so.

This sense of growing constraint could be illustrated in many ways. To this writer, whose particular interest has been the interplay between popular culture and new, nineteenth-century conceptions and agencies of public order, it is clear that there was a palpable narrowing of the limits of what would be tolerated in public and an increasing tendency to suspect the unforseen, the unplanned, the unregulated and the unlicensed on the part of both local and national authorities (the 'state'). Newspapers, writers on social questions, magistrates and new police authorities developed and implemented a new conception of what I term 'base-line' public order in the nineteenth century: the delineation of new thresholds of tolerated public behaviour, individual and collective, and the closer definition of what would be tolerated (and under what conditions) and what would not. This project had as its object the creation of a more ordely, disciplined, regulated and supervised society. What was permitted or tolerated certainly contracted over the long term, and what remained tolerated was likely, by the late nineteenth century, to be more closely supervised, regulated and licensed by the state, counties, boroughs and their agents.

The 1839 Metropolitan Police Act and various provincial improvement acts were charters of this project. Their major objective was the closer and more efficient regulation and organisation of quotidian life. They created regulations and enforcement mechanisms whereby a wide range of acts in public, ranging from the beating or shaking of carpets in thoroughfares and the burning and dressing of corks, hoops, casks and tubs, to the flying of kites, the playing of games to the annoyance of inhabitants, and the blowing of horns and noisy instruments, could be controlled or stopped. The implications for popular culture in the nineteenth century were profound.

Consider that in 1822 the chief magistrate of Bow Street stated that if his officers observed public house violations *they would probably ignore them.*[33] After the 1839 Police Act London pubs had to close at midnight on Saturdays and not reopen until 12.30 p.m. on Sunday.[34] After 1854 Sunday-afternoon closing hours were imposed for the first time; in 1864 weekday closing times were first specified for London and some boroughs; in 1869 and 1872 beerhouses were brought under closer supervision and regulation by the police and magistrates, and unrestricted weekday public-house hours outside London were ended. Evasion of the licensing laws was, of course, a constant problem but, unlike the old Bow Street police, the new police forces *did* take notice and proved keenly interested in the regulation of pubs and public-house life. The earlier closing provisions of the 1872 Licensing Act were greeted with satisfaction by provincial authorities. A circular of police officials showed that although public intoxication did not decrease, and workers hated the measure ('they grumble about being unable to get their beer'), the streets became quieter earlier in the evening. The hours 11.00 p.m. to 2.00 a.m., formerly the worst, were now more tranquil.[35] The 1872 Act was deemed a victory for 'base-line' order. A threshold had successfully been lowered, and the result was better order and increased urban decorum.

Let us carry on with this exploration. Both the 1869 Wine and Beer-house Act and the 1872 Licensing Act placed police and magistrates in a better position to scrutinise and monitor key elements of the urban, working-class recreational nexus. Many music halls operating under excise beer licences were brought under closer control after 1869, and the same was true of working-class dancing saloons. Few serious attempts were made on the whole to actually uproot such establishments. To have done so would have provoked too much resistance and would, in any case, have been a work of Sisyphus.

London had had licensed pubs for music and dancing since the eighteenth century but, until the 1870s, metropolitan beerhouses offering such attractions were exempt from the law. By the 1870s this chink was closed. Municipal boroughs in the West Riding secured improvement acts in the 1860s to accomplish similar purposes. The 1866 Leeds Improvement Act forced all pubs offering music or dancing to secure a licence valid for one year. Penalties for non-compliance were stiff – £5 per day of illegal operation. At a stroke police and magistrates gained a type of leverage over these popular recreational locales which they had never possessed before.

We observed that the pressure exerted on *ad hoc,* open-air sports by the authorities helped to create the new, urban, commercial sporting ground in the 1860s. Most of these operated under excise beer licences. Sporting-ground keepers had hitherto simply paid their fines (if the police managed to get a case), treating them as a cost of doing business, knowing that their chances of losing their licences were remote. Here, too, the constraints we have been discussing narrowed and finally caught up with the migration of open-air sports to the more protected commercial ground. By the 1870s the closer control police and magistrates obtained over beerhouses enabled them to compel sporting-ground keepers to run more respectable operations. Those who continued to permit gambling and other irregularities now stood a much greater chance of being driven out of business. In the nineteenth century — a point we ought not to neglect — the state and its agencies became not only more willing to legislate in such areas, but also proved willing to create and fund enforcement agencies. It had the effects of encouraging elements of popular culture (and those who catered for them) to move in certain directions and not in others, and without the need to engage in frequent bitter frontal assaults and overt repressive activities; of forcing others — especially brutal sports — into more clandestine and invisible channels, where they would inevitably lose contact with a portion of their former publics; and compelling yet others to submit to closer regulation, surveillance and licensing.

Stedman Jones has argued that in the late nineteenth century

> a working-class culture gradually established itself, which proved virtinually impervious to evangelical or ulitarian attempts to determine its character or direction. But . . . this impermeability no longer reflected any widespread class combativity. For the most prominent developments . . . were the decay of artisan radicalism, the marginal importance of socialism, the largely passive acceptance of imperialism and the throne, and the growing usurpation of political and educational interests by a way of life centered around the pub, the race course and the music hall. In sum its impermeability to the classes above it was no longer threatening or subversive, but conservative and defensive.[36]

How many moments have there been when popular culture has not been largely conservative, when it has not lauded the king even in the midst of local rebellions or riots, when it has not contained strong patriotic impulses and sentiments within it, or racist elements for that matter? Occasionally it could be highly aggressive, fusing with a robust popular politics; only rarely was it both aggressive and utopian — posing, that is, the possibility of a social order other than the existing one.

There may be some danger in using the early nineteenth century or the Chartist period as a measure of what came before and after. The turbulence and occasional local rebelliousness of the old eighteenth-century plebeian culture and the millenarian and quasi-revolutionary impulses of the earlier nineteenth century issued in the creation of dense, corporate and fragmented working-class cultures. The world and values of late-nineteenth-century artisans certainly touched those of the dock labourers, northern mill-hand or southern small-town worker, but only at a finite number of points. Some may well have been 'cultures of consolation', although it is somewhat difficult to read the culture of Crossick's Kentish London or Gray's respectable workers in Edinburgh in quite that light.[37] To be sure, all were defensive responses in an important sense, and yet all were *adequate* ones, too. For example, the late-nineteenth-century music hall, as Bailey shows below, contained powerful elements of cynicism, hard-headedness and mockery of the upper classes (as well as Jingoism and sentimentality), which helped its audience to keep a proper psychological balance. Much depends, after all, on whether one expects from the nineteenth-century working class something other than what it did, or whether one thinks it ought to have done (or been) something else.

E.P. Thompson's *Making of the English Working Class* first revealed to many of us what some of the possibilities of exploring popular culture could be. Since then, the percolation into the English-speaking world of continental essays on daily life and popular *mentalités*, and the increasing literacy of historians in the literatures of anthropology and sociology, have given the study of popular culture a certain *cachet* and a sometimes uneasy respectability. Researchers in the field have largely ceased being the recipients of their colleagues' barely concealed fish-eyes: 'It's all very interesting, Bill, and it must be fun, but are you really doing history?' A still-increasing legion of practitioners and theses-in-progress has been called up. Too many, it is now being said in some quarters. Some complain that the study of popular culture can degenerate into a tarted-up form of antiquarianism which evades or ignores the 'big questions' of history or social history: class struggles, social structures, the distribution and uses of power and authority, the realm of politics, and so forth.

The danger does exist. There is nothing particularly useful about spending valuable research time discovering the last date a maypole appeared in a Swaledale village — unless that bit of information is made to speak to some wider questions. To have found out what sorts of uses the ritual or ceremony was put to, how it changed over time, what kinds of local solidarities were expressed or affirmed, who presided over it, which groups in the community participated or withdrew over time, who might have opposed it and why, under what specific circumstances it disappeared (or was made to vanish), and what the after-effects of such struggles were, is no valueless task. On the contrary, such investigations can lead directly into and shed light upon the 'big' social historical questions, and tell us a great deal about social and economic transformations, changing ideologies of social discipline and public order, how structures of power and authority work in specific local contexts, how authority is imposed or negotiated, and so forth.

Studying popular culture in this manner can, in the hands of the best practitioners, generate new concepts in social history from time to time.[38] Popular culture studies can thus serve as excellent entrées into the history of work, urbanisation, religion, politics and public order. They are most valuable, in my view, when consciously undertaken with relations to such other histories in mind.

Notes

1. See P. Bailey, *Leisure and Class in Victorian England* (Toronto, 1978); R. Colls, '"Oh Happy English Children!" Coal, Class and Education in the North-East', *Past and Present,* no.73 (1976), pp.75-99; R.D. Storch, 'The Problem of Working Class Leisure: Some Roots of Middle Class Moral Reform in the Industrial North, 1825-50', in A.P. Donajgrodzki (ed.), *Social Control in Nineteenth Century Britain* (London, 1977).

2. *LM,* 16 Aug. 1863.

3. *LM,* 27 Sept. 1870.

4. *LM,* 3 Jan. 1868.

5. *LT,* 26 July 1856.

6. P. Joyce, *Work, Society and Politics. The Culture of the Factory in Later Victorian England* (Brighton, 1980).

7. R.D. Storch, 'The Problem of Working Class Leisure', pp.156-7.

8. See below, Ch.2.

9. The phrase is David Cannadine's.

10. E.P. Thompson, 'Patrician Society, Plebeian Culture', *J. of Social History,* vol.7, no.4 (1974), pp.393-4.

11. By 'old' popular culture I mean that eighteenth-century popular culture described by Thompson – which was, of course, by no means so old.

12. J. Brewer, 'Theater and Counter-Theater in Georgian Politics: The Mock Elections at Garrat', *Radical History Review,* 22 (Winter 1979-80), pp.7-40.

13. *LT,* 24 Jan. 1835.

14. See below, Ch.5.

15. C. Tilly, *Charivaris, Repertoires, and Politics,* University of Michigan Center for Research on Social Organisation Working Paper No. 214 (1980).

16. D. Thompson, 'Chartism as a Historical Subject', *Bulletin of Society for the Study of Labour History,* 15 (Autumn 1967).

17. P. Burke, *Popular Culture in Early Modern Europe* (London, 1978). Ch.8; B. Kerr, 'The Dorset Agricultural Labourer 1750-1850', *Proceedings Dorset Nat. Hist. and Arch. Society,* vol.84 (1963 for 1962).

18. J. Obelkevich, *Religion and Rural Society: South Lindsey 1825-1875* (Oxford, 1976).

19. See below, Ch.4.

20. H. Cunningham, 'The Growth of Popular Leisure 1780-1840', unpublished paper.

21. See below, Ch.5 and 6.

22. *LM,* 27 Jan. 1866, 22 Aug. 1866, 26 July 1867. See also *LM,* 28 July 1868, for stang riding in Ventnor Street, Leeds.

23. See below, Ch.3.

24. See below, Ch.8.

25. *LM,* 30 Apr. 1869.

26. A. Cohen, *Two Dimensional Man. An Essay on the Anthropology of Power and Symbolism in Complex Society* (London, 1974), p.3.

27. E.P. Thompson, 'Folklore, Anthropology, and Social History', *Indian History Review*, vol.3, no.2 (1977), p.261; W. Reddy, 'The Textile Trade and the Language of the Crowd at Rouen 1752-1871', *Past and Present*, no.74 (1977), p.84.

28. D. Reid, 'The Decline of Saint Monday', *Past and Present*, no.71 (1976), pp.76-101.

29. See below, Ch.7.

30. H. Cunningham, *Leisure in the Industrial Revolution c. 1780-1880* (London, 1980), Ch.6; F.M.L. Thompson, 'Social Control in Victorian Britain', *Economic History Review*, 2nd ser., vol.34, no.2 (1981), p.189.

31. H.F. Moorhouse, 'History, Sociology and the Quiescence of the British Working Class: a Reply to Reid', *Social History*, vol.4, no.3 (1979), pp.485-6.

32. V.A.C. Gatrell, 'The Decline of Theft and Violence in Victorian and Edwardian England', in V.A.C. Gatrell, B. Lenman and G. Parker (eds.), *Crime and the Law. The Social History of Crime in Western Europe Since 1500* (London, 1980), pp.238-370.

33. House of Commons Select Committee on the Police of the Metropolis, *PP* (1822), vol.4, p.26.

34. 'Effects of the Metropolitan Police Act . . . Requiring Public Houses to be Closed on the Sabbath Morning', *J. Statistical Society of London*, vol.4, no.3 (1841), pp.268-9.

35. Lord's Day Observance Society, *The Licensing Act of 1872 . . .* (London, 1874); Leeds Constabulary, *Report and Criminal Statistics for 1872-1873* (Leeds, 1873), p.7. On new legislation regarding fairs and their closer supervision by police in London see H. Cunningham, 'The Metropolitan Fairs: A Case Study in the Social Control of Leisure', in A.P. Donajgrodzki (ed.), *Social Control*, pp.163-84.

36. G. Stedman Jones, 'Working-Class Culture and Working-Class Politics in London, 1870-1900: Notes on the Remaking of a Working Class', *J. of Social History*, vol.7, (1974), p.484.

37. G. Crossick, 'The Labour Aristocracy and its Values: A Study of Mid-Victorian Kentish London', *Victorian Studies*, vol.19, no.3 (1976), pp.301-28; idem, *An Artisan Elite in Victorian Society: Kentish London, 1840-1880* (London, 1978); R.Q. Gray, *The Labour Aristocracy in Victorian Edinburgh* (Oxford, 1976).

38. E.g., the 'moral economy' of the English crowd.

2 THE DECLINE OF THE ORAL TRADITION IN POPULAR CULTURE*

David Vincent

Around the middle of July 1802 a meeting took place between a young Edinburgh lawyer and a Border shepherd and his mother. The lawyer was Walter Scott, who was gathering material for the *Minstrelsy of the Scottish Border*. His host was a self-educated poet named James Hogg, who had been copying down ballads from the oral tradition of his family and community ever since coming across the first two volumes of the *Minstrelsy* in the spring of that year. In Hogg's thatched cottage his mother, Margaret Laidlaw, recited to their guest the traditional ballad 'Auld Maitland'.[1] Scott was delighted, and asked if it had ever been in print:

> 'O na, na sir', she replied, 'it never was printed i' the world, for my brothers an' me learned it an' many mae frae auld Andrew Moor and he learned it frae auld Baby Mettlin, wha was housekeeper to the first laird of Tushilaw. She was said to hae been another nor a gude ane, an' there are many queer stories about hersel', but O, she had been a grand singer o' auld songs an' ballads.'
> 'The first laird of Tushilaw, Margaret?' said Scott, 'then that must be a very old story indeed.?[2]
> 'Ay, it is that sir! It is an auld story! But mair nor that, excepting George Warton an' James Stewart, there war never ane o' my sangs prentit till ye prentit them yoursel', an' ye hae spoilt them awthegither. They were made for singing an' no for reading; but ye hae broken the charm now, an' they'll never be sung mair. An' the worse thing of a', they're nouther right spell'd nor right setten down'.[3]

Hogg published at least three accounts of this meeting,[4] partly because it marked the beginning of his life-long friendship with Scott, and partly because it defined the problem which he would spend the rest of his days trying to resolve.[5] As a child his imagination had been formed by the tales, superstitions and ballads recounted by his mother, and their influence was to pervade the prose and poetry he wrote as an adult. Yet by his teens he was building upon the fragment of schooling he had received in his ninth year, and was starting to make the acquaintance of formal literature. At school he had 'had the honour of standing at the head of a juvenile class, who read the Shorter Catechism and the Proverbs of Solomon',[6] and when his father's eviction from his farm precipitated him into the family calling of a shepherd, he continued his study of the Bible, particularly the Psalms of David, and moved on to the odd volume of theology and classical literature. His first poem was, as he later confessed, 'mostly composed of borrowed lines and sentences from Dryden's Virgil, and Harvey's Life of Bruce'.[7] With increased confidence he began to turn to more indigenous models, but it was not until he met with the *Minstrelsy* and its author that he became fully conscious of the deep division in his cultural identity. It was Scott who made him realise the wealth and vitality of his mother's oral tradition, and it was his mother, in her denunciation of Scott's activity, who dramatised the impact on that tradition of the urban literary culture which the ballad collector represented.

Hogg saw with great clarity that Scott and his hosts in the Ettrick cottage were at once united and fundamentally separated by their response to the oral tradition which was the cause of their meeting. They shared a fascination with the ballads and tales which Hogg and his mother were helping Scott to collect, and were convinced that they stood at a watershed in the history of popular culture; neither the shepherd nor his guest made any attempt to deny Margaret Laidlaw's angry prophecy. At the same time Hogg felt himself too distanced from the oral tradition to completely associate himself with his mother and too much a part of it to merge himself with the world of polite literature, on whose behalf he had invited Scott into the cottage. This paper will concern itself with the conflicting pattern of responses evoked by the concept of the oral tradition, and with some of the tensions and dilemmas caused by its predicted decline as the issues raised in that meeting were worked out during the succeeding century.

I

The term 'oral tradition' had been current for almost two centuries by the time Scott turned his attention to the subject. It was first employed by Bishop Joseph Hall, in the course of a defence of the Anglican Church against the claims of 'Romish Traditions'. He rested his case on the authority of the Bible, 'his Written word', which had been set down that the knowledge of God 'might be preserved entire . . . to the last date of time'. Catholicism, on the other hand, derived its claim from an essentially unreliable source: 'As for orall Traditions, what certaintie can there be in them? What foundation of truth can be layd upon the breath of man? How doe they multiply in their passage, and either grow, or dye upon hazards?'[8] By the late eighteenth century a significant shift of meaning had taken place, although the concept was to retain its association with the Church of Rome until the advent of positivist anthropology in the 1870s. It now defined the difference not between two religions, but between two cultures.

The study of popular culture in Britain begins with the publication in 1777 of John Brand's *Observations on Popular Antiquities,*[9] a revised and extended version of a pioneering collection of customs and superstitions edited by another Newcastle clergyman Henry Bourne in 1725. Bourne's work caused little stir at the time, but when the new edition appeared it attracted widespread attention and led to the founding of the Society of Antiquaries in 1784 with Brand as its resident secretary.[10] Brand was less concerned with the ultimate derivation of his material, which he assumed to be Papist, or heathen, than with the forces which had enabled it to preserve 'at least some *Form* and *Colour* of Identity, during a Repetition of Changes, both in religious Opinion, and in the Polity of States'.[11] The explanation was that these customs and superstitions belonged to the culture of 'The Common People', which had become divorced from that of the educated classes, and was thus immune from the transforming force of literary communication. The vulgar notions and ceremonies he was presenting, 'though erazed by public Authority from the *written Word,* were committed as a venerable deposit to the keeping of *oral Tradition'*.[12] Both in its forms and in its means of transmission, popular culture was essentially illiterate and irrational, the mirror image of the culture of polite society, which now began to look with increasing fascination on the beliefs and modes of behaviour which it assumed it had left behind.

North of the Border, Scott's researches were given added urgency by the imperilled state of his nation. 'By such efforts', he wrote, 'feeble as they are, I may contribute somewhat to the history of my native country; the peculiar features of whose manners and character are daily melting and dissolving into those of her sister and ally.'[13] The possibility of using popular traditions to define and perpetuate a threatened national consciousness had been particularly influential in Germany, where the publication of Herder's *Volkslieder* in 1778 had set in motion a European-wide movement of folk-song collecting.[14]

In Scotland, the revival of interest in ballads had begun in the aftermath of the Forty-five, and much of the subsequent activity has to be set in the context of the political, economic and ideological aggrandisement of England. Yet in essence Scott's approach to the material he was editing was no different to that of Brand and the antiquarians who followed in his footsteps. He assumed that his literate, urban middle-class culture had lost contact with what had once been a common imaginative heritage, which was now to be found only amongst those who had escaped the impact of new forms of communication. The oral tradition made possible his role as a collector, and at the same time created his major editorial problem, that of defining the authentic text. The harder he worked, the more versions he discovered. He explained:

> Such discrepancies must very frequently occur wherever poetry is preserved by oral tradition; for the reciter, making it a uniform principle to proceed at all hazards, is very often, when his memory fails him, apt to substitute large portions from some other tale, altogether distinct from that which he has commenced.[15]

By the middle of the nineteenth century an army of middle-class antiquarians was at work following the guidelines laid down by Scott and Brand, and adding to the material collected in their pioneering volumes. In 1859 William Thoms founded *Notes and Queries* to provide a forum of exchange of material, which continued to mount up in a largely unsystematic form until the establishment of the Folklore Society in 1878. The leading members of this new body were deeply influenced by the new discipline of anthropology, which in turn drew much of its inspiration from Social Darwinism. Their hope was that it would be possible to arrange all known beliefs and customs in a single line of development, proceeding from the earliest forms of society towards the rational civilisation of the present day.

Both the scale and the rigour of the research had been transformed since the beginning of the century, yet the two basic assumptions upon which Scott and Brand had based their work remained intact: that the popular culture under investigation was fundamentally apart from and antecedent to that to which the collectors belonged; and that its central element, the oral tradition, was in decline. Scott was driven on by the fear that the superstitions and ballads of the Borders, 'if not now collected must soon have been totally forgotten', and half a century later William Thoms, in a celebrated article in *The Athenaeum* which introduced the term 'folk-lore' into the English language, invested such research with even greater urgency:

> no one who has made the manners, customs, observances, super-
> stitions, ballads, proverbs &c., of the older times his study, but
> must have arrived at two conclusions: — the first, how much that is
> curious and interesting in these matters is now entirely lost — the
> second, how much may yet be rescued by timely exertion.[16]

II

In the research he undertook for Scott, and in his subsequent creative
and editorial work, there is an equally sharp sensation of discovery in
the response of James Hogg to the culture in which he had been
brought up. He had become aware of the historical identity of a
hitherto private world. In a letter to Scott shortly before their meeting,
he wrote:

> Many, indeed, are not aware of the manners of this country; 'till
> this present age, the poor illiterate people, in these glens, knew of no
> other entertainment, in the long winter nights, than repeating, and
> listening to, the feats of their ancestors, recorded in songs, which I
> believe to be handed down, from father to son, for many genera-
> tions . . . [17]

There was a feeling of pride in the 'manners of this country' which for
so long had been taken for granted by the common people and ignored
by those above them, and this was accompanied by a conviction that
with the dawning of 'this present age' an epoch in the history of popular
culture was drawing to a close.

As more working men began to write about their culture, in articles,
poetry and in autobiographies, a form in which Hogg was himself an
early pioneer,[18] we find an enhanced sensitivity towards their past. Unlike the antiquarians, the self-educated working men were making ever
more sophisticated use of literature and literacy forms to examine the
past of their own community, a past which had formed them and which
still in large part surrounded them. For this reason their analysis of the
decline of the oral tradition was at once more complex and more urgent.

From the perspective of those within the popular culture the anti-
thesis between oral and literary traditions was not as absolute as it

appeared to outside observers. A revolution was taking place, but it contained two important elements of continuity. The first of these was that the labouring poor had had substantial contact with formal literature for well over a century before the period covered by this paper. By 1700, 'illiteracy was everywhere face to face with literacy, and the oral with the printed word'.[19] At this date, about one in six of the least literate section of the community, agricultural labourers, could sign his name in a marriage register.[20] The volume and range of material available to these men and their families were limited, but over the years most households would manage to acquire a few items of literature which would then be passed on to subsequent generations. A survey carried out by the Central Society of Education in the late 1830s concluded that few rural homes were without any sort of reading matter.[21] At best, the libraries would be small: looking back to his native Bingley in the 1820s, the mechanic Thomas Wood recalled that

A cottage library in a fairly well-to-do family would seldom exceed half-a-dozen volumes, and consisted of such works as Dodderidge's 'Use and Progress of Religion in the Soul', Bunyan's 'Works' particularly the 'Pilgrim's Progress', Cook's 'Voyages', 'News from the Invisible world' etc. and a volume or perhaps two, of magazines.[22]

To this list could be added odd broadsides and chap-books bought from the chapmen who had been peddling their wares in country districts since the sixteenth century.[23] The use made of this literature would vary extensively, and some may not have been read at all,[24] but the evidence of the puritan autobiographers and the long history of 'peasant poets' suggest that there had always existed a tradition of serious reading in even the more isolated rural communities. Where Hogg's ambitions were kindled by the example of Burns,[25] his English counterparts could look back to Stephen Duck and his successors.[26] However tenuous it may have been, there was a literary as well as an oral tradition in the culture of the labouring poor.

The second element of continuity concerned the nature of the relationship between the spoken and the written word. Henry Bourne had identified the element of performance as being at the centre of the oral tradition. As he wrote in 1725, 'Nothing is commoner in *Country Places,* than for a whole Family in a Winter's Evening, to sit round the Fire, and tell Stories of Apparitions and Ghosts.'[27] It was assumed that such performances served the function not only of entertainment, but also of preservation. Children listened to their parents, and their children in turn listened to them, and in this way the astonishing longevity of many of the ballads and superstitions could be explained. In the hands of Brand and Scott and their successors, this thesis gained an added dimension. It was now argued that the material had been preserved not only in spite of but because of the absence of the written word. Where the imaginative life of a culture had been committed to print, the oral tradition had decayed. The tradition had only survived, and could only survive, where it was kept entirely separate from literary forms. Yet the accounts given by early nineteenth-century autobiographers suggest a less firm division between the two modes of communication.

Much was conveyed, and continued to be conveyed, through the spoken word. Samuel Bamford, for instance, was able to set his career as a radical politician in the context of the 'rebel blood' of his forefathers, whose exploits had been handed down from father to son since the Civil War.[28] The working-class community had little history other than that contained in its collective memory, and in one sense the autobiographies which began to appear in the early nineteenth century were no more than a formal manifestation of a long-standing process of educating the next generation in the values, achievements and sufferings of its predecessors.[29] As we shall see they wrote at length about the superstitions and tales with which they had become familiar long before they could read. In the countryside the winter nights were still as dark and long as they had been in Henry Bourne's time. However, when they could read, or when they could find someone to read to them, there were two alternative sources of fantasy. The first was the Bible and the classics of religious imaginative literature, particularly *Paradise Lost* and *Pilgrim's Progress,* which could be read at many levels. The second was the chap-books, whose contents were inextricably bound up with the ballads and folk-tales. In his manuscript autobiography, John Clare listed many of the '6py Pamphlets that are in the possession of every door calling hawker and found in every bookstall at fairs & markets whose titles are as familiar with everyone as his own name'.[30] What was striking about his catalogue was the resemblance it bore to the material which the antiquarians were beginning to collect from a supposedly untainted oral tradition. In Clare's childhood there was no differnce in substance between such stories and those told to him by the old women with whom he worked in the fields, whose 'memories never failed of tales to smoothen our labour; for as every day came, new Giants, Hobgoblins, and fairies was ready to pass it away'.[31]

Recent research suggests that at least 80 per cent of the folk-songs gathered in the major collections at the end of the nineteenth century could be traced back to printed broadsides.[32] Whether or not the ultimate source of a ballad or folk-tale was a village bard or a publisher's hack is not always clear and not necessarily very important: by the time it reached the nineteenth century a particular item is likely to have made more than one journey between the printed and spoken form.[33] Even within the oral tradition itself, the performers were often capable of making manuscript copies of their material to guard against failures of individual or collective memory.[34] The presence of the chap-books and family song-books calls into question not only the assumed purity of the oral tradition, but also the means by which it had been preserved. It is possible that the material the collectors sought out from simple rustics might never have survived without the intervention of a formal record.

In their anxiety to demonstrate the gulf between their culture and that of the common people, the antiquarians paid little attention to any factors which might complicate the picture. In 1907 Cecil Sharp published *English Folk Song, Some Conclusions,* which distilled the experience of the nineteenth-century collectors, and in turn deeply influenced the approach of the folklorists of the coming century. In the opening chapter he wrote:

> The expression 'common people. is used in this definition . . . to connote those whose mental development has been due not to any formal system of training or education, but solely to environment, communal association, and direct contact with the ups and downs of life . . . the unlettered, whose faculties have undergone no formal training, and who have never been brought into close enough contact with educated persons to be influenced by them.[35]

In the same way as the pastoral Border culture represented the reverse side of the enlightened world of the Scottish capital, so the West Country communities from which Sharp collected his folk-songs stood for the way of life which the advanced industrial society seemed to have lost for ever. The socialist Sharp and the tory Scott were at one in their conception of a form of society which, if it had ever existed, had disappeared with the Reformation.

For those who had a more direct experience of the changes which were taking place, the elements of continuity had a number of implications. In the first instance, the well-established custom of owning and making some limited use of formal literature ensured that, when the transformation in the availability and exploitation of print took place

in the early nineteenth century, it was seen as an extension of indigenous working-class habits and tastes, rather than an importation, or
imposition, of the values and forms of behaviour of another class.
Those representatives of the middle class who were most sympathetic
to the aspirations of working-class readers assumed that the pursuit of
book knowledge could only be alien to a culture whose traditions were
essentially oral. Henry Brougham summarised their approach:

> One word . . . upon the manner in which learning and improvement
> make their way in society. I think it must be admitted that it
> is always in one way, and that downwards. You begin by making the
> upper classes aware of the value of certain kinds of knowledge . . .
> then . . . the middle parts of the middle class get well acquainted
> with the subject and feel its importance . . . and they try, by their
> exertions and their money . . . to spread to the class below them a
> little of the same feeling, the same love of learning, which they
> possess themselves; and so that lower class gets by degrees impreg-
> nated itself.[36]

In their struggle to define their cultural identity working-class readers
were to encounter many problems but they never doubted that they
were building on their own foundations and not those of another class.

Secondly, the long symbiotic relationship between chap-books and
the oral tradition modified the impact of the explosion of popular
literature triggered by the application of steam power to printing.[37]
To those who were illiterate and were to remain so, the proliferation of
the printed word represented a threat to their jealously guarded possession of a vital means of education and entertainment. At the centre of
Margaret Laidlaw's jeremiad was a deep sense of personal injury. It was
not so much the songs as the singers that were threatened with extinction. But for those who were already accustomed to reading, and
possibly distributing and even writing ephemeral literature, the coming
changes had a familiar aspect. Chapmen could become key transitional
figures. The account left by David Love of Nottingham of his activi-
ies around the turn of the century illustrates the interrelationship between composition, publication and performance which characterised
his business. He began his working life as a travelling bookseller, and
had tried his hand at coal mining and teaching before returning to his
former occupation:

> I then took to my old trade of travelling, and got printed some songs

which I had composed when I kept the school, and sang them at fairs and market-towns; I sold them fast, which gave me encouragement to compose more; and I have made my living by my compositions ever since.[38]

He ended his career in the early 1820s, just as the great metropolitan entrepreneurs in the broadside business were beginning to transform the scale of the printing and marketing side of the industry.[39]

The activities of James Catnach and John Pitts widened the gulf between the publishers on one side and the writers and streetsellers on the other, but some of their material stood in direct line of succession to that of Love and his predecessors. Catnach sought out performers and writers who had knowledge of the old broadsides, and was said by Hindley to have paid men to collect ballads from singers in country taverns.[40] He was, in effect, using steam power and the increasing size and literacy of the urban population to preserve rather than destroy the oral tradition. Broadsides were now only one tributary of a torrent of secular, religious and political ephemera, but they served to introduce those growing up in an industrial society to the songs and tales which for so long had been the staple fare of the imaginative life of the common people.[41]

Finally the vein of creativity which had existed within the popular culture made some contribution to the emergence of a small but vitally important class of self-educated writers and poets in the first half of the nineteenth century. The performer of a ballad or folk-tale had always been dependent on his imagination was well as his memory,[42] and those who entered their repertoire into manuscript song-books, or made their own contribution to the stock of chap-books they carried away from the printer, could be regarded as literary creators. Long before he was introduced to Scott or the world of professional writers, Hogg had gained a local reputation with his pen. He wrote of his literary apprenticeship:

For several years my compositions consisted wholly of songs and ballads made up for the lasses to sing in chorus; and a proud man I was when I first heard the rosy nymphs chaunting my uncouth strains, and jeering me by the still dear appelation of 'Jamie the poeter'.[43]

When he consciously began to write, rather than make *aide memoires* of the verses he had composed in his head while tending his sheep, his first subjects were imitations of the ballads he had been collecting for Scott.

Hogg's transition from 'Jamie the poeter' to the widely published author was only made possible by his contact with formal literature, and such was to be the case with every other working-class poet who left an account of his life; yet time and again we find the future writer beginning his career as the composer of impromptu verses for neighbours, workmates or lovers. The Cornish tin-miner John Harris, who commenced his autobiography with a passage from Hogg's *Memoir*, established his identity as a poet whilst working with his father:

> I used frequently to repeat the rhymes I had written to my mates in the mine. They would put me to stand on a hand-barrow by the cobbing house door, or on a heap of mineral on the floors, and then gather around to hear my verses.[44]

Years before he finally published a poem, the Kettering weaver J.A. Leatherland had 'won some local celebrity as a versifier',[45] and the customary weaver Willie Thom gained the confidence necessary to venture into print from the reputation he had established amongst his peers: 'I had, ever since I remember, an irrepressible tendency to make verses, and many of these had won applause from my friends and fellow-workmen'.[46] An audience had always existed for individuals who through some combination of memory and imagination could entertain those with whom they lived and worked, and it was out of this tradition of performance that the working-class writers emerged.

No working-class autobiographer had any doubt that he had lived through a revolution in his culture. The very presence of their memoirs was evidence of a transformation in the relationship between working men and the printed word. In the view of the Croyden journalist and radical Thomas Frost, the progress in 'mental development and political enfranchisement' over his lifetime had created an immense gulf between his generation and its predecessors. 'Men not yet old', he wrote in 1880, 'may look back upon the days of their boyhood as curiously and as wonderingly as their fathers did upon the age of the Tudors'.[47] Yet Frost was aware that the roots of the popular literature which he helped to write in the 1840s and 1850s reached far back into the centuries before his childhood.[48] If a close examination is made of the oral tradition before it entered the decline which so concerned both the observers and the apparent victims, several important bridges between the old and new can be identified. For self-educated working men, the problem was not so much encompassing two entirely alien cultural experiences as reconciling the elements of change with those of continuity.

III

If the oral tradition largely defined the pre-industrial popular culture, the significance of its decline revolved around the question of superstition. The world of those whose horizons were limited by the oral tradition was suffused with the supernatural. James Hogg's brother William described the atmosphere which surrounded their childhood:

> To a people thus shut up from all human society, it is no wonder to find the days of former years remarkable for superstition. Our mother's mind was well stored with tales of spectres, ghosts, fairies, brownies, voices, &c . . . These tales arrested our attention, and filled our minds with the most dreadful apprehensions . . .[49]

Not only the content but the very *form* of the oral tradition, which might have no visible origin or means of preservation, could be invested with a magical quality: such was implied in Margaret Laidlaw's accusation that Scott had 'spoilt' her songs by breaking their 'charm'. Those, on the other hand, who stood at some distance from the tradition, measured their response to the changes which were taking place in terms of a dialectic between superstition and reason. So much of what might be both gained and lost was contained in the fate of what the Galloway farm labourer Samuel Robinson referred to as 'various kinds of beings of a middle class, friendly or hostile to man according to the class — fairy, brownie, fire or water kelpie etc. — as the case might be'.[50]

A major theme of Hogg's *Memoir* is the search for an alternative education. He emphasises that from his early teens he was acutely aware of a body of learning apart from his mother's tales and songs, and he provides a detailed account of his difficulties in the pursuit of what later working-class autobiographers would call 'useful knowledge'. Such knowledge came from books rather than conversation, and it usually had little connection with the occupational skills which most working men continued to acquire through imitation.[51] Its primary function was to effect a transformation in the consciousness of the reader. William Lovett grew up at the opposite end of Britain from Hogg, in the Cornish fishing village of Newlyn. During his childhood he suffered from much the same combination of imaginative wealth and intellectual poverty, and like Hogg had to make the journey to his country's capital before making real contact with literature. Once there, however, he plunged into the world of books and readers: 'my mind seemed to be awakened to a new mental existence; new feelings, hopes, and aspirations sprang up within me, and every spare moment was devoted to the acquisition of some kind of useful knowledge'.[52] Every auto-biography of a self-improving working man reported this sense of the awakening of a 'new mental existence', as its author first glimpsed the scope of the written word. It frequently amounted to a secular conversion experience.[53] One of the few books Hogg managed to read during his youth was 'Blind Harry's' *Life and Adventure of Sir William Wallace,* of which he became 'immoderately fond',[54] and the anonymous 'Dundee Factory Boy' reported that 'The reading of Wallace opened up a new world to me, and I longed for more mental food to satisfy the cravings of an awakened appetite'.[55]

As they explored their new world self-educated working men travelled far from the oral tradition, yet they retained a fascination with the supernatural, and returned repeatedly to the subject in the commentaries they made on their intellectual journey. The roots of their preoccupation were buried in their childhood. At a time when they were quite unable to distinguish between fact and fantasy, their impressionable minds had been overwhelmed by tales of extraordinary beings and events. Much had merely entertained, but much else had been quite terrifying. In his poem 'Superstition', written in 1814, Hogg described the power of the 'Sovereign of supreme unearthly eye': '. . . she could make the brown and careless boy/All breathless stand, unknowing what to fear;/Or panting deep beneath his co'erlet lie,/When midnight whisper stole upon his ear'.[56] Maturity and reading might undermine belief, but the scars remained.

Even William Lovett, that paragon of all that was rational, was forced to confess to the lingering influence of childhood terrors. As an apprentice ropemaker, one of his duties had been to make arduous journeys to and from the local market:

> But what I felt more severely than the labour inflicted on me was the coming and going along some of these lonely roads by night, for popular credulity had peopled particular spots with ghosts and appearances of various kinds, and in which I was a firm believer. For the numerous stories regarding those nocturnal visitants, told to me in infancy, reiterated in boyhood, and authenticated and confirmed by one neighbour after another, who had witnessed, they said, their existence in a variety of forms, riveted the belief in them so firmly in my brain, that it was many years after I came to London before I became a sceptic in ghosts.[57]

What for many of the antiquarians could be an agreeable flirtation with primitive forms of drama and violence which stood in such sharp contrast to what Scott referred to as 'the monotony of regulated society',[58] was for working-class autobiographers a vital ingredient in their psychological development.

There were, however, general as well as personal reasons for the continuing concern with superstition. Samuel Bamford was born in the Lancashire village of Middleton, which though only six miles from the centre of Manchester had more in common with the culture of Hogg's border country. He devoted a section of *Early Days* to the superstitions which had played such a large part in the life of his community,[59] partly to illustrate his own background, and partly as a means of assessing the progress of his class during his lifetime. By describing such matters, he wrote:

> we are enabled distinctly to perceive the great change which, in a few years, has taken place in the tastes and habits of the working classes: and seeing these alterations clearly set forth, we shall be better able to determine whether or not the labouring classes have been advancing in, or retrograding from, that state of mind, and that body of habit, which are meant by the term, Civilisation.[60]

The investigation of the decline of the influence of the supernatural was a means not just of measuring but of evaluating the historical development of the working class.

At the centre of the analysis was the question of self-control. In his eye-witness account of the history of the West Riding village of Pudsey during the second and third quarters of the nineteenth century, Joseph Lawson discussed at length what he described as 'the galling yoke of superstition'.[61] The body of irrational beliefs and practices represented a yoke to the community both in its direct influence over thought and action, and in the way in which it prevented the assertion of control over the natural and man-made phenomena which it sought to explain. Without a proper understanding of cause and effect, the working class had no hope of coming to terms with the world in which it found itself. 'In proportion as people are deprived of knowledge and are ignorant of the causes of what they constantly see and hear', wrote Lawson, 'their imagination is let loose, and, their reason weak, they become a prey to every false rumour, or popular prejudice and delusion'.[62]

The first requirement was scientific knowledge, or at least a scientific mode of thinking. As William Lovett explained, superstitions took root at the most basic level:

> Of the causes of day and night, of the seasons, and of the common phenomena of nature we knew nothing, and curious were our speculations regarding them. We had heard of 'the sun ruling by day, and the moon by night', but how or in what way they ruled was a mystery we could never solve. With minds thus ignorant, persons need not be surprised that we were very superstitious.[63]

A major problem, though by no means the only one, was that of the health of the community and its livestock. Cut off from trained medical assistance, an elaborate system of folk medicine had developed, sustained by oral tradition, although as elsewhere the transmission of information was assisted and sometimes elaborated by printed material.[64] Throughout the nineteenth century the diseases of the poor kept well ahead of advances in medical care, and consequently the wise men and women and their rituals and potions were slow to disappear. The anonymous 'Suffolk Farm Labourer' wrote:

> In spite of the march of intellect a belief in the efficacy of charms for the prevention and cure of certain diseases is still pretty general among the people of rural districts. There is almost always someone in a village who by 'crossing' the part affected, and whispering over it certain mysterious words, 'bless' or charm away wounds resulting from burns and scalds.[65]

He went on to list a range of regional variations to cures which could be found in every part of Britain.

Folk medicine had always provided psychological and occasionally physical relief, but self-educated working men were aware that progress in preventive and curative medicine was now taking place, and that as long as their community continued to rely on inherited wisdom and ignorance, permanent improvements in its health would be impossible. Although William Lovett later published a school text book on anatomy and physiology,[66] and James Hogg wrote a widely-read treatise on the diseases of sheep, which appeared in the same year as *The Mountain Bard*,[67] few working men could expect to make a direct contribution to the health of their neighbours. Those who became botanists sometimes found that they were pressed into service as herbalists,[68] but the chief function of those who pursued book knowledge was to spread habits of thought which could lead those in need to seek out the best available information rather than turn back to sources which did little good and often much harm.

The health of the working-class population was an important enough subject in its own right, but the struggle of the new wise men against the old had a wider significance. If the labouring population would remain at the mercy of its natural environment until it began to search for its 'causes', so it would never exert any control over the world made by men unless it sought to demystify the sources of power within it. To those committed to political action, the hold of superstition over the community symbolised the obstacles which stood in the way of its emancipation. When Robert Lowery arrived in Cornwall to spread the gospel of the 1839 Chartist Convention, he found the inhabitants ill-prepared for his message:

> They knew little of general society, its state or conflicting opinions. Living in a remote corner of the land, with the ocean almost around them, they had not mixed with the rest of the population. They were very superstitious, and we were assured of ghosts and apparitions in many places.[69]

For working-class writers, the concern with superstition carried a political overtone which was rarely to be found in the works of the middle-class antiquarians.

It can be argued, indeed, that the folk-lore movement, whose growth ran exactly parallel to the emergence of working-class radicalism, represented a reaction against the political threat mounted from below. The study of popular culture and its oral traditions was a means of bringing the classes together on ground emptied of conflict. This process was nowhere better illustrated than by the career of William Hone, a major figure in the histories of both radicalism and anti-quarianism in the first third of the century. In 1817, Hone was the defendant in three prosecutions for blasphemy brought by the Attorney General in an attempt to silence the radical press. His acquittal by London juries humiliated the government and made him the hero of radicals and infidels as the post-war discontent reached its climax.[70] Yet by the mid-twenties this notorious enemy of church and state had found a way of writing about the beliefs and behaviour of the working class which was completely acceptable to 'the "mothers of England" . . . and instructors of youth of both sexes . . .'[71] who now bought his publications in large numbers.[72] Having repented of many of his earlier views, he edited a series of volumes of popular antiquities which made a major contribution to both his ailing finances and the nineteenth-century study of folklore.[73] His final work, *The Year Book*, was compiled and published in the midst of the Reform Bill crisis, and in its pages an anxious middle-class readership could encounter a vigorous, colourful, authentic working-class world which had no apparent connection with the contemporary political unions and riotous crowds.

For working-class radicals, however, the decline of superstition was a matter of the utmost relevance to the pursuit of freedom. By its very nature, the oral tradition ensured conformity to an irrational view of the forces which controlled the existence of the labouring population. Without books and the modes of intellectual enquiry which they promoted, it was impossible to mount any effective challenge to the ideology of the ruling class.[74] Illiteracy and superstition reinforced each other and in turn underpinned the structure of deference which stood in the way of political advance. 'Where you find ignorance among the working men', observed the cobbler and poacher James Hawker, 'you will find them inclining towards the Class. Where you find men who Toil, intelligent men, they incline towards trying to Better the condition of their fellows.'[75]

The prevailing tone of the autobiographers' treatment of the decline of superstition is one of optimism. The inroads of the written word into the realm of the oral tradition held out the prospect of the emancipation of the individual and his class. Yet admist the celebration it is possible to detect elements of doubt and regret which have an important bearing on the overall impact of the changes which were taking place. In the first instance there was the question of the moral values of the labouring population. Most self-educated working men assumed an automatic correlation between intellectual and moral improvement. The further a man stood from the influence of the supernatural, the more chance he had of combating degrading forms of behaviour, such as excessive drinking. Conversely, drink reinforced the hold of superstition to the point when the alcoholic's mind was overwhelmed with demons of every hue.[76] The pursuit of useful knowledge would impart to the reader a dignity and sobriety unattainable to those whose lives were ruled by irrational beliefs and rituals.

There remained the problem, however, of the relationship between self-education and religion. Although the working-class writers were much less concerned than the earlier antiquarians with the supposed Popish features of the oral tradition, they could not avoid the fact that religious forms and practices were inextricably bound up with the world of superstition. The Bible was used for prophecy, churches, churchyards and sacramental objects were invested with magical qualities, and the Devil and all his works were recognised by both oral and scriptural authority.[77] The one autobiographer to have remained almost wholly within the oral tradition, the barely literate Northumbrian wagonway-wright Anthony Errington, proudly related his capacity to turn milk into butter by a combination of prayer and a churning ritual.[78] The two spiritual universes were so closely related that it was not easy to reject one without abandoning the other. 'At this time', wrote Joseph Lawson of Pudsey in the early decades of the century, 'all those who deny the existence of boggards are called infidels and atheists. The Bible even is referred to as a proof of the truth of witchcraft.'[79]

Most autodidacts hoped that they could follow the established Protestant path of constructing a more rational faith on the basis of the Bible and other religious literature. Accordingly they tended to be rather doubtful about the more extreme manifestations of revivalism in which emotion seemed to overwhelm reason. Yet there was a case for arguing that the villagers of Pudsey had the right of it. Some support for their attitude was provided by James Hogg, who, as so often, found himself both welcoming the decline of the oral tradition and deploring its possible consequences. Through his reading and his contact with the Edinburgh literary culture he had moved away from the stark Presbyterian creed of his upbringing, which he savagely parodied in his fictional masterpiece, *The Confessions of a Justified Sinner*. At the same time there remained in him the suspicion that if the dramatised representations of evil which featured so strongly in his background were swept away, then faith in religious virtue would also disappear. He gave expression to his apprehension in the poem 'Superstition', which contained a forthright defence of its subject:

> O! I have seen the door most closely barred;
>   The green turf fire where stuck was many a pin;
> The rhymes of incantation I have heard,
>   And seen the black dish solemnly laid in
> Amid the boiling liquid — Was it sin?
> Ah! no — 'twas all in fair defence of right.[80]

Evil was made concrete that Good might triumph. Abolish the Devil, he argued, and you abolish God:

Sole empress of the twilight — Woe is me!
That thou and all thy spectres are outworn;
For true devotion wanes away with thee.
All thy delirious dreams are laughed to scorn,
While o'er our hills has dawned a cold saturnine morn.[81]

Hogg's fears were fully borne out by the career of a man like the Coventry weaver and naturalist Joseph Gutteridge, whose search for 'more rational conclusions as to cause and effect'[82] eventually led him into a state of complete disbelief. Where the superstitions of Hogg's background had provided an elaborate response to injustice and hardship, Gutteridge's intellectual enquiries ultimately caused him to doubt whether any religious explanation could be found for the sufferings of his family and community.[83] The pursuit of knowledge inevitably represented a secularisation of the reader's outlook, and whilst the great majority of those who wrote an autobiography retained their faith in some form, there was always the danger that in the cold saturnine morn their free thought would finally turn them into Freethinkers.[84]

The second problem was that of the relationship between the oral tradition and the pre-industrial moral economy. Many of the beliefs and observances which preoccupied the self-educated working men embodied economic and social rights which were increasingly threatened. In this context the autobiographers preferred to use the term custom rather than superstition, and in their accounts were far more concerned than the middle-class antiquarians to draw a distinction between the world of the supernatural, and the calendar of rituals and pastimes which relieved the monotony of their working life and provided some defence against the demands of their employers. The 'Suffolk Farm Labourer' divided his material on the decline of the oral tradition into two chapters, one on superstitions, whose disappearance he welcomed, and one on 'Harvest Customs, Harvest Feast, and Tithe Feast', whose erosion was seen as an index of the widening gulf between masters and men. In his neighbourhood, the last load from the harvest field was known as the 'Horkey load', which gave its name to the ensuing celebration:

the 'horkey supper' was always given by the farmer at his own house, but unfortunately a change, not for the better, grew up years after. Many of the farmers' wives did not like the bother of the feast, and gradually the custom grew for the farmers to give a money payment, generally half-a-crown a man, to avoid the trouble of so much cooking.[85]

In the face of the attack by employers in search of more rational forms of production, and the pressure of the more impersonal force of urbanisation, there was little that the self-educated working men could do, save make some permanent record of what was being lost.[86]

The third problem concerned the creative voice of the working-class community. The oral tradition had always provided a vital stimulus to the imagination of the performer and his audience. 'The age of superstition is peculiarly one of poetry', wrote James Burn, 'when men's minds are kept alive by supernatural agencies.'[87] If the child had at times been overwhelmed by the fabulous beings and forces conjured up by the ballads and folk-tales, he would none the less grow into adulthood deeply conscious of the world of fantasy and make-believe.[88] Many of those brought up in this tradition were uneasy lest, once the links with this immensely fertile vein of invention were broken, the creative life of their culture would be permanently impoverished. Hogg's 'Superstition' ended on a sombre note: 'All these are gone', he wrote of the 'sheeted forms' which once had filled his landscape. '— The days of vision o'er;/The Bard of fancy strikes a tuneless string.[89]

Such fears represented only one side of Hogg's response to the changes which were taking place, yet they were genuine enough. What he valued was not only the wealth and vigour of this form of entertainment, but its absolute familiarity. As we have suggested, print was not wholly foreign to the pre-industrial popular culture, but even the most courageous working-class reader felt ill at ease when he first entered the realm of the written word. He would now be faced with unprecedented problems of finding an appropriate voice in which to express himself. For all his achievement, Hogg was often unsure as to language and tone in his writings,[90] and his confusion was shared to a greater or lesser extent by all other self-educated working men.

Underlying such major problems as the choice of books to read, or the style in which to write, was the basic question of vocabulary. Time and again they reached the moment when their first encounter with literature caused them to doubt the adequacy and correctness of their inherited modes of speech. We find, for instance, such self-confident individuals as William Lovett and Thomas Cooper beginning their courses of self-education by attempting to divest themselves of their regional accents which now seemed suitable only for those still locked in the grip of the irrational forces from which they were determined to emancipate themselves.[91] Equipped with at best a minimal command over the basic skills of literacy, they turned in desperation to grammar books and adopted ways of speaking and writing alien to those with which they had once felt so at home.[92] The autobiographer to really triumph over his insecurity was John Clare. He felt compelled to acquire a 'Spelling Book' but, after wrestling with its contents, threw it down in disgust:

> For, as I knew I could talk to be understood, I thought by the same method my writing might be made out as easy and as proper. So in the teeth of grammar I pursued my literary journey as warm as usual.[93]

Almost alone amongst self-educated working men he found a way of infusing his native oral tradition with his wide reading and forged a literary style which was genuinely appropriate to his experience.

IV

Of the three people who talked in the shepherd's cottage in the summer of 1802, it was Margaret Laidlaw who had most to lose. The decline of the oral tradition created a series of new divisions within the popular culture, each one of which put her at a disadvantage in relation to self-educated working men such as her son. It increased the gulf between town and country. The books, the self-improvement societies, and newspapers and publishers were all to be found in the rapidly expanding centres of population. Throughout the nineteenth century, the innovations in popular culture took place in the urban communities. The composition of folk-song was not killed by the industrial revolution, it was displaced from the farms to the factories and mines where it flourished as an expression of the economic and political struggles of the new workforce.[94] Those with youth and ambition on their side could move towards the new opportunities, those trapped on the land were left as silent witnesses of the slow decline of their customs and traditions.

The spread of the written word introduced a new hierarchy into the culture of the common people. The dominant position of those who had heard the most and remembered the most was threatened by those who had the greatest command over the skills of literacy. There now began the long struggle between those who had inherited their wisdom, and those who had learnt it from books. Where once the old had been venerated as the repositories of the experience and imaginative life of the community, the young claimed their place by virtue of their access to richer and more powerful sources of knowledge and entertainment.[95]

The onward march of print also accentuated divisions between the sexes and within families. Margaret Laidlaw's position as a woman and as a mother was under attack. Women had played a major role in the process of preserving and transmitting the various forms of the oral tradition, but they were largely excluded from the opportunities which were being opened up by the greater availability of literature. The self-improvement societies, the book clubs, the newspapers, were increasingly run by men and for men. If women had gained some literacy at school, the opportunity to use it as adults, and to enjoy the power and status which it generated, was severely limited.[96] At home, literacy diminished the influence of parents as schools and private reading endowed their children with skills and knowledge which they could neither control nor understand. Had Scott not been both her social superior and the chief legal officer of the area,[97] Margaret Laidlaw might have expressed her resentment at his intrusion more forcibly. As it was, she must have recognised that there was little she could do to halt the process of change.

James Hogg stood to gain much of what was lost by his mother. In her eyes he represented almost as big a threat as the visiting lawyer. Yet in the end the gulf between mother and son proved less significant than that between the middle-class ballad collector and the self-educated shepherd. This was partly a function of the elements of continuity which can be identified within the revolution which was taking place. Scott's friendship was to play an important part in Hogg's life, but his commitment to the world of books and literary self-expression stemmed from his days as 'Poeter jamie', when he was able to establish himself as a reader and composer on the basis of the materials, traditions and needs of his isolated community. Scott made him aware of how far he had travelled, but the journey had been made alone, using the resources found in his own background.

Furthermore, as the number of working-class readers and writers multiplied in the early decades of the nineteenth century, they found it possible to exert some control over the process of acquiring literacy and literature, and over the means of publication. Hogg himself financed his first volume of poetry by the proceeds of the sale of some sheep he had driven to market in Edinburgh.[98] The amounts of capital put at risk by publishing, particularly by subscription, or by ventures into journalism, such as the unstamped press, could be small, and those who were determined to get into print could do so without the permission of their social superiors. It was not until much later in the century that the state and the church achieved a monopoly over the provision of elementary education, and the publishing trade became so capital intensive as to exclude independent ventures by working-class writers. Until that time, literate working men were subject to great pressures, but were none the less able to embark upon the pursuit of knowledge within the framework of their own cultural traditions.

The distance between the two men was also a functon of Hogg's social and economic identity. If the oral tradition was seen to be the defining characteristic of the difference between the two cultures, the force which held those cultures apart was, and continued to be, class discrimination. Hogg was patronised, even lionised, by the Edinburgh intellectuals, but he was always kept at arm's length, even by his friend Scott, and ended his days a poor man. Until the end of the nineteenth century, there existed no reliable ladder out of the working class via education and book knowledge, and consequently generations of self-educated working men remained subject to the material and social deprivation of their community.[99]

The decline of the oral tradition set up tensions in the popular culture which neither Hogg nor any other self-educated working man in the nineteenth century was fully able to resolve. The world of books offered the individual the possibility of emancipation from the forces which for so long had constrained the thought and action of his community, and at the same time threatened to separate him from vital sources of belief, imagination and historical rights. The pursuit of useful knowledge inevitably involved a withdrawal from the essentially communal process of oral transmission, set the literate apart from the illiterate, and created new lines of demarcation within the working class. In this sense, Hogg's relationship with his mother is perhaps of greater historical significance than his encounter with Scott, for what is notable about that meeting at Ettrick is how infrequently it was repeated during the nineteenth century. Few subsequent working-class writers enjoyed the degree of personal contact with middle-class intellectuals that Hogg was to experience throughout his life. The antiquarians kept their distance from the common people, and for their part the self-educated struggled alone to achieve a synthesis between the oral and literary traditions which now existed alongside each other in the popular culture.[100]

Notes

*I am grateful to George Ewart Evans, Margaret Spufford, Victor Neuburg and George Deacon for comments on an earlier draft of this paper.

1. 'Auld Maitland'. Scott published this version with due acknowledgement to his source, as the opening chapter of the third volume. Walter Scott, *Minstrelsy of the Scottish Border*, 2nd ed. (Edinburgh, 1803), vol.3, pp.1-42.

2. 'auld Baby Mettlin' probably lived at the end of the seventeenth century. See Edith C. Batho, *The Ettrick Shepherd* (New York, 1969 ed.), p.171.

3. James Hogg, *Familiar Anecdotes of Sir Walter Scott* (Edinburgh, 1972 ed.), pp.136-7. There was also present at the meeting William Laidlaw, Hogg's former employer and Scott's future steward, but no relation of Margaret.

4. A shorter account than the one cited above was published by Hogg in 'Reminiscences of Former Days. My First Interview with Sir Walter Scott', *Edinburgh Literary Journal*, vol.2 (1829), pp.51-2 and then reprinted with minor alterations in the version of his 'Memoir' which appeared in the *Altrive Tales* (London, 1832). See also the manuscript account given by William Laidlaw, published as 'Recollections of Sir Walter Scott (1802-1804)', *Transactions of the Hawick Archaeological Society* (1905), pp.66-74.

5. On Hogg see Batho, *Ettrick Shepherd;* Alan Lang Strout, *The Life and Letters of James Hogg* (Lubbock, Texas, 1946), vol.1; Louis Simpson, *James Hogg, A critical Study* (1962); James Hogg, *Selected Poems,* Douglas S. Mack (ed.) (Oxford, 1970); Douglas Gifford, *James Hogg* (Edinburgh, 1976).

6. James Hogg, *Memoir of the Author's Life* (Edinburgh, 1972 ed.), p.5.

7. Ibid., p.82.

8. Joseph Hall, *The Olde Religion* (London, 1628), p.167.

9. John Brand, *Observations on Popular Antiquities: Including the whole of Mr. Bourne's Antiquitates Vulgares, with Addenda to every Chapter of that Work: . . .* (Newcastle-upon-Tyne, 1777).

10. Richard M. Dorson, *The British Folklorists* (London, 1968), pp.10-34.

11. Brand, *Obervations*, p.iii.

12. Ibid., p.iv (Brand's italics).

13. Scott, *Minstrelsy*, p.cxxii.

14. Peter Burke, *Popular Culture in Early Modern Europe* (London, 1978), pp.3-22.

15. Scott, *Minstrelsy*, p.cxxix.

16. *The Athenaeum*, no.982, 22 Aug. 1846, p.863.

17. Quoted by Scott in his introduction to 'Auld Maitland', in the third volume of the *Minstrelsy* (pp.9-10). The full text of the letter is given in Batho, *Ettrick Shepherd*, pp.24-7.

18. For the development of nineteenth-century working-class autobiography, see David Vincent, *Bread, Knowledge and Freedom* (London, 1981), Ch.2.

19. Margaret Spufford, 'First steps in literacy: the reading and writing experiences of the humblest seventeenth century spiritual autobiographies', *Social History*, vol.4, no.3 (Oct. 1979), p.427.

20. David Cressy, 'Educational opportunity in Tudor and Stuart England', *History of Education Quarterly* (Fall 1976), pp.309-12; Lawrence Stone, 'Literacy and Education in England 1640-1900', *Past and Present*, no.42 (1969), pp.110-12.

21. *Central Society of Education, First Publication* (London, 1837), pp.342-59; *Second Publication* (London, 1838), pp.259-60; *Third Publication* (London, 1839), pp.87-139, 368-74. These figures are discussed in more detail in David Vincent 'Reading in the Working Class Home', in James Walvin and John Walton

(eds.), *Leisure in England 1780-1939* (Manchester, 1982).
22. Thomas Wood, *The Autobiography of Thomas Wood, 1822-1880* (1956), p.9. C.f. the very similar list in William Howitt's *The Rural Life of England*, 3rd ed. (London, 1844), vol.1, p.256.
23. The best survey of this world is to be found in Margaret Spufford, *Small Books and Pleasant Histories* (London, 1981).
24. If the CSE findings are accurate, more families must have possessed books than could actually read them.
25. For the impact of Burns on Hogg see *Memoir*, p.11. Also David Craig, *Scottish Literature and the Scottish People* (London, 1961), p.111-35.
26. See Joseph Spence, 'A Full and Authentick Account of Stephen Duck', in Stephen Duck, *Poems on Several Occasions* (London, 1736); Rayner Unwin, *The Rural Muse* (London, 1954), pp.47-109.
27. Brand, *Observations*, p.102.
28. Samuel Bamford, *Early Days* (London, 1849), pp.11, 22. See also William Cameron, *Hawkie, The Autobiography of a Gangrel*, John Strathesk (ed.), (Glasgow, 1888), p.9; Peter Taylor, *The Autobiography of Peter Taylor* (Paisley, 1903), pp.14-18.
29. See David Vincent (ed. & intro.) *Testaments of Radicalism* (London, 1977), pp.1-23.
30. John Clare, 'The Autobiography, 1793-1824', in J.W. and Anne Tibble (eds.), *The Prose of John Clare* (London, 1951), p.19.
31. John Clare, *Sketches in the Life of John Clare. Written by Himself and Addressed to his friend John Taylor esq.*, Edmund Blunden (ed.) (London, 1931), p.48.
32. Robert S. Thomson, 'The development of the broadside ballad trade and its influence upon the transmission of English folksongs', unpublished PhD thesis, Cambridge University, 1974.
33. M. Spufford, 'First steps in literacy', pp.8-12.
34. A.L. Lloyd, *Folk Song in England* (London, 1975), p.24.
35. Cecil J. Sharp, *English Folk Song, Some Conclusions*, 4th ed. (Wakefield, 1965), p.4.
36. Henry Brougham, 'Address to the Members of the Manchester Mechanics Institution, July 31 1835', in *British Eloquence: Literary Addresses*, 2nd Series (London, 1855), pp.180-2. For the attempt by the Society for the Diffusion of Useful Knowledge to put his philosophy into practice, see R.K. Webb, *The British Working Class Reader, 1790-1848* (London, 1955), pp.66-73; R.D. Altick, *The English Common Reader* (Chicago, 1957), pp.269-77; Thomas Kelly, *A History of Adult Education in Great Britain* (Liverpool, 1970), Chs.8 & 11; D. Vincent, *Bread, Knowledge and Freedom*, Ch.7.
37. Victor E. Neuburg, *Popular Literature* (Harmondsworth, 1977), pp.123-234; Louis James, *Fiction for the Working Man* (Harmondsworth, 1974), pp.14-31; S.H. Steinberg, *Five Hundred Years of Printing*, 3rd ed. (Harmondsworth, 1974), pp.277-88.
38. David Love, *The Life, Adventures and Experience of David Love* (Nottingham, 1823-4), p.14. See too the memoirs of the ballad-writer, singer and seller William Cameron (*Hawkie*, esp. pp.57, 91-3). Also Leslie Shepard, *The History of Street Literature* (Newton Abbot, 1973), pp.79-106; V.E. Neuburg, 'The Literature of the Streets', in H.J. Dyos and Michael Wolff (eds.), *The Victorian City* (London, 1976), vol.1, pp.192-4.
39. For Catnach, see Charles Hindley, *The Life and Times of James Catnach, Ballad Monger* (London, 1878); for Pitts, Leslie Shepard, *John Pitts, Ballad Printer of Seven Dials, 1765-1844.*
40. Hindley, *James Catnach*, p.383.

41. 'Wonderful Adventures of the Seven Champions of Christendom', in Louis James, *Print and the People* (Harmondsworth, 1978) pp.195-8. This had been a well-known item since the sixteenth century, and was republished by W. and T. Fordyce of Newcastle in about 1838.

42. David Buchan, *The Ballad and the Folk* (London, 1972), pp.251, 269-70.

43. Hogg, *Memoir*, p. 10.

44. John Harris, *My Autobiography* (London, 1882), p.37.

45. J.A. Leatherland, *Essays and Poems with a brief Autobiographical Memoir*, (London, 1862), p.10.

46. William Thom, *Rhymes and Recollections of a Hand-Loom Weaver* (London, 1844), p.24.

47. Thomas Frost, *Forty Years' Recollections Literary and Political* (London, 1880), p.1.

48. Ibid., Ch.6, 'Popular Literature Forty Years Ago'.

49. William Hogg to James Gray in 1813, quoted in Strout, *James Hogg*, p.8.

50. Samuel Robinson, *Reminiscences of Wigtonshire about the Close of Last Century* (Hamilton, 1872), p.72. 'Their existence', he added, 'was the engrossing topic of conversation whenever a gossiping party met in the winter evening in Galloway, as in all other parts of Scotland; and the district was rich in such lore.' Also W.H.L. Tester, *Holiday Reading. Sketches of La Teste's Life on the Road* (Elgin, 1882), p.3.

51. For the concept of 'useful knowledge', see D. Vincent, *Bread, Knowledge and Freedom*, Ch. 7; Richard Johnson, 'Really Useful Knowledge', in John Clarke, Chas Chritcher and Richard Johnson (eds.), *Working Class Culture* (London, 1979), pp.75-102.

52. William Lovett, *Life and Struggles of William Lovett* (London, 1876), p.35. Also Robert Story, 'Preface', in *The Poetical Works of Robert Story* (London, 1857), pp.v-vi; Benjamin Brierley, *Home Memories and Recollections of a Life* (Manchester, 1886), p.44.

53. David Riesman cites similar conversion experiences amongst the newly literate in Poland, Mexico, the Philippines and the Soviet Union. See 'The Oral and Written Traditions', in Edward Carpenter and Marshal McLuhan (eds.) *Explorations in Communications* (London, 1970), p.113.

54. Hogg, *Memoir*, p.8.

55. *Chapters in the Life of a Dundee Factory Boy* (ed.), J. Myles (Dundee, 1850), p.31.

56. 'Superstition', lines 37-40, in James Hogg, *Selected Poems*, pp.72-80.

57. Lovett, *Life and Struggle*, p.9. Cf. James Dawson Burn, *The Autobiography of a Beggar Boy*, David Vincent, (ed.), (London, 1978), p.68, and the account of Thomas Oliver in *Autobiography of a Cornish Miner* (Camborne, 1914), p.85.

58. Scott, *Minstrelsy*, vol.1, p.lxiv.

59. Bamford, *Early Days*, pp.159-69. See also J.D. Burn, *Autobiography*, p. 66; James, *Print and the People*, pp.18-20.

60. Bamford, *Early Days*, p.132. See also Timothy Mountjoy, *Sixty-two years in the Life of a Forest of Dean Collier* (1887), reprinted in *Hard Times in the Forest* (Colesford, 1971), p.15.

61. Joseph Lawson, *Letters to the Young on Progress in Pudsey during the last Sixty Years* (Stanningley, 1887), p.48.

62. Ibid., p.47.

63. Lovett, *William Lovett*, p.32.

64. F.F. Cartwright, *A Social History of Medicine* (London, 1977), pp.1-39; Bernard Capp, *Astrology and the Popular Press, English Almanacs 1500-1800* (London, 1979), pp.204-14.

65. The 'Autobiography of a Suffolk Farm Labourer With Recollections of

Incidents and Events that have occurred in Suffolk during the Sixty Years from 1816 to 1876' (ed.), 'Rambler', *Suffolk Times and Mercury*, 2 Nov. 1894 – 16 Aug. 1895, part 2, Ch.3.

66. William Lovett, *Elementary Anatomy and Physiology . . . With lessons on Diet etc.* (London, 1851).

67. The book, which was familiarly known as 'Hogg on Sheep'. won a prize from the Highland Society. Its full title was *The Shepherd's Guide: being a Practical Treatise on the Diseases of Sheep, Their Causes, and the Best Means of Preventing Them; with observations on the most suitable farm-stocking for the various climates of this country* (Edinburgh and London, 1807). It was written in a 'homely and plain style' in order to make the latest scientific advances accessible to working shepherds.

68. See the experiences of Joseph Gutteridge in *Lights and Shadows in the Life of an Artisan* (Coventry, 1893), p.78; and Ebenezer Elliott in 'Autobiography', *Athenaeum,* 12 Jan. 1850, p.46.

69. Robert Lowery, *Passages in the Life of a Temperance Lecturer* (1856-7), reprinted in Brian Harrison and Patricia Hollis (eds.), *Robert Lowery, Radical and Chartist* (London, 1980), p.130.

70. Frederick Hackwood, *William Hone, His Life and Times* (London, 1912), pp.132-3; E.P. Thompson, *The Making of the English Working Class* (Harmondsworth, 1968), pp.792-3.

71. William Hone, *The Every-Day book* (London, 1827), vol.2, p.vii.

72. According to Hackwood 80,000 copies of his folk-lore collections had been sold by 1838 (*William Hone*, p.295).

73. The sales of the *Every-Day Book* eventually freed Hone from King's Bench Prison, in which he had been confined for debt. For Hone's debt to Brand, and his extensive influence on subsequent collectors, see Dorson *British Folklorists*, pp.34-43.

74. For a discussion of the relationship between oral tradition and political consciousness see the comments by the Sardinian-born Gramsci, in Quintin Hoare and Geoffrey Nowell Smith (eds.), *Selections from the Prison Notebooks of Anthony Gramsci* (London, 1973), pp.34, 197, 323, 419. For a more general survey, see Jack Goody and Ian Watt, 'The Consequences of Literacy', in Jack Goody (ed.), *Literacy in Industrial Societies* (Cambridge, 1968), pp.55-7.

75. James Hawker, 'The Life of a Poacher', MS, published as *A Victorian Poacher, James Hawker's Journal,* Garth Christian (ed.), (Oxford, 1978), p.91.

76. There was a strong connection between heavy drinking and encounters with the supernatural, especially north of the Border. See, for instance, J.D. Burn's description of the stage-coaches full of 'ugly demons of every shape and form' conjured up by his drunken father as they travelled across empty moorland by night. (*Autobiography,* p.49).

77. The best discussion of the relationship between religion and magic in this period is to be found in James Obelkevich, *Religion and Rural Society: South Lindsey 1825-1875* (Oxford, 1976), Ch.6. See also Keith Thomas, *Religion and the Decline of Magic* (Harmondsworth, 1973), pp.797-8.

78. Anthony Errington, 'Particulars of my life and transactions', MS transcribed by P.E.H. Hair, pp.29-32.

79. Lawson, *Letters to the Young,* p.49.

80. 'Superstition', in Hogg, *Selected Poems*, p.76, lines 118-23.

81. Ibid., p.75, lines 95-9.

82. Gutteridge, *Life of an Artisan,* p.89.

83. Ibid., pp.79-80, 135. See also the spiritual crisis suffered by Thomas Cooper, in *The Life of Thomas Cooper, written by himself* (London, 1872), pp.259-60. Both Cooper and Gutteridge eventually found their way back to a

generalised Christian faith.

84. For a more general discussion of this process, see Susan Budd, *Varieties of Unbelief* (London, 1977), pp.104-23; Edward Royle, *Victorian Infidels* (Manchester, 1974), pp.107-25.

85. 'Suffolk Farm Labourer' Part 2, Ch.2. He was born in 1805, and was referring to the period of his childhood.

86. See, for instance the unavailing attempts of Christopher Thomson (*The Autobiography of an Artisan*, London, 1847, pp.345, 367) and Benjamin Brierley (*Home Memories*, pp. 46-7) to revive dying customs.

87. Burn, *Autobiography*, p.195. The same argument forms the basis of Willa Muir's *Living with Ballads* (London, 1965). See also Buchan, *The Ballad and the Folk*, p.171.

88. Harris, *My Autobiography*, p.14.

89. 'Superstition', in Hogg, *Selected Poems*, p.80, lines 217-8.

90. For a detailed discussion of this point see Gifford, *James Hogg*, p.218-35.

91. Lovett, *Life and Struggle*, p.34; Cooper, *Life of Thomas Cooper*, pp.56-7.

92. See James, *Print and the People*, p.22.

93. Clare, *Sketches*, p.69.

94. See Martha Vicinus, *The Industrial Muse* (London 1974), Chs.2 & 3; A.L. Lloyd, *Folk Song*, Ch.6.

95. For a more general discussion of this point, see D. Riesman, 'Oral and Written Traditions', p.109.

96. See Dorothy Thompson, 'Women and Nineteenth Century Radical Politics, A Lost Dimension', in Juliet Mitchell and Ann Oakley (eds.), *The Rights and Wrongs of Women* (Harmondsworth, 1976), pp.176-98.

97. 'The sheriff of a county in those days', wrote William Laidlaw, 'was regarded by the class to whom at that time Hogg belonged with much of the fear and respect with which their *forbears* had looked up to the ancient hereditary sheriffs, who had the power of everything in their hands.' ('Recollections of Sir Walter Scott', p.70).

98. Hogg, *Memoir*, p. 15; Strout, *James Hogg*, p.25.

99. The point is discussed in more detail in Vincent, *Bread, Knowledge and Freedom*, Ch.7.

100. On the continuation of the oral tradition and its relation to the literate see V.E. Neuburg, *Popular Literature*, Ch.5, 'The Oral Tradition: Some Notes on Survival'; Richard Hoggart, *The Uses of Literacy* (Harmondsworth, 1958), Ch.2, part A.

3 METHODISM, POPULAR BELIEFS AND VILLAGE CULTURE IN CORNWALL, 1800-50

John Rule

I

The study of popular religion needs to be localised. Not only did the level of religious observance in nineteenth-century England vary significantly from one region to another, but the distribution of the various churches and sects followed different patterns. Regional diversity means that one must treat with caution all attempts to write generally of the influence of religion on the working class. In a critique of recent trends in the history of popular leisure it has been suggested that in their attempts to reform traditional recreations evangelicals or temperance reformers were 'purveyors of minority causes'. An historian of the metropolis might well have found that to be the case, but it would be misleading to approach the social history of many smaller and different kinds of community from the same premise. In the mining villages of Durham or Cornwall Methodists of one kind or another could often claim majority support, at least so far as influence went if not membership.[1]

The miners of Cornwall formed an occupational community to which Methodism came early and prospered greatly. By the early nineteenth century west Cornwall had become one of the movement's greatest strongholds. By Methodism we mean to embrace both the Wesleyans and the various splits and offshoots from the parent body: giving, by 1851, 16,691 members of whom just under two-thirds lived in the western mining parts. On census Sunday in that year 113,510 attendances were recorded at the various connectional chapels and churches. Membership statistics are not convertible by some magic multiplier into a measurement of influence, nor are the badly collected ones of attendance in 1851. They do, however, strongly support the impression of a very strong influence which emerges from a large number of sources. In 1842 Charles Barham produced the most detailed and fully researched survey of the early-Victorian mining population we have. He found that the Methodist miners formed a class 'so numerous that its qualities become prominent features of the whole body when it is compared with other communities'. The Anglican clergy would certainly have agreed. 'We have lost the people', complained a vicar in

1833, 'The religion of the mass is become Wesleyan Methodism'. Another explained his modest success to Dr Pusey by stressing the difficulties of working in a county 'wholly given up to dissent and perversity', where there was 'Methodism in every house'.[2]

Two specific aspects of Methodism's influence on the life of the mining communities will be considered. The first is its impact on popular pastimes and the second will be its relationship to popular beliefs.

In the first of these areas it will be argued that the temperance and teetotal movements can be viewed in Cornwall as a 'religious' force extending and amplifying already well-established Methodist sanctions. Recent work in the history of leisure has been criticised by Gareth Stedman Jones for concentrating too much on the role of such agencies and thereby producing a misleading orthodoxy. This stresses the advance of a methodical capitalist rationality and the disappearance or decline of traditional recreational forms. Lurking behind this approach he sees the sociologist's concept of 'social control', a concept which he finds of dubious value. In stressing the concern of the upper and middle classes to impose rational recreation on a working class as part of the process of incorporating it into the capitalist scheme of things, historians of leisure have got things out of perspective. By focusing upon the reforming attempts of evangelicals, Methodists, civic elites and capitalist employers, they have based their analysis only on a reading of the case for the prosecution.[3]

Stedman Jones's strictures are important qualifications and perhaps have already had a deserved modifying effect on the subject. Some recent work shows a degree of dissatisfaction with the simple idea of a successful attack on traditional recreational forms and stresses that the old working-class leisure culture may not only have persisted but even expanded during the first half of the nineteenth century. The baby need not be discarded with the bathwater. If historians have put evangelicals, temperance reformers, Methodists, magistrates, the 'new' police and capitalist employers into a 'sharply delineated foreground', perhaps that is where they should be put. The *central* issue in the history of recreation during this period is the attempt to control and reshape the leisure activities of the working class. Given the stage of development of the entrepreneurial capitalist economy there is no historical mystery about this. Nor is there any need to employ a metaphor of the 'invisible hand' to explain why second-line forces such as Methodism or temperance reform fought what was fundamentally the cause of capitalist employers. In the first place such groups were not wholly separable. In the second, employers' objectives and the motivations of groups like Methodists meshed with and reinforced each other well enough without the need to look for hidden string-pulling or formal alliance.[4]

The confrontation of religion with 'revelry' is not just part of the history of popular recreation: it is central to the understanding of the social history of religion in industrialising Britain. Dr Harrison has pointed out that it was over attempts to dominate popular leisure that the churches and the working classes came most frequently into contact in the nineteenth century:

> Nineteenth-century Christians deplored that recreational complex of behaviour which included gambling, adultry, drinking, cruel sports and sabbath breaking and blasphemy — all of which took place together at the race-course, the drinking place, the theatre, the 'feast' and the fair.[5]

One difficulty with the 'social control' concept is that it is suggestive of the *imposition* of new forms of behaviour upon the working class by *external* forces. This is evidently the case with capitalist employers and order-concious magistrates, but it cannot be wholly so of popular religious movements, for both Methodism and teetotalism elicited significant working-class participation and activity. For all the conservatism of the Methodist 'establishment' and the 'respectability' of its town-chapel elites, in the villages Methodism in its Wesleyan, Primitive and Bible Christian forms had become internalised to a great degree by the beginning of the nineteenth century. In some villages chapel members formed a clear majority of the mining population.

Wesley's *Journal* reveals the extent to which, in its earliest days, Methodism came into conflict with traditional uses of leisure time. He recorded his digust at the 'savage ignorance and wickedness' of colliers near Newcastle in 1743 who assembled on Sundays to 'dance, fight, curse and swear, and play at chuck ball, span-farthing, or whatever came next to hand'. In the town itself he set out to confront the 'crowds of poor wretches' who passed their Sundays in 'sauntering to and fro on the Sandhill'. In Ireland he outfaced a company of revellers and dancers who had taken over his usual preaching place. At Otley in 1766 he made his visit on the local feast day and found a town gone mad in 'noise, hurry, drunkenness, rioting, confusion' to the 'shame of a Christian country'.[6]

The impact of Methodism on traditional pastimes in Cornwall was reinforced from the late 1830s by the temperance and teetotal movements. Dr Harrison has shown the reluctance of church leaders, including the Wesleyans, to become involved in these movements in their early years. This official detachment was not, however, always accepted. Certainly it was not so in Cornwall where an uneasy tolerance of teetotal meetings was ended by a conference ban on their being held in Wesleyan chapels. The immediate effect at St Ives was the secession of 250 members to form the separate Teetotal Wesleyan Methodists. Joined by teetotallers from neighbouring places, they numbered 600 by 1842. Teetotallers could reasonably hope for success in a country which in 1834 had had by far the biggest membership per thousand of the British and Foreign Temperance Society of any country.[7]

Was there a connection between temperance and teetotal success and the pre-existing strength of Methodism? To many working-class Methodists, signing the pledge was an extension of their existing attitude towards strong drink rather than a new departure. The 'saved' drunkards may have been the spectacular signatories, but that does not make them typical. James Tears met with a ready-made response when he first visited Cornwall in January 1838. At his first meeting 150 persons signed, and through 1838/9 his success increased. By February 1839 the Ludgvan society was claiming 800 members out of a population of 2,500. By May the 2,700 members of St Ives were equal to half of the town's population. Similar successes came in towns and villages all over west Cornwall. Dr Harrison had suggested that the 'polarisation' of pub and temperance society was a predominantly urban phenomenon which spread later to the villages. If this was true of agricultural villages it was not so of Cornish mining ones. John Wesley had remarked of the Redruth Methodists as early as 1788 that they were very willing to 'govern the preachers' — a view which was echoed in 1909 when a minister complained that whereas in the towns the minister ruled, 'in the villages the chapel belongs to the people . . . and the people take over the minister as a newcomer attached to them'. The willingness of the local preachers and class leaders to involve themselves in the temperance and teetotal movements was evident, whatever the 'official' views of ministers and church establishment might be. Examples abound in the teetotal newspapers: at St Buryan in 1839 six out of eight class-leaders had joined; at Gwennap 18 and at Germoe the Wesleyan local preachers were reported to have taken up the cause in 'right good earnest'.[8]

The peak of the teetotal agitation in 1839 coincided with the visit to the mining districts of the Chartist missionaries Abraham Duncan and

Robert Lowery. They identified teetotalism closely with Methodism as a common enemy. 'The tee-totallers and the Methodists have monopolised the speakers, and their leaders are against us', grumbled Lowery. Duncan remarked that the Methodists had Cornwall 'divided into districts. The tee-totallers keep their division of territory . . . Between the religious and the tee-total agitation, a considerable amount of enterprise and talent is absorbed'. He found 'Pharisaical cant' omnipotent in every teetotal committee. The link was strengthened by the fact that, in Cornwall, the Bible Christians (Bryanites) were second only to the Wesleyans in number and influence and they were noted enthusiasts for total abstinance.[9] While we can, therefore, accept Professor Bailey's view that by the 1840s 'the single most important agency of recreational improvement was the rising Temperance movement', we must emphasise that in Cornwall by this time it reinforced and amplified long-standing sanctions and pressures.[10]

Behind the changing pattern of recreations in eighteenth- and nineteenth-century Cornwall can be discerned pressures broadly divisible into two main categories: the effects of the capitalistic transformation of the mining industry on the amount of leisure time available to the miners and, secondly, the pressures which can imprecisely but conveniently be summarised as 'evangelical'. This second category covers those who condemned the amusements of the miner on the grounds of inherent brutality, immorality, or general unspecified sinfulness. Such moral reformers usually aimed at substituting 'improving' uses of leisure time for traditional ones. Accordingly they must be considered a counter-attractive as well as a counteractive force.[11] From the mid-eighteenth century humane clergymen had attacked the brutality in many of the amusements of the poor and had been concerned to control the drunkenness which was associated with popular festivities. The Methodists went further: their puritanical distrust of enjoyment led them to regard secular amusement as inherently sinful, while their equally rigid abhorence of idleness made them of similar mind to those employers who for their own reasons condemned time-wasting.

Cornish miners enjoyed many holidays in the eighteenth century which were gradually eroded in the first half of the nineteenth. Holidays not associated with any particular custom were occasions for gatherings at which, apart from side-shows, beer-tents and dancing, the miners indulged in their traditional sports of hurling and wrestling. By the mid-eighteenth century accusations that such gatherings were characterised by excessive drinking, brawling and rowdyism were frequently levelled. Such games could be arranged for any holiday, but were especially associated with parish feasts. Borlase wrote in 1758:

> Every parish has its annual feast, and at such time (however poor at other times of the year) everyone will make a shift to entertain his friends and relations on the Sunday, and on the Monday and Tuesday all business is suspended, and the young men assemble and hurl or wrestle in some part of the parish of the most public resort.[12]

Hurling was not like the modern Irish version, but a traditional form of football played between teams of indeterminate size over several miles of country. Matches were usually promoted by local gentry who rewarded the victors and entertained the players to beer. The object was to carry the silver-encased ball to the goal, often a gentleman's house, in the face of the opposing side seeking to capture it and carry it to their goal several miles in the opposite direction. Sides could number several hundred and contests were rough and bloody:

> 'When this sort of hurling is over, you shall see the Hurlers retire as from a pitched battle, with bloody noses, wounds and bruises and some broken and disjointed limbs, which are all deemed fair play without ever consulting an Attorney, Coroner, or petty lawyer about the matter.'[13]

By the time Borlase wrote (1758) the game was largely confined to matches between teams from the same parish, inter-parish matches having shown a tendency to develop into local wars.[14]

Wrestling was probably a more frequently indulged pastime. It needed fewer participants and less time and space. In the eighteenth century it was also promoted by gentry who offered prizes and bet on results. *Ad hoc* contests frequently took place outside inns. The nature of the sport ensured its survival longer than hurling, which by the end of the eighteenth century was claimed to have become almost extinct. Although the same thing was still being said in 1824, Germoe feast in 1822 seems to have been the last at which it was a central feature of the programme. Primarily a holiday sport, it declined because the occasions for its holding were being eroded. This decline was certainly hastened by the reluctance of a more genteel gentry to promote what Defoe had described as a game fit only for barbarians. Polwhele, a clerical magistrate, thought this was so:

The discontinuance in frequency of such sports, indeed among the common people, is chiefly to be attributed to a change in the habits and manners of their superiors. In Carew's time [c. 1600] gentlemen used to entertain a numerous peasantry at their mansions and castles in celebration of the two great festivals, or the parish feast or harvest home; when at the same time that our halls re-echoed to the voice of festal merriment, our lawns and downs and woodlands were enlivened by the shouts of wrestling and of hurling. Hospitality is now banished from among us: and so are its attendant sports.[15]

Anglican clergymen did to a degree confront the conduct of popular amusements. Temple of St. Gluvias preached against bull-baiting in 1796. Borlase of Ludgvan sorrowed that immoderate 'frolicking and drinking' had made the parish feasts the target of those who would not distinguish between the institution and the 'disorderly observation of it'. The vicar of St Erme was praised for his preaching against wrestling, hurling and other 'robust exercises' which in the 1750s had characterised the parish feast.[16] Methodists altered the tone of condemnation. The sports themselves now seem to have acquired an inherent sinfulness. William Carvosso, a prominant local class-leader, wrote of his youth: 'I was borne down by the prevailing sins of the age; such as cock-fighting, wrestling, card-playing; and Sabbath breaking.'[17] Paying tribute to Wesley, a writer in 1814 listed wrestling and hurling along with drunkenness as the vices of the Cornish, which the broadsheet confessions of James Eddy, hanged at Bodmin in 1827 for a rape and robbery he denied, explains that he got into bad habits in his youth: 'smuggling, Sabbath breaking, adultery, drinking, pilfering, gaming, wrestling etc. and thus got a bad name'.[18] From their first footholds in the county the Wesleys had condemned wrestling. Charles Wesley noted on only his second visit in 1744 that the Gwennap men had been unable to raise men enough for a wrestling match, 'all the Gwennap men being struck off the devil's list, and found wrestling against him not for him'.[19]

Claims for Methodist success in transforming the behaviour of the miners were put forward regularly by the early years of the nineteenth century. In 1802 a writer on the decline of wrestling — 'every old inhabitant of this county can tell you how very much it has declined' — argued that although the magistracy had done much to control 'assemblages of riot and murder', the contribution of the Methodists had been a substantial one.[20] Six years later an Anglican clergyman gave them the larger share of the credit for the fact that 'desperate wrestling matches . . . and inhuman cockfights . . . and riotous revellings' were becoming rarer.[21]

The tone of Methodist condemnation was strong. An advertisement in the *West Briton* in 1821, inserted to disuade match promoters from endangering the souls of miners, claimed that if converted miners were asked why they did not attend, they would reply that it was because of the commandment: 'Whether ye eat or drink, or whatsoever ye do, do all to the glory of God'. A letter in 1829 asked the miners:

Why do you not go to the wrestling? For eight good reasons Because I can employ my time better. Because it is throwing my money away. Because I wish not to be seen in bad company. Because I would not encourage idleness, folly and vice. Because I should set a bad example. Because God has forbidden it. 'Abstain from *all* appearance of evil' . . . Because I must soon die.[22]

Although regularly denounced from the pulpit wrestling did survive, but the decline of open patronage drove it into closer alliance with the publicans.[23] Inns and beershops continued to play a significant role in the recreational life of many miners. It was noted in 1839 that no sooner did mining operations commence in a district than a beershop was opened to induce the 'honest but thoughtless' miner to spend his money by drawing him into 'haunts of vice' — pubs offering skittles, quoits and pitch and toss. Pay days, it was complained, were frequently spent in the beershops in weekend-long celebrations, and work itself offered customary opportunities for drinking. When a boy first took on a man's work a treat was expected and promotion to sump-man, pit-man or captain carried the like obligation.[24]

The view that the second quarter of the nineteenth century was a 'bleak age' before a post-1850 reconstruction of popular leisure needs qualification. As Dr Cunningham has pointed out, there were respects in which it was rather a period of vigorous growth of popular leisure.[25] Robert Storch has suggested that one reason that temperance reformers such as Joseph Livesey saw a desperate need for the 'moral improvement' of the masses was the real profusion of pub-centred gambling and sporting activities in early Victorian cities. If there had not been a variety of other popular indulgences, the counter-attractive side of temperance reform would not have needed so much emphasis.[26]

The Rev. Thomas Collins took the children of the Camborne Wesleyan Sunday School on a seaside trip in 1849 to give them pleasure and to remove them from the influence of a 'noisy, revelling' fair. He even composed a special hymn for the occasion:

> We rejoice, and we have reason,
> Though we don't attend the fair;
> Better spend the happy season
> Breathing in the fresh sea air.
>   Happy Children!
> What a number will be there!

To coincide with another fair he held special evening services to 'guard our young people'.[27] The annual tea-treat for Sunday scholars had become a widespread insititution by the 1820s. Teas were followed by recitations of amazing length from prize scholars and there was much flag waving, banner carrying and processioning.

In the early days the Methodists had represented a minority culture distinguished from their neighbours by their attitudes and behaviour. Their activities centred on the chapel with its services, revivals, meetings, love-feasts, watch-nights and hymn singing. By the nineteenth century it had grown from a minority culture into one which imparted generally observable traits to the mining community. With growing strength, confrontation between Methodists and 'revellers' became more frequent. Even before the end of the eighteenth century, Sithney Methodists were confident enough to try and drown the noise of the feast by singing psalms and were stoned for their pains.[28]

By the early years of the nineteenth century Methodists were strong enough to move from their village strongholds into the towns and the fair as well as the feast became an area of confrontation. The Wesleyan minister at Camborne held services on the fairground in 1840. Nor did the annual games escape. At St Austell the Primitive Methodists held a camp meeting on the site on the Sunday before the games. They offered fervent prayer that God might stay 'the prevalence of vice, and abolish the Sabbath desecrating custom'. One of the intending umpires was actually converted and although the games were held, they were so in a more retired place on the outskirts of the town.[29]

Counter-attractive measures were used on a greater scale by the teetotallers. Miners were marched around behind banners and bands, their thirsts quenched with gallons of weak tea and their need for excitement and involvement met by meetings dominated by the passionate oral rendering of hard-won struggles with temptation. The distance between the Methodists and the recreational patterns of the old popular culture had been widened as gentry patronage had given way to publican promotion. Opposition was now carried to the point of fanaticism. The abstainers' banner at a Penzance rally proclaimed simply: 'Eight thousand drunkards die annually and go to Hell'.[39]

Attempts had been made before to deal with the drinking of the lower orders. A Society for the Suppression of Drunkenness had been formed at Redruth in 1805 to exert pressure on local officers of the peace to enforce laws against drunkenness and to offer rewards to informers.[31] But this was an attempt of the socially superior to enforce sobriety on their inferiors: teetotalism enlisted the poor themselves in the campaign against the public house. As Dr Harrison has pointed out: 'Tee-totallers transformed temperance meetings from occasional gatherings of influential worthies . . . into counter-attractive functions enabling working men to insulate themselves from public-house temptation.' In this way a bond between the middle-class and working-class 'respectables' was consolidated.[32]

In 1838 the teetotallers held a grand field day at Redruth. Following a sermon in the market place the members marched behind a band through the streets with flags, ribbons and banners flying. They returned to the market place where about 300 took tea before leaving once again behind the band for the Methodist chapel where at a large meeting many new members were joined.[33] The observance of the annual feast at Ludgvan in 1839 was a major departure from precedent. It was celebrated by teetotallers who, after meeting in the church-town, marched three miles through the village. The local newspaper recalled the scene twelve months previously:

> the parish was one scene of revelry and drunkenness: and it seemed as if destruction had taken hold of the four corners of it. There were four public houses and twelve beershops: and in these no less than £6000 was annually spent in intoxicating drinks. At present it is a rare thing to see a man drunk, unless he comes from another parish. Not a quarter part of the money is spent on drink; and those who formerly wasted their time and their earnings in the ale-house, are found decently clothed, with their families in places of religious worship.[34]

The excitement of bands and processions, the encouragement of a sense of direct personal involvement and the invitation to the working man to be a hero (at least for the moment that he signed the pledge or testified to his salvation from drink) were designed to wean workers from traditional recreations and old patterns of living. A mile-long procession of Rechabites through Camborne and Redruth in 1841 was described by a local diarist as 'a very grand sight indeed'. He also commented that a wrestling held at the same time near the Brewery was 'very slightly attended'.[35] Two years later an even longer and more grand procession of Rechabites and teetotallers perambulated Redruth before assembling for an open-air meeting at Plainanguarry — literally 'playing place' in the Cornish language, that is a site for the holding of popular amusements from time immemorial — followed by tea in a local chapel. After the tea a crowded meeting completed a successful day. The diarist could not resist concluding his entry for that day by noting that a drunken miner returning from a spree on the mineral train fell off and had his hand cut off.[36]

A glance at the Whitsun weekend of 1844 is instructive on the extent to which the alternative provision of counter-attractions had succeeded in winning adherents. Whitsun was a traditional holiday period favoured in particular by travelling fairs. It is to be expected that teetotallers would have made a special effort during it. Truro fair was reported ill-attended in comparison with previous years. A local newspaper commented especially on the absence of young people, noticeably of the mine-girls who from 'time immemorial' had been accustomed to attend the fair in their 'ill-assorted dresses, in every variety of colour'. Camborne fair was also badly attended despite fine weather and as good a supply of amusements as usual. In contrast, the other side did really well. At Rudruth the Rechabites and teetotallers held a festival which was celebrated with 'more than usual gaiety', with large crowds thronging the streets until late evening. At Hayle the abstainers mustered a parade with three bands.[37]

By the early 1850s organised railway excursions added to the counter-attractions. One, in 1852, carrying the Camborne teetotallers to the sands of Hayle in 76 trucks, was celebrated in song:

Steam is up and we are ready;
See the engine puffing goes!
Keep your heads cool, and be steady
Mind your cups and mind your clothes.

Apprehension was in order, if a local news report is to be believed, for on the return journey the engine ran out of steam and the excursionists took the chance of raiding an orchard alongside the track.[38]

Building on pre-existing Methodist attitudes the teetotal movement may have had greater success in Cornwall among the miners than it had among most occupational groups. The tightness of the mining villages with those disproportionately large Methodist chapels which are still the visible reminders of a great culture influence suited the hold as well as the spread of religious movements. By 1864 an outsider could describe Cornish parish feasts as a 'sorry sight' where the offerings of drinking, sack races and donkey derbys had ceased to attract the mass of the people. He attributed this to the success of temperance in removing 'the great object of attraction':

> The majority derive far more amusement at assisting in the numerous tea drinks connected with the Sunday Dissenting Schools . . . the drinks are also held on a variety of occasions, thus if a chapel has to be repaired, or a new one built, or a missionary meeting to be held, the same ceremony accompanies it.

Plain fare was compensated for by 'intellectual' plenty, for the speakers were many and their orations lengthy.[39] Others commented in similar vein. 'Wrestling is almost discontinued, except as a publican's speculation', remarked one. 'But the spirit of aggregation rather finds a vent in camp-meetings, temperance parties, and monster tea-drinkings'.[40]

The assessment of success of religious and temperance reformers in their contest with 'revelry' must be impressionistic: influences of this kind cannot be measured easily. Probably the initial 'novelty' element of teetotalism wore off to an extent, and people went back to old ways to join again those who had never left them. It is not easy to judge how rapidly this happened, for as the novelty wore off so too did the inclination of the local press to report temperance activities. Perhaps we can balance the picture we have so far given with examples of revellers inflicting the bitter taste of failure on abstainers. In 1845 Thomas Trevaskis, a Bible Christian known as the 'Temperance Father of the West', was defeated by the forces of revelry at Padstow. In the previous year he had spoken against the oldest of all the Cornish festivals, the Padstow Hobby-horse. He had described its celebration as a scene of 'riot, debauchery and general licentiousness – a perfect nuisance to all the respectable inhabitants of the place', and backed his condemnation with the public offer to substitute a fat bullock to be roasted on the day for the next seven years:

> To the Proprietors of the Hobby Horse of Padstow. This is to give notice that on or about the end of the month. I shall offer you the bullock, according to promise. It is for you to consult against that time, whether you will give up your vain practice of the Hobby for the more rational amusement of eating roast beef.

On the 1st day of May he drove his bullock into town. The people persisted in their preference for irrational amusement and, with a hail of stones, drove him out of town, bullock and all.[41]

Trevaskis was not the only Bible Christian to confront the celebrators of the 'hoss'. In 1846 some members of that sect bound for Canada as missionaries were much disturbed when some Padstow men among the crew rigged up their own 'hoss' from canvas. The rider and his helpers galloped about the deck in the time-honoured tradition of the ceremony and endeavoured to blacken the faces of all who had not prudently retired below decks. One of the missionaries stood his ground, but received a blackened face despite the poker which he brandished in defiance of such satanic revelry.[42]

In 1843 the teetotal societies of east Cornwall had arranged a meeting on the slopes of Roughtor on the Bodmin Moor. Despite damp, misty weather 3,000 persons attended. The following year they tried to repeat their success. This time 10,000 attended, but the increase was not entirely accounted for by teetotallers, far from it. The publicans of the neighbouring parishes, who had been impressed with the size of the last crowd, seized the opportunity. They attracted many people by promising that they too would come to Roughtor with booths, stalls, donkey-riding and other amusements. A day which was to have been a great demonstration of strength by the abstainers instead earned for itself the unlikely name for a teetotal rally of the 'Roughtor Revels'. It was small consolation that one of the publicans was subsequently fined for selling outside the area of his licence.[43]

Such setbacks show the incompleteness of teetotal success, but they should not be allowed to detract too much from the very real impact which the movement had. Many of the moral reformers may seem quaint, many of the incidents of confrontation amusing, but it should not be forgotten that the recreational reformers were in deadly earnest. If we shift our focus from the community to the individual we enter a realm of internal mental conflict: the hard and painful balancing of enjoyment against damnation. The struggle was for more than the leisure time of the miner. It was for commitment to a changed style of life. An account of the religious revival of 1824 notes: 'Among the vile and profane tinners that have been subdued . . . is a noted wrestler. . . [he] thanks God that among all the prizes which he has won he has now the best'.[44]

II

The second aspect of the influence of religion on the life of the mining communities which will be considered is the relationship of Methodism to pre-existing popular beliefs and attitudes. Certainly there is much to support Dr Harrison's suggestion that Christian attempts to dominate their leisure brought the working classes most clearly into contact with the churches. But there is a danger in this approach to popular culture. Gareth Stedman Jones has, as we have noted, stressed the dangers of a 'social control' perspective which neglects to consider the class expression of the workers themselves.[45] Labour historians, already accustomed to see Methodism as an inhibition on the growth of popular radicalism and as a carrier of the work disciplines of industrialism, tend to view it as an external force attempting to shape the working class into respectability. This is not an incorrect perspective, but it is not a complete one. Whatever it was in the towns, village Methodism was not completely dominated by the middle class. Teetotalism was not new in many aspects of its working-class activism. Village Methodism through its local preachers and class leaders had from its formative years gloried in the participation of working people. Those who impressed the virtues of sobriety and industry on the Sunday scholars and those who contested with the ale-houses were as likely to be neighbours and work-fellows as they were social superiors.

It has already been argued that the enormous success of teetotalism in Cornwall was in greatest measure due to the fact that the county had long been a great Methodist stronghold. If the reasons for Methodism's success among the miners are examined, then it appears that with its dark areas of superstition and its anti-intellectualism it was less in conflict with many traditional forms of belief and action than a self-reliant rationalism would have been. A traditional Methodist historiography which offers a universal-panacea theory of the movement's success in west Cornwall distorts the true picture. According to this tradition the 'depraved' tinners lived without fear of God and without the benefit of 'experimental religion': swearing, fornicating, drinking, fighting, wrecking, smuggling, profaning the Sabbath with an unconcerned regularity and in general living a life of unchecked sinfulness.[46] Then came John Wesley, whose teaching filled every moral, spiritual and social need of the hitherto deprived Cornish.

Such explanations are, to say the least, partial. Even had the Anglican church really been inadequate in every way since the

Reformation, it would be difficult to believe that the common people of west Cornwall lived for two centuries in a moral and cultural vacuum, facing the changes of fortune and harsh demands of the world with a self-reliance and certainty out of keeping with their level of sophistication and the narrowness of their intellectual horizons, or else living in unsupported misery, reeling from a fate they could not begin to understand and finding oblivion only in alcohol or relief in mindless violence. They were not, of course, without religion. Village people living to a large extent outside the culture of literacy came to possess a background of beliefs, partly religious, partly magic, against which they sought to understand the realities of existence: both the ups and downs of life and those calamities like fire, flood, fever or storm which pressed so heavily on people living close to the margins of subsistence. Dr Obelkevich has shown how the 'religious realm' of the labourers of south Lincolnshire in the nineteenth century reached beyond Christianity to 'encompass an abundance of pagan magic and superstition'. In addition, popular religion included conceptions of Christian doctrine which were adapted and transformed as they passed from the church to the cottage.[47]

In Cornwall the miners and fishermen among whom Methodism grew so rapidly both pursued occupations in which the role of luck was considerable. Fishermen were not only dependent upon wind and tide, but in some seasons the migrating shoals on which their livelihood depended failed to appear in their usual abundance. Miners paid under the tribute system were remunerated according to the value of the mineral ore which they raised, and chance played a large part in determining whether their place in the mine was a good or bad one.[48] Both miners and fishermen faced unusually high risks of death or injury. Small wonder that they attributed power over the sea or the mine to other agencies than those which ruled on land or above ground. Fishermen would not put to sea if a clergyman were seen near their boats and miners would not permit the sign of the cross to be made underground.[49]

Underground spirits were known as 'knockers'. Related to the piskey (pixie) they were said to be in the spirits of Jews who had worked the mines in Roman times. Morally neutral, they brought good or bad fortune according to the treatment they received. They could indicate the location of good ores by knocking with their hammers, but they could bring injury or death to those who treated them with hostility or scepticism. Above ground in the everyday life of the community, changes in fortune could be explained by the struggle of good with evil spirits. Sometimes a human agency, the witch, was involved, especially in small communities in which a personal relationship between the bewitcher and the bewitched could be identified. A clergyman of considerable local standing and literary reputation claimed in 1826 that within his memory there had been conjuring persons and cunning clerks. Every blacksmith had been a doctor, every old woman a witch. In short all nature had been united in 'sympathising with human credulity; in predicting or in averting, in relieving or in aggravating misfortune'. He went further to claim that some of the rusticated clergy reinforced popular superstition by pretending to the power of laying ghosts and hinted that he could name some whose influence over their flocks was largely attributable to this pretence. Well into the nineteenth century Curate Richards of Camborne was reputedly seen by miners attempting to lay the ghost of the recently dead squire with a whip. Some saw utility in popular superstition, fearing that when finally removed from the popular mind 'religion would languish if not expire'. 'The decline of superstition', one remarked, 'has made the people very irreligious'.[50]

More sophisticated clergymen had little sympathy. They could not, as Obelkevich had pointed out, avoid being hostile to what they regarded as 'a mass of dimly perceived beliefs that were deviant at best and heathen at worst'.[51] The Rev. William Borlase reprimanded a parishioner who claimed to be able to recover lost or stolen goods by conjuration. He warned him not to meddle with the 'dangerous mysteries of the lower world' and to refuse all intercourse with the devil. While Methodists tended to confine their attribution of powers to God and the devil, and were said in 1817 to be under their 'soul-subduing' power emancipating the miners from the 'terrors of imagination', much evidence suggests that not only did that 'emancipation' take a long time, but while it was being pursued many elements from Methodism itself were being taken up and absorbed into the very popular culture with which it was contesting.[52]

Methodism did not so much replace folk-beliefs as translate them into a religious idiom. Neither witchcraft not spirit-agency as an explanation of events precludes commonsense empirical observation. Men die because they happen to be at a moment in time under a fall of rock. What needs explaining is why that man was in that place at that time. Witchcraft, as Max Gluckman has observed, explains that singularity of misfortune which the agnostic or scientific mind prefers to see as 'chance'.[53] In modern British history no church of comparable weight has allowed a greater degree of comprehensiveness or frequency to devine or satanic intervention than did early Methodism. The idea of an omnipotent deity and a malicious devil can explain singularity of misfortune as well as can witches or evil spirits. The retributive anger of God can explain the most widespread of disasters.

The credulousness of the miners was an essential feature of their ready acceptance of the teachings of John Wesley. They could be responsive to his message not because he demanded a new and rational view of the world, but because he did not. Methodism did not ask that a man fully understand his environment. He need only realise that what was incomprehensible to him had purpose for a God who owed him no explanation. Not that good furtune necessarily followed the good, for the tests of faith could be very stiff. After all, the rewards which the wicked might reap in this world were as nothing compared with the retribution awaiting them after death. The hand of God was seen in everything from bee stings to earthquakes: 'That God is himself the author and sin the moral cause of earthquakes; (whatever the natural cause may be,) cannot be denied', wrote John Wesley. Preaching once at St Just, he was troubled by the sun in his eyes, but a cloud suddenly appeared from nowhere and covered the sun. 'Is anything', he remarked, 'too small for the providence of him by whom our very hairs are numbered?' The evangelical *Cornish Banner* published an account of the East Wheal Rose mine flood of 1846. Among the 1,260 persons employed there, it concluded, many surely had been of 'a very wicked and abandoned character'. The flooding of the mine was viewed as 'a judgement' and as 'a loud appeal' to other miners: 'Be ye also ready; for in such an hour as ye think not, the Son of man cometh!'[54]

The hand of God could be seen in the varying fortunes of the miner working on tribute. If he did well it was Providence which blessed his labours; if not, then it was his faith which was being tested. In matters such as disputes over the siting of chapels the wishes of the Lord were ascertained by the casting of lots. Divine intervention was never more dramatic than when the Lord's people were safeguarded. The Helston class was meeting when one of its members had a premonition of danger. They left straightaway, just before a spark ignited some gunpowder stored in an adjacent room. 'So', Wesley concluded, 'did God preserve those who trusted in him'. Conversely the suffering or demise of an adversary also showed God's power. With no small degree of satisfaction Wesley recorded the suicide of a Cornish clergyman who had opposed the Methodists and in his journal for 1757 we find:

His wife promised Mr P. before he died that she would always receive the preachers, but she soon changed her mind. God has just taken her only son, suddenly killed by a pit falling upon him, and on Tuesday last a young strong man, riding to his burial, dropped off his horse stone dead. The concurrence of these awful providences added considerably to our congregation.[55]

Such attitudes prevailed into the nineteenth century. In 1839 a Primitive Methodist minister entered in his diary a blow-by-blow account of God's dealings with his opposers:

Looking over the way God has lead me it is mysterious. I have been here four years. My opposers have so far been put down. When I came into the circuit 264 members now 970. Enemies put down and others that opposed suffered. Bromsle ill Penzance, Coulson gone out of his mind, Elias wife ill two years, Moon ill Penzance, Mr Blazey died suddenly, June 24th 1838, the day I should be removed he wrote against me. He was Mayor of St Ives. Strange mother died, sister died, brother-in-law drowned. Mary Pollard lost 6/-. Cheel married old woman . . .[56]

A book published in 1837 relates a tradition that when Charles Wesley visited the St Just society it was suffering severe persecution from Squire Eustick. Wesley pronounced, 'The man who has troubled you this day shall trouble you no more for ever.' Within a few weeks the squire died insane. The impression made on the popular mind was a strong one. Significantly, the popular memory recorded in 1837 differs from Charles Wesley's own account. He recorded that he asked 'that the door might again be opened, and that he who hinders might be taken out of the way as God knew best'. Eustick certainly died soon after and it is not difficult to see how Charles Wesley's more guarded statement became transformed into the unequivocal pronouncement which popular tradition attributed to him.[57]

The starkness of many aspects of Methodist theology enabled it to be woven in existing folk-beliefs, the more especially since its regular interpreters were not the educated Wesleys but the local preachers and class leaders. Such men could be regarded as the interpreter, or even agency, of God's will, just as witches or conjurers were agencies through which darker powers operated. At their simplest the powers of intercession attributed to a local preacher might amount to no more than a belief that through prayer he could secure fine weather for feast days.[58]

Such interminglings were especially evident in the nineteenth century in those rural areas being freshly evangelised by the Bible Christians. In one village the bullock of a local farmer-preacher died. Suspecting an old women of ill-wishing it, he roasted its heart and had his suspicions confirmed when the old woman woke up screaming. Both he and the woman were members of the Bible Christians and the burning of the heart was accompanied by a reading from the Bible. A miner from the same sect who was thought to have powers of conjuration was reprimanded by a fellow miner whose pig he had failed to find: 'Ah William, you are not so pious as you used to be, or you could have instantly told me where to find my pig'. A folklorist of the late nineteenth century records an ill-wishing in 1870 which is remarkable not so much for its lateness as for the fact that the woman regarded as responsible was a 'blackslider'. Since marriage she had ceased to attend chapel. In a village where Methodists were dominant, it is not surprising that a woman who reacted against their influence – she had called them a 'set of duffans and back-biting and undermining hypocrites' – was regarded as having at least some link with the forces of evil.[59]

Obelkevich has remarked on the central role of the devil in popular culture, and certainly in Cornwall the influence of Methodism gave him a special importance. The holder of a Cornish living in the 1850s noted the frequency with which his parishioners reported dreams of Jesus and the devil: 'these are real persons to the Cornish mind, and their power is respectively acknowledged'.[60] Although physical manifestations of God, Father or Son, were rarely reported (though one convert at a Bodmin revival did see Christ no less than three times with his naked eye), sightings of the devil were frequent. Even sophisticated Methodists, like the distinguished philosopher Samuel Drew, believed they had seen the devil, or at least his messenger. Satan or his agent was usually bestial in form, described as ressembling a large shaggy dog or bear, always hairy and with eyes that glowed fiercely red.[61]

Billy Bray was the best-known miner-preacher of the Victorian era. Once passing a shaft where some miners had been recently killed, he became convinced they would materialise from the invisible world. They did not, but approaching a second shaft which had to be crossed on a narrow bridge he became even more convinced that the devil awaited him on the bridge. He explained:

The devil! who is he? what can he do? The devil is a fallen angel! He was turned out of Heaven by God! He is held in chains! I am

Billy Bray! God is my heavenly Father! Why should I fear the devil? ... Come on, then thou devil; I fear thee not! Come on Lucifer, and all demons! Come on, old ones and young ones, black ones and blue ones, fiery and red-hot ones, come on devil and all thy ugly hosts!

Bray got so used to the devil's attempts to frighten him or lead him astray than he familiarly referred to him as 'Old smutty face'.[62]

John Wesley himself believed in ghosts and witches. By substituting the devil and his bestial messenger for 'knockers' and piskeys, Methodism did not substitute reason for superstition. By and large it successfully translated that superstition, but the triumph of the religious idiom came only after a period of intermingling of Methodist and folk-beliefs. Methodist superstition matched the indigenous superstition of the common people. Perhaps it was not intended, but the match in Cornwall was sufficient to contribute to the consolidation of one of their strongest congregations.[63]

A folklorist found in the late nineteenth century that the circles of standing stones, relics of Cornwall's stone-age culture, had come to be regarded as petrified young people who had sported on the Sabbath. Here we have together, superstition, divine retribution and condemnation of 'sport'.[64]

Notes

1. G. Stedman Jones, 'Class expression versus Social Control? a critique of recent trends in the social history of "leisure"', *History Workshop,* no.4 (Autumn 1977), p.165.

2. *Report of the Royal Commission on Child Employment,* PP ((1842), vol. 16, Report of Charles Barham, p.760; H. Miles Brown, 'Methodism and the Church of England in Cornwall 1738-1838', unpublished PhD thesis, University of London, 1947, p.170; *Old Cornwall* (1961), vol.5, pt.12, p.519.

3. Stedman Jones, 'Class expression versus Social Control', pp.162-3.

4. For a most useful recent survey see H. Cunningham, *Leisure in the Industrial Revolution* (London, 1980); Stedman Jones, 'Class Expression versus Social Control', p.165.

5. B. Harrison, 'Religion and Recreation in Nineteenth-century England', *Papers presented to the Past and Present Conference on Popular Religion* (7 July 1966), p.2.

6. John Wesley, *Journal* (Everyman ed., 1906), vol.1, pp.420, 425, vol.2, pp.99, 265 (entries dated 1 Apr. 1743, 10 July 1743, 15 May 1749 & 4 Aug. 1766).

7. B. Harrison, *Drink and the Victorians. The Temperance Question in England 1815-1872* (London, 1971), p.180; M.S. Edwards, 'The Tee-total Wesleyan Methodists', *Proceedings of the Wesleyan Historical Society* (1961),

vol.33, pts.3-4, pp.66-7; Harrison, *Drink and the Victorians,* p.109.
    8. H.L. Douch, *Old Cornish Inns* (Truro, 1967), pp.108-9; T. Shaw, *History of Cornish Methodism* (Truro, 1967), p.78; R. Currie, *Methodism Divided* (London, 1968), pp.30-1; *Cornwall Tee-total Journal* (Feb., Apr. and May 1839); B. Harrison, 'Pubs' in H.J. Dyos and M. Wolff (eds.), *The Victorian City. Images and Realities* (Paperback ed., London, 1976), vol.1, *Past and Present/Number of People* pp.161-2.
    9. British Museum Add. Mss. 34,245, vol.A, vol.148; Harrison, *Drink and the Victorians,* p.180.
    10. P. Bailey, *Leisure and Class in Victorian England. Rational Recreation and the contest for control, 1830-1885* (London, 1978), p.47.
    11. I discussed the pressures stemming from the new disciplines imposed by the mines in 'Some social aspects af the Industrial Revolution in Cornwall', in R. Burt (ed.), *Industry and Society in the South West* (Exeter, 1970), pp.71-106.
    12. W. Borlase, *Natural History of Cornwall* (Oxford, 1758), pp.300-1;
    13. R . Heath, *A Natural and Historical Account of the Islands of Scilly and Lastly a General Account of Cornwall* (London, 1750), pp.437, 441.
    14. Borlase, *Natural History,* p.300.
    15. Ibid., p.304; R. Polwhele, *The Old English Gentleman* (London, 1797), p.114 (footnote); Douch, *Cornish Inns,* p.50; R. Polwhele (ed.), *Lavington's Enthusiasm of Methodists and Papists Compared* (London, 1833), pp.cxxi-cxxii. For a general argument see the section 'The Withdrawal of the Upper Classes', in P. Burke, *Popular Culture in Early Modern Europe* (London, 1978), pp.270-81.
    16. L. Bettany (ed.), *Diaries of William Johnstone Temple* (Oxford, 1929), p.187; Borlase, *Natural History,* p.300; 'Account of a Tour in Cornwall', Pendarves Mss. Cornwall Record Office, Truro; R. Pococke, *Travels through England* (ed. J.J. Cartwright for Camden Society, London, 1888, reprinted 1965), p.136.
    17. B. Carvosso, *A Memoir of Mr. William Carvosso* (London, 1837), p.32.
    18. *Cornwall Gazette,* 19 Mar. 1814; Broadsheet in County Record Office, Truro.
    19. Charles Wesley, *Journal* entry for 4 Aug. 1744 (reprinted in J. Pearce, *The Wesleys in Cornwall* (Truro, 1964), p.49.
    20. *Cornwall Gazette,* 18 Sept. 1802.
    21. R. Warner, *A Tour through Cornwall in 1808* (London, 1809), pp.300-1.
    22. *West Briton,* 2 Nov. 1821, 24 July 1829.
    23. Anon., *Letters from West Cornwall written in 1826* (London 1861), p.71.
    24. 'Drinking Customs of the Cornish Miners', *Cornwall Tee-total Journal,* vol. I, no.9, supplement August 1839.
    25. Cunningham, *Leisure in the Industrial Revolution,* p.9.
    26. R. Storch, 'The Problem of Working-class Leisure. Some Roots of Middle-class Reform in the Industrial North', in A.P. Donajgrodski (ed.) *Social Control in Nineteenth-Century Britain* (London, 1977), p.153.
    27. S. Coley, *Life of the Rev. Thomas Collins* (London, 1871), pp.297-9.
    28. R. Polwhele, *Anecdotes of Methodism* (London, 1801), pp.28-9.
    29. *West Briton,* 3 July 1840; J. Petty, *History of the Primitive Methodist Connexion* (London, 1880), pp.28-9.
    30. Douch, *Cornish Inns,* p.109.
    31. R. Polwhele, *History of Cornwall,* vol.7 (London, 1806), p.100.
    32. B. Harrison, 'Religion and Recreation in Nineteenth-century England', *Past and Present,* no.38 (1967), p.106.
    33. 'A Redruth Diary', *Old Cornwall,* vol.5, p.178.
    34. *Cornwall Gazette,* 1 Feb. 1839.
    35. 'A Redruth Diary', p.103.

36. Cornwall County Record Office. Mss. Diary of Thomas Nicholl, entry 5 June 1843.

37. *West Briton,* 31, May 1844.

38. D. St. J. Thomas, *A Regional History of the Railways of Great Britain* (London, 1960), vol.I, *The West Country,* p.104. Mr Thomas and other popular historians of the railway like to claim that the refrain was: Happy Camborne, Happy Camborne/Where the railway is so near/And the engine shows how water/Can accomplish more than beer. Sadly it was not so sung. The last two lines of the refrain are an added parody. See *Old Cornwall,* vol.2, pt.5, p.42. On the thin line separating 'respectability' and 'unrespectability' among the working class see P. Bailey, '"Will the Real Bill Banks Please Stand Up?" Towards a Role Analysis of Mid-Victorian Working-class Respectability', *J. of Social History,* vol.12 (1979), pp.336-53.

39. 'Social Condition of the Cornish Miner', in *Western Morning News,* 10 Aug. 1864.

40. *Quarterly Review* (1857), p.34.

41. *West Briton,* 31 May 1844; L. Maker, *Cob and Moorstone* (London, 1935), p.48.

42. Shaw, *Cornish Methodism,* p.69.

43. Douch, *Cornish Times,* p.111.

44. Methodist Archives. Fletcher-Tooth Correspondence, John Radford to Mrs Tooth, 30 Jan. 1824.

45. Stedman-Jones, 'Class Expression versus Social Control'. For an evaluation of the concept and its relevance to nineteenth-century Britain see introduction by A.P. Donajgrodzki to *Social Control in Nineteenth-century Britain.*

46. For example: 'There is no more splendid page in the Methodist annals than the transformation of Cornwall. Quite apart from the viciousness and lawlessness which prevailed; there was almost a total ignorance of religion. Churches were unattended, and the very phraseology of religion had become obsolete.' (M. Edwards, *John Wesley and the Eighteenth Century* (London, 1935), p.160.)

47. I researched this subject area in my post-graduate days (see my unpublished thesis, 'The Labouring-miner in Cornwall, c.1740-1870: a Study in Social History', University of Warwick, 1971, pp.240-607). The systematic and perceptive study of Dr Obelkevich seems to suggest that I was on the right lines and that a more thorough investigation of Cornwall would produce conclusions generally in line with his. J. Obelkevich, *Religion and Rural Society: South Lindsey, 1825-75* (Oxford, 1976), pp.258-61.

48. For a detailed account of the tribute system see Rule, thesis, pp.34-71.

49. R. Hunt, *Popular Romances of the West of England* (London, 1881), p.349.

50. R. Polwhele, *Traditions and Recollections,* vol.2 (London, 1826), p.605; *Old Cornwall,* vol.2, no.2 (1931), p.3; Mss. Journal of Christopher Wallis, County Museum, Truro, entry 7 Nov. 1795.

51. Obelkevich, *Religion and Rural Society,* p.262.

52. P.A.S. Pool, 'William Borlase', *Journal of the Royal Institute of Cornwall,* New Series, vol.5, pt.2 (1966), p.151; C.S. Gilbert, *Historical Survey of Cornwall,* vol.1 (Plymouth, 1817), pp.104-5.

53. Max Gluckman, *Custom and Conflict in Africa* (Oxford, 1955), pp.83-4.

54. John Wesley, *Works* (London, 1830-1), vol.7, p.386; *Journal,* entry 6 Sept. 1755 (from Pearce, *Wesleys in Cornwall,* p.123). *Cornish Banner* (1846), p.57.

55. John Wesley, *Journal,* entries 7 and 13 Sept. 1755 and 5 Sept. 1757 (from Pearce, *Wesleys in Cornwall,* pp.124, 126-7).

56. J.C.C. Probert, *Primitive Methodism in Cornwall* (Redruth, 1966), p.68.

57. R. Treffry Jnr, *Memoirs of Mr John Edwards Tresize* (London, 1837), p.31; Pearce, *Wesleys in Cornwall,* entry 21 July 1746, p.55.

58. *Cornish Magazine,* vol.2 (1898), p.224.

59. 'Social condition of the Cornish miner', *Western Morning News,* 16 June 1865; W. Bottrell, *Traditions and Hearthside Stories of West Cornwall* (Penzance, 1873), pp.285-6.

60. Obelkevich, *Religion and Rural Society,* pp.276-9; W. Haslam, *From Death into Life* (London, n.d.), pp.52-3.

61. *Cornish Guardian,* 30 Mar. 1853; J.H. Drew, *Samuel Drew — The Self-taught Cornishman* (London, 1861), pp.33-4.

62. F.W. Bourne, *The King's Son. A Memoir of Billy Bray* (London, 1898), p.70.

63. On Wesleyanism and superstition see E.P. Thompson, 'Anthropology and the Discipline of Historical Context', *Midland History,* vol.1, pt.1 (1971), pp. 54-5.

64. Hunt, *Popular Romances,* p.177.

4 'PLEASE TO REMEMBER THE FIFTH OF NOVEMBER': CONFLICT, SOLIDARITY AND PUBLIC ORDER IN SOUTHERN ENGLAND, 1815-1900*

Robert D. Storch

I

'Please to remember the Fifth of November.
Up with the ladder, down with the rope
Please give us a penny to burn the old pope.[1]

Southern market and county towns were largely passed over by many moulding forces of nineteenth-century history — rapid urbanisation, factories, trade unionism, Chartism and other popular movements — and they have been generally passed over by social historians as well. A literature on social structure, class relations, local politics and economic change hardly exists. One must, therefore, travel across this terrain with neither an Ordnance Survey map nor even a rudimentary sketch provided by a crossroads rustic. Nevertheless this study may open, if not a window, perhaps a peephole into some processes of cultural and social change in this region.

The Fifth of November was once the most important occasion on the popular calendar in many small southern towns. Its celebration involved the youth and young manhood of labouring, craft, shopkeeper and tradesman elements. At both the beginning and end of our period — though in different ways — the upper classes provided patronage or a moral sanction, and sometimes physically participated. One major theme will be the impact of local elites through the withdrawal and subsequent re-extension of patronage.

Most eighteenth-century incorporated towns held official celebrations whose features were official processions, the provision of drink, wood and fireworks, and the mingling of elites and plebeians round the bonfire. Respectable tradesmen often held their own tavern dinner, sometimes preceded by a separate procession. Some of these survived into the nineteenth century — in Hampton, Middlesex, for example, to 1878. Lewes and Great Torrington churchwardens paid for wood, gunpowder, ringers and flagbearers, and the Guildford corporation patronised a popular demonstration at least through the 1780s. Until

71

a brief Liberal capture of the reformed corporation in the 1830s, the Exeter Guildhall was illuminated and mayor and corporation marched in solemn procession to the cathedral to give thanks for James I's deliverance. In Chelmsford and Battle gentry patronage lasted until the 1850s.[2] Attempts had been made in the 1780s, largely resulting from concern about fire danger, to suppress bonfires which were not built and monitored by official elements; but there were few moves to stop Fifth-of-November celebrations entirely.

The Fifth had been of interest to the upper classes because it was a commemorative rite marking the failure of a plot which, in their view, could have changed history and suppressed 'English Liberty'. It symbolised the survival of certain institutions − even the nation itself.[3] Despite the progressive withdrawal of the upper classes, the early-nineteenth-century southern populace continued to believe that demonstrations were prescribed by the highest authority. Many a reformer would have to point to the 'mistake . . . respecting the subject. It is thought . . . that it has the sanction of the laws. [But the] legislature was too wise . . . to adopt anything so ridiculous.'[4]

Late-eighteenth-century small-town authorities, fearful of fire danger, made widespread attempts to suppress bonfires made by plebeians in the narrow streets of town centres, but they apparently gave no thought to entirely withdrawing either their physical presence or their patronage until the French Wars. Wartime hysteria, new concerns about public order and social discipline, official repression and the spectre of an artisan-based, Painite radicalism made the upper classes increasingly wary of patronising or participating in popular revels.[5] As the Fifth more and more became a vehicle for the vilification of local figures, this withdrawal became permanent. When official participation ceased, manifestations were left to be exclusively mounted by plebeian elements. This helps to account for the appearance in the nineteenth century of new phenomenon, the bonfire societies or gangs, whose function was to organise and stage bonfires and give direction to the crowds they led. Nineteenth-century demonstrations thus frequently became riotous, prolonged struggles between magistrates, police, bonfire societies and crowds. Attempts to stop them evoked violence and threats. In 1867 the mayor of Exeter was told:

> it will be to your sorrow if you dare . . . interfear [sic] with our rights and usage which has not been interfeared [sic] with for centuries. Fine one if you dare; look out for your shrubery [sic] and

your cot [sic] if you do when you little think of it.[6]

Even where popular manifestations were countenanced by gentry or town authorities, two distinct (but linked) 'versions' existed. In Exeter the official version consisted of church-bell ringing, official processions, prescribed sermons and illumination of municipal premises; the plebeian version centred upon the assembly in the cathedral yard, with its bonfires, tumult and effigy-burnings. But the former could never completely define the form or content of the latter, which drew on nearly the entire repertoire of plebeian public expression. The Fifth was marked by a general breakdown or reversal of the customary order and was a classical day of licence. A carpenter or butcher could appear as a woman or archbishop, disguise himself, carry arms, discharge fireworks and burn local big-wigs in effigy. In Durham, it was thought, nobody could be hanged on the Fifth; Lincolnshire farmers believed that on the Fifth they could shoot in the landowners' preserves, immune from all processes of law.[7] Like Basle Fasnacht, Guy Fawkes possessed

The . . . elements of a ritual of reversal . . . masks, aggresive music performed . . . by . . . organised and fantastically disguised groups of people . . . pictorial and verbal invectives against representatives of law and order as well as against fellow-citizens who notoriously manage their business on the edge of legality . . .[8]

The Fifth increasingly drew on a rich symbolic tradition of popular justice. The bonfire gang frequently decided the figure(s) to be burned in effigy. Those burned could be remote figures (the Pope), offenders against local standards of behaviour, or outsiders[9] threatening to upset neighbourhood affairs. Procedures could be highly formalised. In Horsham and Reigate the shoemakers publicly proclaimed the victim: 'An effigy . . . was on Crispin Day hung on the signpost of one . . . of the Public Houses . . . until the 5th of November, when it was taken down and burned.'[10] In Devon effigies were often paraded to rough music — whistle and kettle or tinpot bands. After 1850 the Fifth increasingly incorporated *actual* domestic charivaris for adulterers, irresponsible fathers and child-abusers in Devon.

When authorities decided to withdraw their patronage or attempt abolition they often found it impossible to draw the entire community along, for the Fifth continued to be supported by elements of small-town society extending beyond the labourers and artisans composing the bulk of the crowds. Sections of the provincial lower middle classes

— frequently the Tory section — never accepted that manifestations should cease; others would argue for reform not abolition. As magistrates and mayors attempted to abolish, transform or encourage the privatisation of the Fifth,[11] they often manufactured crises of communal solidarity and public order problems which evaded resolution for decades. In some old, stable Tory towns such as Exeter, the will to crush the popular demonstration was always feeble; besides, in such places, arcane upper-class quarrels could be easily transmitted to crowds and taken up by them. Effigies of the Bishop of Exeter were occasionally burned, as well as Tractarian or ritualist local clergy. Crowds often redirected their fury to the Church of England from the Church of Rome, burned effigies of tax inspectors, unscrupulous tradesmen, unpopular employers, police or magistrates. Manifestations spilled over into tarring and feathering, the burning of unseaworthy boats, or food price disturbances.[12]

II

Guy Fawkes demonstrations ranged from the small, rural gathering round the fire,[13] through rowdy free-form crowd scenes, to formalised corteges with elaborate banners, music or rough music, specially designated leaders or orators,[14] effigy burning and the dragging of tar-barrels through the streets. Bonfires and effigy burnings were usually held on a specific spot: in Exeter the cathedral yard, in Guildford opposite Holy Trinity, in Lewes before the County Hall. Attempts to move the locale often met with fierce resistance.

After two decades of fruitless attempts by Brighton authorities to restrict manifestations to the Steine, the High Constable tried to suppress them entirely in 1834. Bludgeon-carrying men smashed the windows in the High Constable's hotel, observing, 'When Mr. Sarel was constable he kicked the barrel himself and give the men 10s to git beer'.[15] Early in the century effigies almost always represented either the Pope or Guy Fawkes, but later included foreign enemies (the Czar, Nana Sahib), prominent criminals (Maria Manning, Müller), and local employers, policemen, moral offenders and clergy.

A specifically nineteenth-century development was the formation of secret or semi-secret bonfire gangs, known as 'Guys' or 'Bonfire Boys'. They apparently developed in Sussex, Surrey and Devon after the Napoleonic Wars and in Essex in the 1850s. By the 1880s most Sussex or Devon towns had their societies, but by then few were still secret and many were patronised – and occasionally reformed – by the middle classes to play a role in the increasingly denatured demonstrations of that period. The classic scene of 125 years ago saw the preliminary perambulation of the town by children begging coppers; but after dusk the young men, led by grotesquely disguised Bonfire Boys, came out to do the serious business. Some towns (Guildford, Chelmsford, Exeter) had only one gang; elsewhere (Lewes, Rye) there were several, based on wards or neighbourhoods of the town. What one might now observe on the Fifth is thus a fragment of a once larger whole, the rump of a popular féte which was once much more than a mere children's begging occasion.

Who composed Guy Fawkes crowds and the bonfire societies? The data below were compiled on 103 persons in 23 incidents appearing in courts in ten Sussex, Devon, Surrey and Essex locations between 1833 and 1877.[16] They suffer from the usual uncertainties: the 2 per cent unemployed is undoubtedly understated; 4 per cent are seemingly middle class, but in view of contemporary police practices this too may be understated. The vast majority were, of course, artisans and labourers and represented a clear cross-section of the trades of southern market and county towns.

Table 4.1: Occupations of Arrested Guy Fawkes Demonstrators, 1833-77

Accountant	1	Lads, boys	5
Baker	1	Militia officer	1
Barber	1	Painter	3
Bricklayer	1	Pauper	3
Broker	1	Plasterer	1
Cabinetmaker	1	Poulterer	1
Carpenter	5	Rag dealer	1
Carter	1	Railway servant	1
Cooper	1	Sailor	3
Cork-cutter	1	Shoemaker	3
Farmer	1	Smith	3
Fitter	1	Stableman	2
Foundryman	2	Sweep (master)	1
Gardener	4	Tailor	4
Grocer's asst	2	Unemployed	2
Groom	1	Unknown	23
Labourer	20	Women	1

Participants were largely young males. The average age of 16 persons treated for injuries at the hospital in Exeter in 1881 was 21; the average age of those arrested in a Colchester manifestation in 1875 was 19.[17]

The second question is more difficult because of the secrecy of the bonfire societies. These groups drew in the sons of shopkeepers and tradesmen, and received much financial and moral support from adults. Because many 'Guys' came from this stratum, occupations of those arrested in crowds led by them probably did not exactly mirror the composition of the societies. This was especially true in Guildford, Exeter and probably Lewes. Occasionally gangs were occupationally based. In Harwich and Maldon shipwrights formed their own parties and paraded with draft tools; in Rye the frequency of boat burnings and tarring and feathering indicated a large involvement of the fishing and marine population. We observed that in Horsham the bonfire gang was based on journeymen shoemakers. In Kingsteignton, whose major industry was clay-digging, the Guys were 'a set of clay-cutting roughs'. Similarly, in the shoemaking town of Crediton their identity was plain 'from their . . . proportions and . . . aprons'. In much larger centres (e.g. Exeter) they represented a wider cross-section of trades.[18] Workers in recently implanted new industries, such as electric engineering in Chelmsford, remained aloof until middle-class elements transformed the Fifth into an officially sanctioned town festival in the 1880s.

The leadership of the Exeter society ('Young Exeter') was both identifiable and respectable. Young Exeter appeared in the 1820s and was headquartered in Waterbeer Street near the business of its leader, John Eyre Kingdon. Kingdon was a prosperous Tory coal merchant, street politician and founder of the Volunteer Artillery. The elaborateness of Exeter demonstrations and effigies bespoke an ability to raise large sums of money. Young Exeter never resorted to the theft of wood or other materials. It decided identities of effigies, fabricated them, announced the order of the march, firmly led the crowds and tried to prevent spillover from the cathedral yard into the city streets. It was frequently compliant to the wishes of Tory city authorities, protesting against the rare attempts to move demonstrations from the yard to an open field, but volunteering as special constables to prevent violence.

Kingdon retired in the 1860s and was probably succeeded by the master carpenter James Cossins, who reported that he 'received the subscriptions' for many years.[19] By the 1870s, having forsworn effigies, Young Exeter was judged too complaisant in some quarters and another gang, styling itself 'Young Guys', appeared. Little is known about them, but elsewhere in Devon Young Guys groups, standing for the mounting of demonstrations in the old way — effigies and all — appeared at this time. In 1879, when Exeter authorities for the first time attempted to stop the manifestations, Young Exeter stood aloof, leaving the Young Guys to preside over what turned into a riot.[20] Before the 1870s there *were* limits to Young Exeter's complaisance. Even in 1867 when demonstrations threatened to be accompanied by social turbulence it refused to totally forgo them. In general, city authorities felt that Young Exeter in its mid-Victorian heyday was useful, both leading the 'roughs' and keeping them in check. Exeter manifestations were well planned, organised and highly formalised. Authorities knew with whom to negotiate and revels were kept to the cathedral yard and out of city streets. Support extended into the city's governing elite. Many 'in authority . . . freely gave their cash', and former mayors and prominent Tory politicians disported themselves in the yard in their youth.[21]

Manifestations were more contested elsewhere, but membership of the gangs was similar: workers, artisans and 'sons of respectable tradesmen'. Support occasionally also came from elements even higher. After the Lewes riots of 1846 a reliable source claimed that 'nephews, cousins and connections of . . . the principal inhabitants were among [the rioters], and the legal, mercantile, landed and other interests were . . . represented'. The liberal *Sussex Advertiser* compiled a list of respectable persons placing themselves 'on a par with the lowest of the low'.[22] The vitality of the Fifth in the south rested upon a kind of plebeian solidarity between artisan, lower-middle-class and labouring elements which elsewhere had disappeared with the eighteenth century or, in parts of industrial England, manifested itself in quite new ways — in phases of the Chartist movement, for example.

Secrecy and anonymity were sometimes preserved by intimidation, but pressure to keep mum was surely intense apart from this. Shopkeepers' and tradesmen's sons were deeply involved; their opinions very likely mirrored their fathers' and many of the latter would have wanted to minimise personal conflict within face-to-face small-town petty business circles.[23] Perhaps this helps to account for the prolonged inability of magistrates and police to penetrate the Guy phenomenon. Rarely were Guildford Guys captured. In 1863 a shopkeeper's son was accused of being a Guy and stoning a policeman. A parade of young clerks, compositors and printers testified to his innocence and he was acquitted, although the magistrates claimed he was on their secret list.[24] Finally in 1865 four Guys were unmasked: two painters (aged

29 and 23), a coachsmith's labourer and a cooper (aged 26). Most were said to be tradesmen's sons. No doubt the Guildford Guys as a whole were much like them.[25]

Bonfire gangs made and conducted bonfires, organised processions, identified persons to be vilified, constructed effigies, directed crowds and collected funds. Marked off by distinctive dress, they were usually masked and carried bludgeons as symbols of their authority. In Guildford they appeared in 'fantastic costumes, with masks . . . or with their faces painted', frequently with a kind of helmet, but somtimes in a white-smock uniform; in Exeter they wore white jackets and trousers, south-wester hats and high boots; at Little Waltham blackened faces, turned coats and elongated hats were worn;[26] the original Lewes costume was a striped guernsey shirt.

The Fifth remained a plebeian occasion. In the southern towns a small-town plebs remained in being, occasionally uniting as consumers or on patriotic or Protestant issues, and continuing to employ older forms of protest and festivity: the anonymous tradition, 'counter-theatre' and direct action.[27] Guy Fawkes remained squarely within an older tradition or repertoire of collective action and expression which was characterised by:

a tendency for aggrieved people to converge on the residence of wrong-doers and on the sites of wrongdoing . . .

the extensive use of authorised public ceremonies and celebrations for the acting out of complaints . . .

the rare appearance of people organised voluntarily around a special interest, as compared with . . . whole communities and constituted corporate groups.

the recurrent use of street theatre, visual imagery, effigies . . . and other dramatic devices . . .

the frequent borrowing — in parody or in earnest — of the authorities' normal forms of action . . .[28]

Eighteenth-century popular manifestations were occasionally highly politicised. They had links with small-town popular radicalism in Sussex and, apparently, there were huge demonstrations during the Wilkes affair in Newcastle and elsewhere, with burnings of anti-Wilkes effigies.[29] Certainly in its colonial American version the Fifth became 'a unified, politicised celebration' used by Boston artisans to 'execute' anti-British effigies in the 1760s.[30] The connection of this older repertoire of expression and action with popular radicalism probably lasted through the 1830s. On the Fifth of 1831, Huddersfield crowds solemnly burned a bishop-effigy. An orator denounced the established church as a blood-sucker, to shouts of 'fair play for the people', 'end of all monopolies', and 'the roast beef . . . of Old England'. In 1833 an effigy of a police spy was paraded through Bethnal Green:

> Listen all who would be free,
> Every child of Liberty,
> Listen to the tale I tell —
> Treachery! as false as hell,
> Is amongst us; so we beat
> The effigy of foul deceit
>   [The Effigy is beaten]

> 'Tis a holiday for Guy,
> He was better than a spy!
> Wretched villain — who would flood
> The bosom of the earth with blood!
> Would hang the lover of the cause,
> of Equal Rights and Equal Laws! —

> Sneak, a tyrant's will to please —
> Sells his soul for bread and cheese
> To the Tyrants, who enslave
> Us from the cradle to the grave:
>   [The Effigy is beaten]

Huge crowds applauded as the effigy was hanged, cut down, the head smeared with ochre and impaled on a stick, and the body cast into the fire.

> Then all, circled in a ring,
> Warm with Liberty — we'll sing
> 'Rule, Britannia rules the waves,
> Britons never will be slaves!'

In 1833 both the Cold Bath Fields anti-police riot and the affair of Popay the spy occurred. Elsewhere in London that year guys were labelled 'Rowan' 'Mayne' and 'Justifiable Homicide' — perhaps referring to the killing of constable Culley in Cold Bath Fields — but there were *also* unemployed demonstrations whose effigies brought out angry Irish crowds and ended in English-Irish street rows. No wonder the police commissioners cracked down hard in the 1830s:

> Not a squib went fiz, nor a rocket whiz
> As the Guy to the gallows was hurried
> the mob were afraid of the New Police
> And therefore were deucedly flurried.

> Few and short were the jokes they flung
> For fear of the laws did them twitch hard
> But they steadfastly gazed on the Guy as he hung
> And bitterly thought of Sir Richard.[31]

But popular radicalism was already disentangling itself from these older forms. One year later unionists tried to prevent the annual football melee during the Derby turn-out in the name of 'Union Morality':

> Magistrates cannot put a stop to it nor military put :t down. But you . . . my brothers of the union, you must do it . . . A monstrous thing it is that several thousands . . . should waste their energy on deeds like that . . . Your 'Betters' have been foremost in this Fete, halloing you like brute dogs to the strife.

Unionists organised a counter-event, a sober, solemn trades procession, headed by a banner reading 'Let Prudence Be Our Guide'.[32] The earlier, explosive, nosiy and chaotic forms did not disentangle themselves from popular radicalism all at once, but the Derby vignette pointed strongly to that detachment.[33] Most mid-century Chartists or trade unionists set themselves firmly against such old-fashioned popular blowouts. They would have seen no particular value in Guy Fawkes: hooting and shouting through the streets, going the rounds of the houses of the prominent, capering in grotesque costumes, and burning effigies of local figures would have been seen as beneath a worker's dignity and certainly no part of a radical politics. Our southern localities were never great Chartist or union strongholds in any case, remaining locked into older repertoires of collective expression long after they shrivelled elsewhere. The Fifth remained a form of expression which continued to be used by a small-town plebs: Crediton shoemakers, Bradminch papermakers, and the miscellaneous tradesmen and journeymen of Lewes,

Exeter or Guildford, where industry and the composition of the labour
force changed very little.

Whatever the former links of the Fifth to popular radicalism in the
south, they were clearly severed by the early nineteenth century,
leaving behind a certain residual defiance of authority, a truncated and
deformed conception of popular rights and No Popery and patriotic
rhetoric. This patriotic element persisted strongly. Demonstrations
usually concluded with the national anthem, and the Crimean War and
Indian Mutiny saw the mounting of fervent patriotic displays. Southern
bonfire gangs always proclaimed themselves the true patriots and
loyalists; their rhetoric was replete with insistence on the rights of loyal
subjects (usually to mark the Fifth), anti-Romanism and reference to
Roast Beef, Plum Pudding and Malt and Hop Utopias. Guildford Guys
regarded interference with a bonfire as a kind of treason and warned
the police:

> Not with us loyal subjects
> For to dare to interfere
> Whilst drinkin' to our Prince's Health
> In a mug o' good old beer.[34]

Patriotic elements were also present in eighteenth-century popular
radicalism but by the 1850s or 1860s they had subtly rearranged
themselves, becoming, by then, more compatible with a certain type of
street Toryism than anything which passed for contemporary
radicalism.

Apart from massive outpourings during the 'Papal Aggression' in
1850, reference to national issues and politics completely dropped out.
Never was a prime minister vilified, nor any national figure except
Parnell and the home secretary in the 1872 liquor Licensing
controversy. Even in the 'Papal Aggression' case, the hidden agenda was
frequently to denounce local Tractarian clergy. Compared to the highly
politicised charivaris and carnivals of early- and mid-nineteenth-century
France[35] this might seem meagre stuff, but the Fifth was not
depoliticised in the nineteenth century — if anything the opposite. It
continued to contain strong elements of political comment and social
protest, but its references and targets became *exclusively local.* Nor did
it survive as a fête *tout court,* but grew in scope, intensity and the uses
to which it was put after 1815.

This can be illustrated by examining the issues agitating our passed-
over districts and the nature of the targets of the bonfire gangs: the

Pope and Guy Fawkes – the ancient targets of popular southern Protestantism; opponents of the celebration of the Fifth; those wishing to alter the form of demonstrations; and transgressors of various types – moral offenders, employers, officious policemen and violators of trade customs. Finally, there were occasions when the rites of the Fifth commented on issues affecting the general interests of the poor.

The Fifth probably acquired its character as an all-purpose vehicle for vilifying a large range of offenders only in the nineteenth century.[36] Most very-early-nineteenth-century demonstrations displayed effigies of Popes and Guy Fawkes only. Through the 1820s this was the case in Hastings, for example. Although the old effigies never disappeared, by the 1860s there were new ones: England's foreign enemies, and, most importantly, local malefactors. By the 1870s masked Hastings butchers and flymen routinely displayed effigies of unpopular employers or customers.[37]

Popular Protestantism remained a chief animating force. Like communism in small-town America, Romanism was the more fearful for being so abstract and remote. The re-establishment of the Catholic hierarchy gave an enormous fillip to popular demonstrations. Even in London the police stood aside as effigies emerged from places as unlikely as the stock exchange. In Battle all elements in the community rallied to the bonfire, forcing its erstwhile patron Sir Godfrey Webster, who had contemplated disassociating himself from the Fifth, to make an appearance and continue his patronage. It also played a major role in facilitating the great compromise at Lewes between the bonfire gang and authorities, which shortly institutionalised the Fifth in its most contested locality. In the popular view, 1850 marked the 'licensing' of Guy Fawkes in its 'traditional' form by the Lewes authorities. In its No Popery version, the Fifth demonstrated against hostile external forces supposedly threatening English liberties; the freedom to mark it became 'a charter of the town, failing to preserve which Britons become slaves'.[38] But attacks on Catholics or their chapels were very rare. Where violence occurred, it was usually aimed at Tractarian or ritualist clergy. In 1865 cavalry were mobilised to prevent the burning of a Folkestone parish church; in 1868 crowds tried to fire St Michael's and burned effigies of both Pope and parish clergy. At Teignmouth in 1858, preceded by rough music, a woman confessing to a priest and a Puseyite priest talking to a devil were paraded on a wagon. Of a piece with such incidents were the Exeter Surplice Riots, the burning of Bishop Philpotts and the mobbing of Rev. J. M. Neale at Lewes in 1857.[39]

Those who opposed Guy Fawkes out of opposition to ultra-Protestant bigotry, or a bourgeois conception of local pride or public order, could be roughly handled. In November 1863 Guildford Guys

> assembled . . . suddenly . . . and attacked the House of Mr. Weale, one of the Magistrates. They [were] armed with hammers, axes and stones and . . . demolished the whole of the windows . . . frames, shutters and doors . . . Having done this, they . . . repaired to the house of . . . the late Mayor, and . . . demolished the front of his house . . .[40]

Ridiculing, intimidating and burning effigies of prominent locals were serious matters in small communities, 'The sanction of ridicule' E. Lloyd Peters observed, 'sears the soul.'[41] In Devon the Fifth occasionally imitated the charivari, and was increasingly used to censure the *same behaviour* as the charivari proper. Exeter did 'not usually [meddle] with . . . domestic sins on Guy Fawkes Night', but elsewhere it was frequent – especially after 1850. In Teignmouth in 1855 we observe this merging of charivari into the rites of the Fifth. Accompanied by rough music, a car passed with three effigies: 'One, suspended on a gallows, had the inscription "S.D.R" . . . the other two – one . . . a man, and the other . . . a woman, – had over them . . . "Double-face", and "Poor Lucy".' In 1859 effigies of a man, woman and child were paraded; over the trio a banner read:

> Am I in this poverty to stop?
> Come and own your child you fop.

In Exmouth effigies were dumped and burned on offenders' doorsteps, a borrowing from the fearsome Devon 'stag-hunt' ritual. Similarly in parts of Sussex child-abusers were hanged in effigy on the Fifth, beaten up or had their property smashed.[42]

The Fifth was occasionally used to comment on issues of general concern to the poor. Agricultural labourers burned 'Free Trade' in the shape of a skeleton at Boreham, Essex, in 1887. There were protests against the 1872 Licensing Act at Farnham; in Exeter it was feared that the home secretary might be burned, but he got off with choruses of groans. There were Fifth-of-November protests against the hiring of foreign labour in Newhaven ships. In 1885 Wellington shopkeepers paraded an effigy of a farmer who sold provisions directly to the public. Consumers prevented the burning, smashed shop windows and cheered the farmer.[43] In Horsham unpopular labour practices imposed by employers upon journeymen shoemakers were criticised. In Rye unseaworthy vessels were confiscated and consumed on the bonfire. In 1880 ten boats 'were seized, freighted with barrels, and dragged . . . through High Street'. Exeter journeymen coachmakers were burned in the cathedral yard if they refused to conform to trade custom. Starting in the 1870s shop assistants burned employers refusing to join in early closing. An Eastgrinstead shopkeeper 'sporting two faces' was burned. In Rye a banner with dolls attached was paraded: 'These are the misers who stopped Early Closing – Old Cocky the Jew, Jarvis, the toy-dealer, Tommy, the sugar-dealer'. In Bridgwater the effigy of a foreman (labelled 'Old Boss') was hanged from a gallows, while crowds smashed his windows and demolished his wall. Even the early-twentieth-century novelist-socialist, the decorator Robert Noonan, resorted to making an effigy of a hated foreman carpenter who had disparaged painters' skills. It was done as a prank, and not (apparently) on the Fifth, but still in the old south-coast tradition! The Fifth could even be used to mount acts of individual rebellion. In 1887 an inmate of the Chelsea Workhouse was charged with complaining about the food and making an effigy of the workhouse master 'to bring [him] into contempt'. The police court filled with laughter as the magistrate told the master: 'public characters like you don't mind little ridicule. It is the penalty of greatness.' For one day even the most powerless mustered a bit of leverage![44]

Food-price riots in Oxford and Devon in 1867 proceeded directly from Fifth-of-November manifestations. With a loaf selling in Teignmouth at 8½d, a procession headed by a man wheeling a pig in a wheelbarrow paraded, smashing bakers' and butchers' windows and shouting 'Drop the Bread! Drop the Meat!' They warned that if food did not drop by Guy Fawkes day there would be worse. Large-scale disturbances broke out in Exeter on the eve of the Fifth. Next day much of the county erupted. In Credition the bonfire society lit the fire and rolled a tar-barrel through the main street, the signal for the sacking of bakers' shops. All night long 'disguised leaders' led rioting crowds. In Devon provisioning was still imbued with persistently held beliefs regarding the conditions of a just social order. Was it not natural for these disturbances to erupt on the Fifth, or for Teignmouth crowds to state that justice was expected by the Fifth or they would secure it themselves?[45]

Were bonfire societies tools in the hands of parties or manipulated by local political factions? One expects Tories to have been more sympathetic and, in general, this was true; but it is difficult to show that Guy Fawkes crowds were manipulated for narrow party purposes. In Lewes, as one would expect, mid-century liberals had little sympathy with bonfire gangs. George Bacon, the liberal *Sussex Advertiser* editor, fiercely opposed them and suffered burning in the shape of a pig. After the mid-century institutionalisation of the Fifth, conservative Lewes tradesmen and shopkeepers became even more closely identified with the bonfire societies.[46] Young Exeter was led, as we saw, by a populist Tory coal-merchant. Liberal opinion before 1850 held aloof, supporting Catholic emancipation, abolition of the Fifth-of-November prayer and discontinuance of official processions. But in the 1840s the liberal *Western Times* became obsessed with Puseyism and supported the mounting of a monster manifestation in the 'Papal Aggression' year. It occasionally even suggested candidates for burning, and rejoiced that 'the populace can blow off the steam of its honest indignation in a . . . display of . . . effigies'. Exeter Tories occasionally paraded effigies of liberal council candidates on the Fifth, always to the *Western Times'* hypocritical outrage; but certainly between the 1840s and 1870s the Fifth became an increasingly common procession, stripped, as it became, of many of its overtly anti-Catholic overtones.[47] In Guildford, where liberals held as aloof as in Lewes, members of the upper classes were attacked by the Guys irrespective of party. Tories in fact got the worst of it, the conservative hold over the borough being so thoroughgoing that anyone in authority was bound to be a Tory![48] Local Tory elites were perhaps more apt to recommend reform rather than abolition of Guy Fawkes demonstrations, but the case of Guildford will show that Tory authorities could seriously attend to the question of public order when they concluded things had got out of hand.

Attempts by Exeter authorities to alter or suppress demonstrations were infrequent. In 1853 a high Anglican mayor tried to remove them to an open field with no success. The rare attempts to ban them (in 1867 and 1879) precipitated riots and the calling out of the army. Exeter manifestations were led by respectable persons and infrequently spilled over into city streets. Popular involvement was massive. In Lewes and Guildford petty-bourgeois elements supported demonstrations and had links to the bonfire gangs. As the following studies show, it was hard to overwhelm huge crowds with force; but, more importantly, it proved difficult to detach many small tradesmen and shopkeepers from their old plebeian alliance with those below in support of the Fifth. There was thus, for a long time, no moral consensus – even among many of the propertied – on the issue, and when it did emerge the outcome was frequently reform, not suppression.

III

Patronage tended to set limits on disorder and symbolise the underlying solidarity of the community around certain ideological bits and pieces. Its withdrawal signalled a rupture in that solidarity and removed limits on manifestations. Consider the contrast between Witham and nearby Chelmsford.

In Witham there was conflict with High Street shopkeepers fearful of fire and damage at least since 1815[49] A bonfire gang, led by a shadowy figure calling himself 'Prince of Wales', developed in the 1850s. Demonstrations were always held near the George Inn in the town centre, and were preceded by processions, solicitations of beer and wood foraging. Effigies were never used. As in Guildford, unpopular figures suffered direct property damage instead.[50] There were serious disorders or actual riot situations on at least nine occasions between 1859 and 1890. The county police could do little, vacillating between repressive action and refusals to commit themselves, arguing that if enough force were consistently concentrated to forestall demonstrations, other points in Essex would have to be stripped and left unattended. Tradesmen near the bonfire site suffered property loss when police refused to act, but when there was intervention damage and violence could be even more severe.

In 1873 the fire was prevented by twenty Essex police at the cost of a riot and the wounding of two constables. In 1875 there was a brief reform effort. Fireworks, torches, wood and a field were provided by middle-class elements, but the crowds followed the bonfire gang instead and the evening ended in a house siege and attacks on the police. In 1881 the Chief Constable personally led a large force and the result was another riot.[51] Throughout the century the Fifth in Witham remained unchanged, weathering both occasional applications of force and rare attempts to patronise and transform it.

In contrast, before 1860 the Fifth in Chelmsford was patronised by local gentry and militia officers. Revellers were provided with wood, fireworks and a field away from the centre. In the 1850s a 'be-masked and be-clubbed band' emerged, which paraded with bludgeons and torches; but money and the field were still supplied for a bit of commotion, drunkenness and patriotic display.[52] After the 1860 manifestation patronage was suddenly withdrawn amid mutterings about 'roughs and their disguises'. It is difficult to account for this. The ban may have originated with the board of health, which had recently assumed local government functions, or it may have been a reaction to the deletion of the Fifth-of-November service from the prayer book.[53] Whatever the cause, the results were startling.

The withdrawal of space and money forced crowds into the streets, and the bonfire gang now had to raise what it needed by confiscation. For nearly thirty years the order of the day would become property damage, theft, violence and burnings in effigy. This deterioration of public order was manufactured by many of those who professed the greatest interest in its preservation. One section of the local middle classes became frightened by the spiral of violence and property damage, complaining not only that 'life was not safe, but that property is not desirable in Chelmsford ... in the nineteenth century'.[54] Some wished for the importation of metropolitan police, which home secretaries were almost never willing to grant.[55] Yet others continued to support some kind of demonstration, arguing that if the lower classes 'must have a fire it would be much better to provide one ... as in former years.'[56] After the riot of 1864 reformers collected £20 and secured an open site, but when the fire died the Guys, 'dressed in fantastic costumes', descended on the town. The affair ended in bitter complaints that the fire was not adequate and charges of peculation.[57]

Over the next twenty years things spiralled out of control. The largest outburst of violence since Chelmsford was seized by sectaries on 5 November 1641[58] occurred in 1866. An inflammatory handbill purportedly released (and later disowned) by the Chelmsford Protestant Association asked:

What can be the reason
Why gunpowder treason,
Should ever be forgot?
Inhabitants of the Chelmsford!
Let us rightly commemorate the
MERCIFUL AND MIRACULOUS discovery
of the DIABOLICAL and COWARDLY
plot of the 5th of November, 1605,
when certain Popish Gentlemen ...
sought to overthrow the PROTESTANT
constitution of the country. Surely
there is cause still to
REMEMBER THE FIFTH OF NOVEMBER ...

On 31 October and 1 November prominent opponents of the Fifth were besieged in their houses and the Guys exhorted a mass meeting to 'keep up the old charter and stick to their rights'. Afterwards crowds were regaled with beer and they went up the town smashing the windows of unpopular tradesmen and the magistrates' clerk. On the Fifth itself violence was only averted by calling dragoons from Colchester.[59] By the 1880s vilification of individuals and effigy burnings, attacks on millers and occasional arson became dominant features, the press fearing that caricatured persons would hire private gangs to crack heads and law and order would cease to exist.[60]

The last great outpouring before reform came as close to being tolerated as any since the end of gentry patronage. The villain of 1887 was the tax inspector William Davis, who seized and auctioned the barge of James Brown, a coal merchant. Sixty prominent Chelmsford businessmen held their own vilification rite — an excessive Victorian dinner concluding with a silent toast to Davis. On the Fifth an elaborately decorated barge was paraded, reflecting contributions from quarters perhaps unaccustomed to finance bonfire celebrations.[61] The 1887 manifestation was the last. By the 1880s the middle classes were gripped by the consciousness of no longer being passed-over. An electric engineering industry appeared, Crompton's Arc Works alone employing 1,000 hands. The borough was incorporated, and in 1888 the first elections were held under the charter. This year was also chosen to end Guy Fawkes disturbances. It was argued that respectable Chelmsford should invest in good order, insert itself into the celebration, fund and organise it, and change its character. A number of those involved in the incorporation campaign had eaten Brown's dinner and drunk the silent toast to Davis.

On the Fifth a bill announced a grand torchlight procession, monster bonfire and 'town carnival' for the *ninth*. At its centre were 400 costumed persons (faces blackened) flanked by marshals. The mayor and corporation marched in person to the field. Middle-class women were turned out and seated in a 'ladies enclosure'. After the fire the mayor urged speedy dispersal to prove 'Chelmsford is orderly to the backbone'.[62] By the early 1890s manifestations on the Fifth had dwindled and the transfer to the ninth was completed. Excursion trains brought visitors to witness Chelmsford's slick, lavish and orderly 'democratic march'. Working-class respectability joined in enthusiastically: the volunteers marched along with the fire brigade and the Arc Works' 'Band of Brigands'. The former Guys (apparently) marched as well, flanked by marshals, in an orderly fashion four-abreast.[63] All associations with the Fifth slowly dissolved, while a carefully controlled and patronised opportunity to indulge the people's fondness for fancy dress and bonfires was provided.

The patronage formerly extended by the gentry was thus reassumed by the middle class both to symbolise a certain bourgeois ideal of class harmony and to create a nineteenth-century standard of proper public decorum.

In Guildford demonstrations continued unbroken through the Napoleonic Wars,[64] gained momentum and reached a crescendo of disorder, intimidation and property damage in the 1850s and 1860s. Magistrates campaigned for suppression in the 1820s with unexpected results. In 1827 there were 'fires, and consequent malicious . . . feeling against . . . the magistrates' and informers.[65] In 1828 there was the 'Gasworks Plot'. Three young members of 'a Club . . . held at the Bowling Green' plotted to plunge the town into darkness on the Fifth, but convictions were not obtained and the general conspiracy of silence discouraged the magistrates.[66] In 1843 the latter made the first effort to suppress the Fifth since the Gasworks Plot with equally discouraging results. According to George Peters, a young carpenter and (probably) a Guy, the police came to the Queen's Head (a Guy pub) to say that 'if they kept out of mischief' they could set off their fireworks and no notice would be taken. The magistrates, meanwhile, posted bills forbidding demonstrations, which the Guys ignored, claiming nobody had been convicted for a long time and the police had signalled that they would not be molested. But on the Fifth the police acted and arrested William Chennell and George Loe (the latter dressed up in a soldier's cap and coat with corporal's stripes). The two were fined £3 each for setting off fireworks in disguise. Chennell and Loe refused to pay and were sent to Kingston gaol. The same day their fines were paid by subscription, and they were brought back in triumph to the cheers of a large crowd and a band of music. Later that night the windows and window frames of the mayor, ex-mayor and superintendent of police were destroyed by angry crowds led by Guys who considered that they had been oppressed by the magistrates and betrayed by the police.[67]

The Guildford borough police was small, incapable of crowd control, and became increasingly intimidated; the Guys informed themselves of the attitudes of local notables, rewarded supporters with immunity from attack, punished opponents with property damage, immobilised the authorities and never shrank from violence. After several gentlemen instigated a grand jury presentment in 1848 jury secrecy was breached; there were a number of house sieges and the mayor and grand jury were accused of making marked men of the complainants.[68] Attacks were made on property of corporation members and policemen, which contributed to their notorious lassitude. The police superintendent habitually locked his men in the station on the Fifth and plied them with bread and beer. While Guildford was briefly policed by Surrey (1851-4) the magistrates tried to avoid all responsibility; in future the Surrey Constabulary would routinely refuse aid.[69] A shopkeeper described Guy fund-raising techniques:

> I was call'd to my door by a mob many of whom wore masks and were . . . armed with most formidable bludgeons. The leader . . . demanded money. I told him I had none . . . He then shook the [box?] more violently and . . . a movement among the mob . . . told me that the most prudent course was to comply . . . This . . . Black Mail . . . must be well known to the . . . Authorities . . . and no steps . . . have been taken . . . *I must ask . . . you will not let my name be known to the Authorities . . . or my house will not be safe . . .* [70]

Henry Peak, Chartist son of a London shopkeeper, arrived in 1851 to find

> A great fire . . . burning . . . Every shop window . . . was barricaded; and wet straw and manure heaped [up] to prevent the penetration of fireworks; . . . these being immense squibs . . . 12 or 15 inches . . . being chiefly loaded with gunpowder . . . curiosity drew me towards the fire, where a . . . lawless crowd was gathered; the chiefs . . . fantastically dressed . . . were . . . the 'Guys' Society . . . who gave orders to the mob by means of a horn [whose] blasts . . . were understood and acted upon . . . [71]

The plight of Guildford respectability was aptly summed up in verse:

> Last year, remember
> Just 'fore November
> I pitched into the Guys right slick;
> But one fine morning,
> I got a warning,
> Which made me do the other trick.
> No broken panes have I to mend,
> Because d'ye see, I'm Guy Fawke's friend.
>
> I wrote an 'article',
> Of which every particle

Praised up the Guys and the days of yore.
When men were not punished
Nor yet admonished
If they smashed a window or broke a door.
No broken panes have I to mend,
Because d'ye see, I'm Guy Fawke's friend.[72]

In 1853 Surrey police reinforced by metropolitans forestalled demonstrations, but in 1854 – with both Surrey and London police gone – disorders redoubled.[73] Houses of tradesmen who had served as special constables in 1853 were surrounded and stoned and the Riot Act was read. 'A stranger', wrote one observer, 'would have imagined himself in a country disturbed by anarchy and red republicans . . .'[74]

Manifestations could not have persisted so long *in the form they took* without support from respectable persons. Support of some adult employers, family loyalty – and perhaps the experience of parents as Guys – outweighed, for a time, demands for a nineteenth-century standard of public order. By the 1860s all changed. As a reforming mayor relentlessly prosecuted an anti-Guy campaign, the violence level escalated, raising doubts in some minds and converting to opposition more and more of the supportive or tolerant.

Guildford attracted no new, advanced industry. Although linked by railway to London since 1845 – and destined to become a bedroom suburb by 1900 – Guildford in the 1860s still remained a market-town dependent upon an agricultural hinterland. Yet the campaign to suppress Guy Fawkes unfolded just as Guildford was experiencing a building boom and beginning to attract 'new gentlemen' – like mayor P. W. Jacob, a Tory Somerset man – with shallow roots in the area, persons who would have had nothing but contempt for the old-fashioned disorders of what was still, in many ways, an eighteenth-century town. The growing party of order found an uncompromising leader in Jacob, who in 1863 secured a mandate to remain until the Guys were quelled. The consequent escalation of violence produced changes of heart in some quarters, more fortitude in others, more middle-class solidarity and confidence, and a determination to use force in whatever quantity necessary.

Just prior to Jacob's election the Guys fatally blundered. Pointedly omitted from the official celebration of the Prince of Wales' marriage, they disrupted official festivities, fed a bonfire with corporation-owned hurdles, besieged a prominent surgeon's house and battered in his doorplate.[75] Complaints now filtered into *The Times'* letters section, embarrassing public figures and businessmen who feared that the town's reputation and prospects were severely damaged.

In 1863 Henry Piper, Jacob's predecessor, procured infantry and dragoons and swore in hundreds of specials — including 'as many of the suspected characters as possible' — and the Volunteers.[76] On 4 November troops arrived to ominous quiet. Col. Gray

> was . . . struck with the peculiar quiet . . . unusual on the arrival of Troops, and am . . . led to credit the report . . . that there was a meeting oɪ the downs . . . Those composing the meeting . . . will either light it [the bonfire] to-morrow night without the Town or defer it . . . until the troops be withdrawn.[77]

The Riot Act was read — although there was no riot! — and streets were cleared, but when the troops returned to Aldershot (21 November) the Guys erupted, nearly demolishing the premises of Piper and another magistrate.[78]

Upon taking office Jacob acted quickly; he fired the head constable, replaced him with the appropriately named Surrey inspector John Law, and increased police manpower by 65 per cent.[79] With Guildford now invested by police and specials on the Fifth, the Guys came out on election day in 1864 and 1865 — in the way of warning to Jacob and new councillors. 'It was hard', a Guy wrote, that 'such muffs as is our magistrates' shoud 'hinder a bonfire'.[80] Jacob's firmness bespoke a new consensus among local notables, and the enhanced ability to mobilise specials itself indicated increased confidence in the magistrates' nerve.

The Guys made one desperate last stand. On Boxing Day eve 1865 they assembled and crossed the Wey bridge, yelling their cry 'Loo, Loo, Phillaloo Muster!' — which 'could never be forgotten by anyone who ever heard it'. A policeman was stoned, beaten and left for dead, but four Guys were apprehended, taken to Horsemonger Lane Gaol and tried at the Assizes. Three were sent to prison.[81] The Boxing Day riot had deflating effects: identities had been revealed, and the prison terms were discouraging. For a few years the Guys abandoned Guildford entirely and demonstrated in Godalming,[82] where the Fifth was similarly suppressed in 1870. By 1870 the press could laconically note: 'scarcely a squib' in Guildford.[83]

The 1860s and 1870s saw a county-wide offensive against unreformed manifestations by Surrey police and magistrates which produced brief, violent reactions in Chertsey, Farnham and Croydon.[84]

In Reigate authorities negotiated reform. In 1890 the watch committee offered a tolerated and expensive demonstration in return for good order. As at Chelmsford the middle classes came forward, mobilising working-class respectability in turn. The resulting 'Bonfire Carnival' was so huge that the Guys were lost in its mass. Turning out were Cyclists' Brigades, tradesmen's advertising floats, Foresters and Oddfellows, postmen and representations of the cartoon figure Alley Sloper.[85] There were similar reforms in Dorking, Nutley and Walton.[86] By 1890 the Fifth in Surrey had been either suppressed or thoroughly transformed by middle-class money and organising skills.

IV

The commonest outcome in the 1870s and 1880s was a rush by local elites and middle-class reformers to establish patronage and to shear demonstrations of personal or political references. Guy Fawkes manifestations rested upon a delicate relationship between bonfire gangs and accompanying crowds which could be broken in a number of ways: by forcibly suppressing the Guys; by penetrating the societies; or by swamping them through a massive infusion of patronage, the physical reappearance of the upper classes, and the turning out of works' bands, friendly societies and other elements of working-class respectability which had hitherto remained aloof. Manifestations persisted past the turn of the century, but were increasingly mounted by official or middle-class-penetrated societies working hand in glove with local authorities, as at Chelmsford, Reigate, Eastbourne, Teignmouth and other hitherto disturbed localities.[87] Money now tended to be politely solicited, scrupulously accounted for and surpluses donated to charities.

Why did so many manifestations unravel between 1870 and 1890 after persisting and growing for so long? One point of view holds that workers were divided over the perpetuation of 'traditional' forms. Changes in industrial, community and working-class organisation ultimately produced a 'letting-go' as new types of collective action and organisation appeared.[88] But in our southern region industrial change was slow, and newer forms of working-class organisations remained feeble. Guildford was typical. There were only two minor strikes in the nineteenth century and the labour force remained totally unorganised.[89] Little stirred in most of these Mugsboroughs until after 1900. The Toryism of the Hastings fishermen, against which Tressell had to contend, was typical of most of these places.

The working-class exponents of the Fifth did not suddenly abandon it. Others did. The Fifth rested not only on an intimate relationship between Guys and crowds, but on a similarity of perspective which extended to elements of the lower middle classes. First the gentry and town elites had pulled away in the early nineteenth century or before; but by the 1870s that crucial section of tradesmen and shopkeepers which had once made bonfire rites an old-fashioned plebeian occasion noticeably pulled back. Such people were more likely to call for reform and regularisation of the Fifth and not its suppression, but their pulling away left a freer field for the mobilisation of the force *or* the preparation of the reforms which ended the older popular version. Working-class respectability sometimes played a subsidiary role, rushing enthusiastically into reformed celebrations — but *only* when the lead was given in other quarters. Even in Ashford and Folkestone where friendly and temperance societies played a key (but subaltern) role in reform, it was done in consultation with middle-class reformers and backed by infusions of their money.[90]

Whatever the case was elsewhere, the southern middle classes were major catalysts of popular cultural change. It was their outlook which was more radically changed and widened by nineteenth-century experience. They were quick to see what kinds of public-order changes were appropriate when new industry moved in (as in Chelmsford) or when the Devon coast and West Surrey became fashionable places to live or holiday. Moreover, they read the national press, which familarised them with new standards of public order and social discipline advocated or imposed in the great urban centres.[91] The suppression or reform of the Fifth was thus a result both of the changing attitudes and strategies of local middle-class elites and of the progressive unravelling of a common, small-town plebeian culture. This experience was traumatic, quite apart from the effects of depression. Abandoned and isolated (and having little of a trade union or Chartist experience to remember or build upon anew), turn-of-the-century working-class life in our Mugsboroughs became characterised by that demoralisation, desperation, and ugly, petty, small-town wage slavery described by George Meek and Robert Noonan.[92]

Whether the Fifth was destroyed or reformed depended on local constellations of circumstances, and on the degree to which (and speed with which) a consensus among elites and petty property-owners could be forged. This was, no doubt, a complex process (as is the history of all relations of authority), and not to be understood until the history of petty-bourgeoisies and class relations in the south is researched. But it is clear that by the 1890s local elites were fully in control and self-confident as never before. Occasionally their authority was established or demonstrated by force, but usually it also had to be struggled or even negotiated for, using a broad armoury of physical, ideological and moral weapons.

Despite its perhaps surprising nineteenth-century vitality, a certain fragility was nevertheless built in to the old popular culture of which the Fifth was a component. It remained prone to being abandoned by segments of its exponents, or smashed, transformed or folklorised[93] by its foes. It has been argued that the nineteenth-century contest between police and criminals was won by the former because they devised and applied new strategies and techniques to criminals, whose outlook and methods did not keep pace.[94] The old bonfire gangs were similarly handicapped. Once they assimilated the ideologies and techniques of both order and reform, and once shopkeeper-tradesman support began to fray, the authorities (with occasional help from the army or metropolitan A Division) could wear or batter down the Fifth, or negotiate and pay for its capture and sanitisation.

Finally, a few words about the Fifth as a public-order problem. Protection of property and control of public spaces were core public-order concerns of Victorian authorities. Precisely these were put in question by the street blockages, unregulated discharge of fireworks, fires in confined streets, unpredictable crowd movements, theft of wood, extortionate solicitation and outbursts of effigy burning, window smashing and house sieges. Guy Fawkes went to the heart of the Victorian problem of order and forced southern authorities to think hard about both its definition and its imposition. There were few objections to fireworks and processions *per se*, as long as they were officially or respectably organised or sanctioned. After all, the business of whole towns halted for jubilee celebrations, marriages of royals or newfangled town carnivals. Regarding the Fifth, the object was to end a *popular* version of the event and stop everything unsanctioned, unlicensed and unforeseen. This could be done either by suppressing the Fifth entirely, or by leading the Guys 'into a proper channel', using Guy Fawkes 'for one of those reunions of class with class . . . '[95] on the model of Chelmsford or Reigate.

Historians must confess their limits at a certain point. Readers will be left with any number of questions. How did the forms and uses of the Fifth in the seventeenth or eighteenth century differ from those described here? Whatever the case, despite earlier precedents and traditions they took on new forms and uses in the nineteenth century. Were links to local party politics more complex than I have made out? Quite possibly. These questions must be left to others who might wish to remember the Fifth of November, to track it backwards or plunge deeper into its nineteenth-century incarnation.

Notes

*I am indebted to Richard Price, Alfred Young and John Walton for comments, John Field for useful references and Anne Strong Storch for research assistance.

1. J. Cossins, *Reminiscences of Exeter Fifty Years Since* (Exeter, 1877), p.66.
2. Some eighteenth-century details courtesy Kathleen Wilson; G. Heath, *Hampton in the Nineteenth Century* (n.p., 1973), p.18; A. Beckett, 'Lewes Gunpowder Celebrations', *Sussex Co. Magazine*, vol.2 (1928), p.486; J.K. Green, *Fireworks, Bonfires, Illuminations and the Guy Riots* (Guildford, 1952), pp.1-2; W. Hooper, *The History of Great Torrington in the County of Devon* (Sutton, 1948), pp.144-5; H.L. Parry, *The History of the Exeter Guildhall and the Life Within* (Exeter, 1936).
3. See R. Da Matta, 'Constraint and License: A preliminary Study of Two Brazilian National Rituals', in S. Moore and B. Myerhoff (eds.), *Secular Ritual* (Assen/Amsterdam, 1977), pp.244-6.
4. *SA*, 10 Nov. 1823.
5. On this process see J. Brewer, 'Theater and Counter-Theater in Georgian Politics: The Mock Elections at Garrat', *Radical History Review*, 22 (Winter 1979-80), pp.7-40; E.P. Thompson, 'Patrician Society, Plebeian Culture', *J. of Social History*, vol.7 (4) (Summer 1974), pp.382-405.
6. *Exeter Gazette*, 5 Nov. 1867.
7. *Notes and Queries*, 7th Ser., vol.6 no.24, (Nov. 1888), pp.404-5.
8. P. Weidkuhn, 'Carnival in Basle: Playing History in Reverse', *Cultures*, vol.3, no.1 (1976), p.31.
9. See V. Bailey, 'Salvation Army Riots, The "Skeleton Army" and Legal Authority in the Provincial Town', in A.P. Donajgrodzki (ed.), *Social Control in Nineteenth Century Britain* (London 1977), pp.231-53.
10. H. Burstow, *Reminiscences of Horsham* (Horsham, 1911), p.76; W. Hopoer, *Reigate: Its Story Through the Ages* (Guildford, 1945), pp.173-4.
11. See the method of celebration recommended to the bourgeois paterfamilias in *Illustrated London News*, 8 Nov. 1851.
12. My unpublished paper 'Popular Festivity, Social Protest and Public Order: The Devon Food Disturbances of 1867'; R. Swift, 'Food Riots in Mid-Victorian Exeter', *Southern History*, vol.2 (1980), pp.101-27.
13. See opening of Hardy's *Return of the Native*.
14. On such figures see R. Pinon, 'Qu' est-ce qu' un Charivari', in *Kontakte und Grenzen. Probleme der Volks-Kultur-und Sozialforschung* (Göttingen, 1969), pp.393-405.
15. *Brighton Herald*, 8 Nov. 1834.
16. Various reports in *Brighton Guardian, Brighton Herald, SA, Surrey Standard, WST, Guildford Journal, Surrey Gazette, WT, WEPG, CC*. Reports used only if *batches* of cases uniformly gave occupation.
17. *WT*, 7 Nov. 1881; *CC*, 12 Nov. 1875.

18. *CC,* 11 Nov. 1868, 8 Nov. 1878; *White's History, Gazeteer . . . of Devonshire* (Kelley reprint of 1850 ed., New York, 1968); *WEPG,* 11 Nov. 1867; *WT,* 7 Nov. 1867; Quarter Sessions Depositions. Epiphany 1868, Devon Record Office 3/4B/9C.

19. *EFP,* 8 Mar. 1871; *WT,* 9 Nov. 1850, 9 Nov. 1875; Cossins, *Reminiscences,* p.68.

20. *WT,* 6 Nov. 1877, 8 Nov. 1877 (Exmouth Young Guys), 7 Nov. 1879.

21. *WT,* 6 Nov. 1878; Cossins, *Reminiscences,* p.68.

22. 'An Old Inhabitant' [M.A. Lower] , *Observations on the Doings in Lewes on . . . the Fifth of November, 1846* (Lewes, 1846), p.10; *SA,* Nov. 1852; J. Etherington, 'The Lewes Bonfire Riots of 1847', *Sussex History,* vol.1, no.6 (1978).

23. Suggestive is E.L. Peters, 'Aspects of the Control of Moral Ambiguities . . .', in M. Gluckman (ed.), *The Allocation of Responsibility* (Manchester, 1972), pp.116-17.

24. *WST,* 28 Nov. 1863.

25. *Guildford Journal,* 3 Apr. 1866.

26. 'Supt. Law's Story', *The Keep,* 2 (Jan. 1913), p. 2; *WT,* 6 Nov. 1880; *CC,* 11 Nov. 1870.

27. See E.P. Thompson, 'Eighteenth Century English Society: Class Struggle Without Class?', *Social History,* vol.3, no.2 (1978), p.158.

28. C. Tilly, *Charivaris, Repertoires, and Politics,* University of Michigan Center For Research on Social Organization, Working Paper no.214 (1980), p.5.

29. E. Foner, *Tom Paine and Revolutionary America* (New York 1976) pp. 12, 14; Newcastle information courtesy K. Wilson.

30. A. Young, 'Pope's Day, Tar and Feathers and Cornet Joyce, Jun. From Ritual to Rebellion in Boston, 1745–1775' (Mimeo).

31. *Poor Man's Guardian,* 19 Nov. 1831 (Huddersfield); *Destructive and Poor Man's Conservative,* 23 Nov. 1833 (Bethnal Green), 16 Nov. 1833 (Rowan-Mayne effigies), 9 Nov. 1833 (Unemployed, English–Irish rows); *Notes and Queries,* vol.12, 3 Nov. 1855, p.341.

32. *Pioneer,* 1 &22 Feb. 1834.

33. See Dorothy Thompson's comments on the decline of direct action and folk violence in areas strongly touched by Chartism. *Bulletin of Society for Study of Labour History,* 15 (Autumn 1967).

34. *WST,* 14 Mar. 1863.

35. R. Bezucha, 'Mask of Revolution: A study of Popular Culture during the Second Republic', in R. Price (ed.), *Revolution and Reaction: 1848 and the Second French Republic* (London, 1975), pp.236-53; Tilly, *Charivaris, passim.*

36. Although John Walter informs me that it was occasionally so used in the seventeenth century.

37. T.S. Brett, Manuscript History of Hastings and St. Leonard's, vol.9, Hastings Public Library; *Hastings and St. Leonard's Observer,* 8 Nov. 1878, 6 Nov. 1880.

38. Manuscript Diary of Henry Peak, vol.D in Guildford Public Library: S942-21; *SAE,* 9 Nov. 1850; *SA,* 12 Nov. 1850: *SAE,* 11 Nov. 1865.

39. *Folkstone Chronicle,* 11 Nov. 1865, 9 Nov. 1867, 28 Nov. 1868; *WT,* 4 Nov. 1848, 13 Nov. 1852, 13 Nov. 1858, 9 Nov. 1866; *SA,* 24 Nov. 1857; R. Newton, *Victorian Exeter* (Leicester, 1968), pp.55-7, 117.

40. P. Jacob to Home Office, 22 Nov. 1863, in Public Record Office [henceforth PRO] HO 45 OS/7443/21.

41. Peters, 'Aspects of the Control of Moral Ambiguities', vol.22, p.113; E.P. Thompson, '"Rough Music": Le Charivari Anglais', *Annales,* vol.22, no.2 (1972), pp.285-312.

42. *WT,* 8 Nov. 1879, 10 Nov. 1855, 12 Nov. 1859, 11 Nov. 1864; T. Brown,

'The Stag-Hunt in Devon', *Folklore*, vol.62 (June 1952), pp.104-9: Burstow, *Reminiscences*, pp.76-7.

43. *ECC*, 11 Nov. 1887; *SAE*, 11 Nov. 1865, 9 Nov. 1867; *SA*, 9 Nov. 1872; *WT*, 8 Nov. 1872; 7 Nov. 1885; *E. Sussex Journal*, 13 Nov. 1888.

44. Burstow, *Reminiscences*, p.77; *E. Sussex Journal*, 9 Nov. 1880; E. Goodsell, 'Reminiscences of Rye Bonfire Boys', *Sussex Co. Magazine*, vol.3 (1929), p.754; *WT*, 7 Nov. 1846, 9 Nov. 1866; *Hastings and St. Leonard's Observer*, 8 Nov. 1878, 6 Nov. 1880; *SAE*, 8 Nov. 1890; F.C. Ball, *Tressell of Mugsborough* (London, 1951). Shop assistants were a volatile element in late-nineteenth-century small southern towns. Appearing masked to execrate their employers on the Fifth in the 1870's, they provided the earliest socialists recruits in Hastings after the turn of the century. See Ball, *Tressell of Mugsborough*, p.61; *Devon and Exeter Daily Gazette*, 7 Nov. 1887 (Chelsea pauper).

45. Storch, 'Popular Festivity, Social Protest and Public Order'.

46. Etherington, 'The Lewes Bonfire Riots'; G.E. Brent, 'The Immediate Impact of the Second Reform Act on a Southern County Town. Voting Patterns at Lewes Borough in 1865 and 1868', *Southern History*, vol.2 (1980), pp.171-2.

47. *WT*, 10 Nov. 1832, 13 Nov. 1841, 11 Nov. 1854, 8 Nov. 1856; *WEPG*, 13 Nov. 1841.

48. Liberals occupied few council seats until 1870. There was not one liberal mayor in the period 1832-75.

49. *Power Plot Anniversary, 1819. Witham in an Uproar!* Broadside in Chelmsford Public Library: WBp/821; *CC*, 9 Nov. 1876.

50. *CC*, 9 Nov. 1866, gives a good description of Witham proceedings.

51. *CC*, 7 Nov. 1873, 12 Nov. 1875, 11 Nov. 1881.

52. *CC*, 12 Nov. 1847, 9 Nov. 1855.

53. On the board see *History of the Incorporation of the Borough of Chelsford* (Chelmsford, 1889); deletion of the Fifth of November service (1859) acted as a cue to stop manifestations. See judges' or magistrates' speeches in *Leeds Mercury*, 24 Nov. 1859, and *Guildford Journal*, 4 Apr. 1866.

54. *CC*, 11 Nov. 1864.

55. *CC*, 9 Nov. 1866. A clear statement of government policy is in PRO HO 45 OS/7443/5.

56. *CC*, 13 Nov. 1863.

57. *CC*, 10 Nov. 1865.

58. B. Ryves, *Mercurius Rusticus . . .* (London, 1685 ed.), p.31.

59. Bill and account of events in *CC*, 9 Nov. 1866.

60. *CC*, 11 Nov. 1870, 12 Nov. 1875; *ECC*, 11 Nov. 1887.

61. See Durant cuttings, Chelmsford Public Library: AA/025/175; *ECC*, 11 Nov. 1887.

62. *ECC*, 16 Nov. 1888.

63. *ECC*, 8 Nov. 1889, 7 Nov. 1890, 11 Nov. 1892.

64. See capsule history sent to Home Office. Mayor of Guildford to Home Office, 12 Nov. 1852 in PRO HO OS/5128.

65. Green, *Fireworks*, p.2.

66. 'Recorder's Opinion Whether Rowdyism on November 5th can be the Subject of Criminal Prosecution (1828).' Manuscript in Guildford Muniment Room, BR/CP/8.

67. *SA*, 14 & 21 Nov. 1843; anon., *Rambles Round Guildford* (Guildford, 1857), p.151.

68. *SA*, 14 Nov. 1848.

69. Green, *Fireworks*, p.3; *Surrey Gazette*, 9 Nov. 1852; P.F.P. Braure (?) to Home Office, 26 Oct. 1863. PRO HO 45 OS/7443/6; Capt Hastings to Mayor, 22° Oct. 1863, PRO HO 45 OS/7443/5. Manuscript Minutes Guildford Watch Commitee, entries 10 May 1853, 3 Oct. 1854.

70. M. Dowlen to Home Office, 6 Nov. 1862, in PRO HO 45 OS/7324.

71. Peak Diary, vol.D., pp.273-5.

72. *Guildford Journal*, 11 Nov. 1862.

73. Justices' Clerk to Home Office, 15 & 25 Oct. 1853, in PRO HO 45 OS/5128; *Surrey Gazette*, 8 Nov. 1853; *SAE*, 12 Nov. 1853, 11 Nov. 1854.

74. *Surrey Gazette*, 7 Nov. 1854, *SAE*, 11 Nov. 1854, 10 Nov. 1860.

75. *WST*, 14 Mar. 1863; G. C. Williamson, *Guildford in the Olden Times* (London, 1904), p.185.

76. This worried the Home and War Offices. Parliament opposed use of volunteers in civil disturbances. See War Office to Home Office, 7 Nov. 1863, PRO HO 45 OS/7443/13.

77. Lt Col. Gray to War Office, 4 Nov. 1863, PRO HO 45 OS/7443/12.

78. *WST*, 7 Nov. 1863; Green, *Fireworks*, p.4; PRO HO OS/7443/3, 4, 5, 7, 21.

79. Manuscript Minutes Guildford Watch Committee, entries 26 Nov., 11 Dec. 1863.

80. *SAE*, 5 & 8 Nov. 1864, 11 Nov. 1865.

81. Williamson, *Guildford . . .*, p.184; *SAE*, 30 Dec. 1865; *Guildford Journal*, 9 Jan. 1866, 3 Apr. 1866 (Assize Report).

82. For Godalming see *SAE*, 10 Nov. 1866, 9 Nov. 1867.

83. *SRA*, 12 Nov. 1870.

84. *SRA*, 26 Oct., 9 Nov. 1872 (Chertsey), 9 Nov. 1872 (Farnham); *SAE*, 11 Nov. 1876 (Croydon); E. Smith, *Farnham. The Story of a Surrey Town* (London, 1971), p.89.

85. *SAE*, 8 Nov. 1890.

86. *Guildford Journal*, 12 Nov. 1870, 12 Nov. 1888; *SAE*, 8 Nov. 1890.

87. For the Capture and sanitising of Paris carnival see A. Faure, *Paris Carême-Prenant. Du Carnival à Paris au XIXe Siècle, 1800-1914* (Paris, 1978).

88. G. Steadman Jones, 'Class Expression Versus Social Control? A Critique of Recent Trends in the Social History of "Leisure"', *History Workshop Journal*, 4 (Autumn 1977), p.169.

89. R. Sykes, 'Politics and Electoral Behaviour in Guildford and West Surrey', unpublished PhD thesis, University of Surrey, 1977, pp.59, 64-5.

90. C.S. Burne, 'Guy Fawkes Day', *Folk-lore*, vol.23, no.4 (1912), pp.412-13. Burne was reminded of old Corpus Christi processions by reformed, turn-of-the-century, southern demonstrations in which friendly societies participated.

91. D. Philips, '"A New Engine of Power and Authority": The Institutionalization of Law Enforcement in England, 1780-1830', in V.A.C. Gatrell *et al.* (eds.), *Crime and the Law* (London, 1980), pp.155-89; R.D. Storch, 'Policing Daily Life in the Victorian City', in H. Diederiks (ed.), *Crime, Law and Law Enforcement in the Atlantic World* (Washington, forthcoming).

92. G. Meek, *George Meek. Bath Chairman. By Himself* (London, 1910). Noonan indicated that the Fifth had become a pathetic begging procession of the Hastings unemployed by 1910.

93. On folklorisation, the recuperation of popular festivals 'as formal entities . . . presented as spectacles, exclusively for the "showing"' and as 'Objects of consumption', see M. Mesnil, 'The Masked Festival: Disguise or Affirmation', *Cultures*, vol.3, no.2 (1976), p.24.

94. V.A.C. Gatrell, 'The Decline of Theft and Violence in Victorian and Edwardian England', in V.A.C. Gatrell, B. Lenmann and G. Parker (eds.), *Crime and the Law*, pp.276-8.

95. *SRA*, 12 Nov. 1870.

5 THE LANCASHIRE WAKES IN THE NINETEENTH CENTURY

John K. Walton and Robert Poole

I

On the eve of the great migration of the rapidly developing textile industry into the steam-powered factory and the town, the nascent cotton district of south and east Lancashire had a rich and varied calendar of popular holidays, traditions and customs. Samuel Bamford listed those that prevailed during his boyhood in Middleton, a weaving and mining village a few miles north of Manchester, in the early-nineteenth century. The year began with the Christmas holidays, which lasted for several days from the first Monday after New Year's Day. Shrove Tuesday was a holiday, and mid-Lent Sunday was observed with cymbalin cakes and mulled ale. Easter saw heavy drinking, dancing, 'pace-egging' and a mock mayor ceremony, and it concluded on the Wednesday with 'White Apron Fair', when the local women displayed themselves in all their finery. May-Day was used for the ritual settling of grudges, and Whitsuntide was a further occasion for dancing and drinking, with many villagers visiting Manchester Races. But, we are told, ' "The Rush-bearing" was the great feast of the year.' This was held on the anniversary of the dedication of the church, usually the third Saturday in August, when rushes were ceremonially carried from the outlying hamlets and strewn in the parish church to act as a floor-covering during the coming year. The rushes were brought piled up in special constructions on carts conducted by stalwart men, and accompanied by music and morris dancers. Often the carts came into conflict, and the fighting which also accompanied the other popular festivals was particularly prevalent at rushbearing. But this was also a time for hospitality, with houses being cleaned and whitewashed, and ale brewed to welcome relatives and friends from other villages. Fairground amusements ('flying-boxes and whirl-a-gigs') arrived to take advantage of the crowds, and such delicacies as nuts and Eccles cakes were sold from baskets or stalls, while public houses were packed with drinkers and dancers. Despite its commercial side, the last great holiday of the year laid great emphasis on home-based hospitality and conviviality. For most people it lasted four or five days, but a few contrived to keep up the pace for a full week. After this, only the Guy

Fawkes celebrations on the Fifth of November interrupted a long spell of steady work until the Christmas holidays began the cycle again.[1]

Customs varied, but Middleton was representative of most of the Lancashire textile district at this time. Almost everywhere the parish church anniversary, the summer 'rushbearing' or 'wakes', formed the climax of the recreational year. The same was true of many other areas of England, from the village feasts of West Yorkshire to the West Country revels, and from the wakes of the Staffordshire Potteries and the Black Country to those of rural Northamptonshire.[2] In some places on the fringes of the cotton district, especially in the north, pleasure fairs without religious overtones occupied the place of the wakes, although they came to be covered by an indiscriminate use of the term in late Victorian times. In parts of Lancashire, as elsewhere, Whitsuntide had strong claims to primacy; but the wakes generally met a wider range of needs than any other festival.[3] At Middleton it expressed family, village and parish identity through conviviality and ceremony, provided a legitimate outlet for conflicts between individuals and groups, and an opportunity for the display of skills, hospitality and possessions. It induced a relaxed atmosphere in which high spirits and pent-up emotions could be expressed in horse-play and sexual encounters, and it prepared the villagers for the long autumnal evenings of 'wakin' time', when work in the loomshops began by candlelight and continued through the shortening days as the weavers insured themselves against a hard winter.[4]

The quickening pace of social and economic change during the first half of the nineteenth century put these local festivals under severe pressure. The Lancashire textile towns grew with unprecedented speed, engulfing some villages and drawing migrants from them all, especially as handloom weaving entered the final stages of its decline in the 1830s and 1840s.[5] Throughout the period, indeed, the weavers were losing their ability to participate in their established local festivities, as falling piece-rates meant working longer hours to maintain even a frugal standard of living which left little room for hospitality and social life. Factory workers, on the other hand, were forced by fines and dismissal threats into much more regular attendance.[6] Employers' political economy preached long working hours and the devotion of free time to self-improvement, often of a narrowly practical and individualistic kind; while a wider sector of the workforce came under the direct or indirect influence of a repressive evangelicalism, which insisted that the devil should not be allowed to find work for idle hands.[7] As the new police began to intervene in working-class recreations in the

1840s, and as employers began to make their presence felt as magistrates, legal coercion could be used more effectively in support of evangelicalism and urban discipline.[8] Attempts were made to suppress or control popular recreations wherever drinking, fighting, blood sports and commotion appeared to threaten property, authority, morality or rationality as interpreted by landowners, employers and their allies.[9]

The wakes were vulnerable to these changes on all counts. Their convivial and hospitable aspects were at risk during troughs in the trade cycle. They contained elements which were threatened by moral disapproval, factory development, and the encroachment of urban development on the space available for recreation. They could be perceived as threats to property, public order and commercial interests. Landowners, employers and local government might seek to undermine them, while 'rational recreations' might be promoted by religious bodies and other agencies of improvement as alternatives. In the longer term, commercialisation of recreations, which followed from other economic changes, might compete with wakes or transform them from within.

In the late 1840s Bamford believed that pressures of this kind had been too much for the village culture of his boyhood. He considered that 'Most of the pastimes and diversions which I shall describe are no longer practised, – some of them not even known, – by the youthful population of the manufacturing districts at the present day.'[10] Despite all the evidence of older recreations having been undermined, Bamford's perceptions are probably misleading, especially with regard to the wakes. The form taken by the industrial revolution in Lancashire left ample room for continuities alongside the obvious changes. Small and medium-sized cotton firms persisted strongly amongst the large, and many employers came from landed backgrounds, giving rise to a variety of paternalistic regimes which could extend tolerant and openhanded patronage to traditional sports and holidays.[11] In any case, although factory work was the norm amongst children and adolescents, most people graduated to other occupations in their twenties, and unrevolutionised sectors such as building, labouring and handicrafts continued to employ a clear majority of the adult male labour force.[12] Moreover, the centres of factory industry recruited their populations mainly by short-distance migration, and the tendency at an early stage for towns to crystallise into distinct neighbourhoods, often centred on particular factories, helped to promote a sense of continuity and community which was still more apparent in the many surviving industrial villages.[13] Even the larger cotton towns remained manageable social systems into which most of the inhabitants could become well-integrated, and this remained the case even when populations grew beyond the hundred thousand mark in late Victorian times. Although factory work was only a passing phase for most people, factories bred a community of experience and expectation in their surrounding areas, and this helped to ensure that stern factory rule-books remained unable to prevent workers from 'running off' at holiday times or when unusual attractions appeared in the neighbourhood.[14] In the same vein, the efforts of the new police to put down boisterous gatherings and traditional sports were commonly resisted, sometimes violently and often successfully.[15] Surface changes mask underlying continuities; as Patrick Joyce remarks:

> In the transition to a more stable and organised urban life the legacy of older and more violent spontaneous ways was a powerful one. The 1850s and '60s was still a time of hard drinking, hard sports and hard gambling . . . the debt to rural life was still a considerable one.

On this argument, the attempts at repression by the 'improving' middle class, and the allied efforts to build a substitute culture of self-improvement and 'rational recreations', came to little; and what really wrought the important transformation in popular recreations were the new commercial influences of the later nineteenth century: the musichall, professional sport, the popular press and the seaside holiday.[16]

This argument is secondary to Joyce's purposes, and he does not develop it at length or in depth. Indeed, he does not even mention the wakes and other calendar customs, and most historians of recreations in the industrial revolution have been guilty of similar neglect.[17] Brian Harrison has suggested that, 'The railway excursion and the consequent rise of the seaside holiday resort killed the Lancashire wakes and civilised the local fair'; but this question-begging formula, which distorts the actual pattern of events in almost every respect, again lies at the periphery of a different argument.[18] Robert Malcolmson, who did focus directly on wakes and fairs, pointed out that though 'gatherings which were largely plebeian, and unashamedly devoted to pleasure', came under threat from those in authority, 'it should be emphasized that their decline was gradual and relatively gentle; by the mid-nineteenth century it was only moderately advanced'. E. P. Thompson has even suggested that 'Until the first decades of the nineteenth century . . . the people clung tenaciously to their customary wakes and feasts, and may even have enlarged them both in vigour and extent.'[19] These comments carry more weight, but the speculative and cautious mode of expression reflects a lack of systematic research on wakes in specific kinds of economic setting. Confidence in Malcolmson's generalisations is undermined by the premature and over-ambitious nature of his attempt to examine popular recreations at national level in the absence of previous local and regional studies; but apart from Hugh Cunningham on the London fairs and Douglas Reid on the observance of St Monday in Birmingham, there have been few subsequent attempts to repair the omission, and the wakes themselves have been practically ignored.[20] Peter Bailey's Bolton case-study in his *Leisure and Class in Victorian England,* with its emphasis on 'rational recreations', is not very helpful for our purposes, despite its other virtues.[21]

The continuing neglect of the wakes is surprising, for their boisterous, communal nature makes them an ideal touchstone for assessing the extent of the survival of pre-industrial attitudes to leisure and community in early industrial society. The survival of wakes and other festivals need not in itself be an index of continuity, and the historian must look for changes in context, content and function even when the persistence of a customary holiday is superficially well-attested. If we bear this in mind, a study of the Lancashire wakes has obvious value in testing the extent and significance of continuity in popular recreations in a region where industrialisation and urban growth came early and spectacularly.

How did the pressures we have described affect the Lancashire wakes during the nineteenth century? This is a difficult question to answer even within the limited confines of the cotton district. Our main source must be the local press, but newspapers adopted no consistent policy in reporting on wakes. For most of the period, Tory newspapers were more likely to take a positive interest than Liberal/Nonconformist ones, but the case of the *Stockport Advertiser* illustrates the potential problems. It enthusiastically advertised the entertainments put on by publicans at local wakes in the 1820s, but then fell almost completely silent on the subject until 1838, when it began to report spasmodically on a few of the more prominent festivals. Coverage improved slowly, and the publication of a list of local wakes in 1867 revealed the existence of over a dozen whose survival could not have been deduced from the paper's wakes reporting.[22] Clearly, one cannot date the disappearance of wakes by the silence of the sources, which may merely reflect a change in editorial policy (although the widespread absence of wakes reporting during the cotton famine is significant). Moreover, the content of reports is often suspect. Accounts often use a conventional phraseology, whether approving, disapproving or neutral, which conveys little or nothing of the content or atmosphere of the event, and cannot be used to support anything beyond the most basic kind of continuity.[23] These problems, and the sheer scale of the subject, prevent us from offering at this stage a quantified profile of the fate of wakes in the Lancashire textile district in this period. But we can point to the strong survival of important elements of the traditional wakes in many places well into the second half of the nineteenth century; and we can bring out the inadequacy of simple explanations of decline, by discussing the kinds of pressures which were brought to bear and the responses to them.

II

We can point to several distinguishing features of wakes in early-nineteenth-century Lancashire: the rushcart, with its attendant morris dancers; the widespread attachment to heavy drinking in association with blood sports and fighting; the fairground attractions of stalls, exhibitions and primitive children's rides; and the association with hospitality and domesticity as relatives and neighbours, dressed in their best clothes, were welcomed into newly swept and whitewashed houses. By the end of the century the surviving wakes were more straight-forwardly commercial occasions. The fairground and the public house dominated proceedings for those who stayed at home, while the railway excursion or extended seaside visit supplemented and then displaced local attractions in the affections of the working-class population. But this transition was a slow and piecemeal process, and even the manner of seaside holiday observance presented tangible continuities with the older form of the wakes as a celebration of local identity.

The wakes remained strongly associated with blood sports until the late 1830s, and it was this aspect which brought them under the earliest and most direct attack. Bull-baiting was effectively made illegal in 1835 and cock-fighting in 1849, although in many parts of the country the magistrates had been able to suppress them earlier.[24] In Lancashire, this legislation tipped the scales against bull-baiting, although successful enforcement sometimes took several years. Eccles, whose wakes attracted many Mancunians and made a special feature of the sport, did not survive the decade as a bull-baiting venue.[25] At Halshaw Moor (where the 'wakes' was a commercial venture sponsored by a publican and initiated as late as 1827) and Radcliffe, bull-baiting was also put down by the late 1830s, while at Rochdale it seems to have been abandoned in the town itself as early as 1820, but to have persisted much longer in the out-townships of Cutgate and Bagslate.[26] Significantly, the last strongholds of the sport seem to have been in similar isolated settlements of handloom weavers and miners. Gee Cross and Godley Hill, across the Cheshire border near Hyde, are cases in point. They were unruly hamlets famous for quoits, skittles, prize fighting and all kinds of blood sports, and they defended their collective identities against outsiders with a barrier of dialect and incomprehensible nicknames. At Gee Cross the first attempts to abolish the wakes bull-baiting were met by an effective threat of mass resistance, and a pertinaceous constable had his trousers slit and his shirt pulled through at the back to represent a tail.[27] Even here, though, the coming of the much-resented county police force seems to have marked the beginning of the end, and, as in the great Staffordshire strongholds of bull-baiting, the sport was effectively suppressed almost everywhere by the mid-1840s.[28] Cock-fighting, not necessarily associated with wakes, was easier to conceal and persisted much longer. Several Preston public houses were still notorious for it in the early 1850s, and elements of the patronage bestowed on the sport by successive Earls of Derby persisted in Bury at about the same time, when Sunday morning mains were being held at the Earl's brick-and-tile works.[29] Gentry patronage in some areas (though not in Preston's beerhouses) no doubt helps to explain the strong, if covert, persistence of cock-fighting through the nineteenth century and beyond, though it becomes increasingly difficult to identify it directly with the wakes, which were perhaps too public and becoming too well-policed for this kind of activity. Much the same applied to prize-fighting and the various sports associated with terriers and fighting dogs.[30]

The Lancashire wakes had thus lost their association with blood sports by mid-century. In itself this seems to have done little to reduce their attractive power. Halshaw Moor and Radcliffe were able to meet the need for alternative attractions after the loss of their bull-baiting and, as at Barrowford, horse racing was introduced in its stead.[31] In any case, the prohibition of blood sports involving animals did not imply that a decline would take place in the equally gory battles between men, which continued to be a prominent feature of wakes celebrations.[32] Fighting at the wakes was particularly noticeable in connection with rushcarts, which were a notable feature of the wakes within a twenty-mile radius of Manchester, embodying the oldest traditions of the festival and surviving with remarkable tenacity into late Victorian times in some areas.[33]

The rushcart itself was a distinctive and often elaborately decorated arrangement of rushes rising up to twelve feet above the cart on which it was built. It was almost confined to south-east Lancashire and north Cheshire, though a less elaborate form of rushbearing survived elsewhere, especially in parts of rural Lancashire and Cheshire, north Derbyshire and the Lake District, well into the nineteenth century.[34] The rushcart was for many years a symbol of village solidarity. Its building was a collective enterprise, with the younger men taking the lead in collecting subscriptions and doing the manual work, while their elders used their skills and experience in supervising the construction, and the women prepared the banners and costumes and set out the various symbols of communal wealth on the 'sheet' draped over the front.[35]

By the early-nineteenth century the rushcarts were beginning to lose their association with the parish church and to become an end in themselves, as the adoption of flagged floors rendered the rushes unnecessary to the comfort of the worshippers. The rushcart survived the loss of its (often residual) practical justification, however, and persisted in its more important role as the expression of the collective pride and prosperity of a small community. This was displayed through the time and skill which went into the preparation of the cart, the quality of plate, ornaments and other precious possessions which were set out on the white linen cloth at the front, and through the impression created by the men who pulled the cart and the morris dancers who escorted it, all wearing clothes specially prepared for the occasion.[36] There might be as many as a dozen rushcarts at a single wakes. As rushcarters were expected to drink plenty of ale, and as they had charge of such an important symbol of communal identity, it was not surprising that competition between rushcarts occasionally found expression in a pitched battle. Fighting between the crews of rival rushcarts remained normal in Oldham into the 1840s, and in Rochdale it continued unabated into the cotton famine.[37] This violent ritual produced an annual tally of 'broken limbs' and 'broken heads', which was not confined to the rushcarters. These set-piece confrontations stood out amid the general violence of the wakes, which only began to wane in the 1850s and 1860s.[38]

The rushcart remained a prominent feature of the wakes in several parishes and outlying villages into the 1880s and beyond, from Hyde to the Oldham area and Saddleworth, and it survived beyond mid-century in many more. Almost all of the rushcarts after 1880 had, however, to be resuscitated by a group of interested people. By this time complaints had long been voiced that the rushcart had ceased to be a genuine feature of communal village life, and had degenerated into an excuse for individuals to extort contributions from onlookers in order to enjoy a drunken spree.[39] But the simple fact of survival conceals important changes in the significance of the custom and the way in which it was experienced.

Complaints about the degeneracy of rushcarts were common throughout the Victorian years. They came from outsiders rather than participants. To a Rochdale Sunday-school teacher in 1869, 'the vain, useless, insignificant, contemptible rushcart' represented 'ungodliness in all its forms'.[40] To the Oldham diarist Edwin Butterworth they were simply 'monuments to childish barbarism', condemned to imminent extinction by progress.[41] His view was more typical. The rushcart, it was said, was a survival from the rustic past which had outlived its social and practical usefulness to become an excuse for debauchery, 'got up . . . for the sole purpose of getting money to spend in drink'.[42] This was probably neither more nor less true than it had ever been, but it suggests a theme worth pursuing: as the rushcart tradition lost its practical justification and communal roots it became less of a community ritual and more of a petty enterprise concerned with raising cash.

In 1864 an *Oldham Chronicle* correspondent catalogued some of the ways in which the local rushcart tradition had declined in vitality:

Instead of — as in former times — a muster of fifty grown men pulling at the 'waiges',[43] it is only youths that will do the work now. The shafts of the carts, or waggons, are not now, as formerly, held up by some half-dozen men, but a horse is made to serve instead . . . Instead of the cart sheet . . . being covered with watches, silver plate and all the other valuables that could be mustered, the cart is now ornamented with materials of less value. The rivalry of display on the part of the various rushcarts is apparently a thing of the past. This is not much to be regretted . . . more than once it has resulted in fighting, in the carts being pulled over, and not infrequently in broken heads. At a fight of this description, some years ago, a man was killed, and others seriously injured. Now the greeting is a nod or a shake of the hand.[44]

These symptoms of anaemia were apparent almost everywhere by this time, and were accompanied by an increasing preoccupation with collecting funds as rushcart building came to cost more in time and money. The rushes themselves were becoming harder to find by mid-century as towns spread and farmland was drained, and it took time to gather them from distant marshy moorland. It might take nine hours and many miles walking to collect the rushes and between six and eight hours to build the actual rushcart, and the necessary communal effort and goodwill seem not to have become so readily forthcoming. Boys were sometimes paid for rush-gathering, but special long rushes were required to 'bolt' the top of the cart and at Uppermill, at least, their selection remained a man's job. In 1890 several men went up on the moors early on the Sunday before the wakes, and in their search for rushes 'all the party got over knee-deep in the bog, some of them sank up to their thighs, whilst one sank up to his waist, and had to be hauled out'. This would not have been a congenial job for townsmen, and the pool of potential rush-gatherers must have been dwindling throughout the nineteenth century. It was small compensation that the used rushes remained saleable in some places for, although the church no longer wanted them, they could often be sold at the end of the wakes and a publican could sometimes be found to buy up the whole rushcart, presumably as an attraction for his customers.[45]

The supply of skills and motivation was declining in other respects, too. By the late 1870s a spate of attempted revivals found rushcart builders in short supply, and this suggests a failure to pass on skills in the previous generation. In turn, this meant a further rise in expenses, if only in the form reported from Oldham in 1879 when 'Bill o' Tom's' was able to demand payment in brandy instead of the customary beer.[46] Fife and drum music, too, was giving way to the more expensive brass band, and morris dancers rattled their collecting boxes with growing urgency; in 1880 some forty of them began practising their dancing six weeks before the wakes in Ashton.[47] All this reflects a growing attention to organised display which cumulatively increased the cost of presenting a rushcart to a more sophisticated and demanding public. At Middleton in 1865 a particularly elaborate rushcart cost £7 to build, and the Uppermill rushcart of 1890 cost £9, £1 of which went to the builder. But this was only one element in the overall cost, and the total expenses of the revived Withington rushcart in 1886 came to £35, covering hire of morris dancers and horses, rent of land on which to build the cart, and a good meal for all concerned. Despite these heavy overheads, the rushcart still made over £30 profit on the collection.[48]

All these expenses posed problems for the dwindling number of rushcarters. We can identify three ways in which rushcarting changed after mid-century, apparently in response to these pressures. One unpromising approach was to put less effort into manufacture and display. Gorton in 1851 produced only one rushcart, a small affair 'destitute of ornament, either of flowers or silver plate'.[49] Secondly, where a rushcart was not possible, people might compromise by displaying other kinds of cart, although we cannot be sure how far this was an alternative to a full-scale rushcart and how far it was intended as a supplement. In Oldham in the 1850s and 1860s the smaller carts and garlands might be got up by adults or children, and there was no clear dividing line. Rushcarts came to be increasingly outnumbered by the much smaller 'grove carts', which contained only decorative arrangements of garlands and branches in imitation of the top-piece of the rushcart; by 'Adam and Eve carts', which were similar but carried pairs of children with bodies blackened in homage to an ancient custom; and by isolated teams of morris dancers. As well as being simply rushcart substitutes, other types of cart could be significant displays in their own right. In the mid-1830s coal carts laden with 'enormous pieces of coal' and proudly drawn by enormous miners began to appear at Oldham Wakes, and other trades joined in at different times. The 1863 wakes saw a 'dirt cart', attended by men employed in earth-moving for the cotton famine relief committee. Others of the mobile displays were described as 'mere abortions', and all must have involved less investment of time and money than the traditional rushcart. In this respect they were undoubtedly signs of the times.[50] Thirdly, as costs rose and participation declined, the publican played an increasingly important role as patron. One reason for this seems to have been the decline of hospitality to rushcarters from gentry and employers as attitudes hardened during the first half of the nineteenth century. Subsequent interest was very limited, although James Dearden, Lord of the Manor of Rochdale, tried to stimulate a rushcart revival there in mid-Victorian times, offering a guinea for each rushcart to appear at his house and ten guineas for the best. This unusually hard-headed antiquarian venture was remarkably successful in the short run, attracting twenty rushcarts.[51] Millowners were even less forthcoming. In 1869 the Leeches of Grosvenor Street Mills in Stalybridge provided the material and labour for a well-dressing revival, but we can find no comparable examples of rushcart patronage.[52] Significantly, too, rushcarting attracted little support in newly developed areas. Under the circumstances, publicans were often happy to step in to support an attraction which tended to strengthen the wakes, which were generally a profitable institution for them. There was nothing new about the association between publicans and rushcarts, but it certainly became stronger as the problems of the rushcarters increased. By the mid-Victorian period most of Oldham's rushcarts were being built at public houses, a donation of £1 from the landlord being typical. As the rushcarting tradition began to lapse in the later nineteenth century, it was often the publicans who sustained and revived it, as at Droylsden in 1851, Saddleworth in 1861, Hollinwood in 1864 and Uppermill in 1890.[53] The pub, with its yard or garden, provided the space to build the rushcart; it offered a convivial social centre for the rushcarters; and it ensured a measure of financial support. At the Bridge Inn in Saddleworth these elements were combined in one event in 1878 when the rush collectors were rewarded by the landlord with a dinner.[54] As in the case of so many declining sports and entertainments, the publican brought the rushcart under his capacious wing; and in so doing, he confirmed its unfortunate image in the eyes of 'progressive' and nonconformist opinion.

The survival of the rushcart thus depended on its adaptation to an environment in which commercial influences were becoming inescapable. Even so, the tradition retained much of its old identity. It was still a collaborative venture, carried out mainly by young men now but with essential help from older people, and its continuing success depended on the acceptance of the rushcart by those who gave donations. The pub had always been at the centre of rushcarting, and the increased importance of the publican was a change in degree rather than in kind. What stands out, indeed, is the determined nature of the attempt, admittedly organised by a committed minority, to sustain a tradition which looked increasingly anachronistic and absurd in its details to most outsiders.

The apparent decline of the hospitality tradition as a central feature of the wakes poses similar problems of evidence and interpretation. Bamford remembered Sunday as 'the great day for hospitality', with relatives and friends arriving from a distance. 'Even decent strangers who apparently had no fixed place of visitation, would be frequently called in as they passed the open door and invited to partake with the family and their guests.'[55] At Barrowford in the early nineteenth century 'almost every door was open, and a white cloth on the table which could be seen from the street seemed to say, "come in and welcome".'[56] Such open hospitality probably declined early. At Slaithwaite, in the West Riding, which was locally famous in mid-

Victorian times as the last outpost of the old style of wakes, hospitality seems to have been limited to relatives and established friends by the 1860s, although houses were cleaned for the occasion and enormous meals of roast beef, pickled cabbage and currant pudding dominated Monday and Tuesday as well as Sunday. Neighbours who preferred a seaside holiday were 'dubbed as snobbish, selfish and disloyal to old customs'.[57] In Lancashire the railway excursion habit caught on much earlier and more thoroughly, and the conservatism of Slaithwaite became a by-word even in the West Riding, where changes of this kind came more slowly.[58] But the tradition of hospitality on wakes Sunday never disappeared from the Lancashire textile towns, despite the fact that those who could best afford it were increasingly tempted away on seaside holidays, especially in the last quarter of the nineteenth century, and even though many of those who attended the wakes locally were outsiders drawn in by fairground attractions and general jollity. The hospitality tradition at Eccles Wakes, for example, survived the official abolition of the festival in 1877 and there is no doubt that here, as with rushcarting, strong continuities persisted alongside the visible changes well beyond the middle of the nineteenth century.[59]

As the older communal elements of the wakes underwent a slow, piecemeal and sometimes erratic transformation and decline, commercial entertainment became more important in its own right. As with the rushcart, the publican played a central part. He had often been the organiser of the old blood sports, some of which were on a commercial footing with bulls being hawked around from wake to wake; and the grounds of the larger pubs had long been the venue for such rustic sports as climbing the greasy pole, eating scalding porridge, smock racing and chasing the greased pig. Publicans sometimes organised festivities of their own which they dignified with the title of 'wakes'.[60] They also capitalised on the demand for entertainment for visitors to the wakes, especially as home brewing and special beer-selling privileges at wakes time declined. They offered singing rooms and sometimes dancing saloons, and played some rather original kinds of 'sacred music' for the large numbers of Sunday visitors.[61]

The publicans continued to do well out of the wakes, though they suffered increasingly from the competition of the seaside. The fairground stallholders and entertainers had a similar experience. Like the publicans, they had already featured among the attractions of the wakes in Bamford's Middleton; and the visible pattern of wakes observance inland shifted steadily towards the fairground, as towards the pub, for most of the nineteenth century. The attractions became more varied and ingenious as time went by, but the fairs found room for local stallholders as well as for itinerant specialists. The change from muscle power to steam power on the rides, the introduction of shooting galleries and 'sea on dry land', and the evolution of the peep-show into the magic lantern and then into the primitive cinema of 'Wall's Ghost Show' and the like — all these developments kept the fairground attractive without significantly changing its functions.[62] The most important change in the eyes of contemporaries was summed up by a complacent editorial in the *Burnley Express* in 1888:

> Few will assert that in our system of holiday-making we are less wise than our progenitors. Compare our excursions to the seaside . . . our cricket matches, and even our fairgrounds with the morris dancing, the old English games and the drunken brawls which were the chief characteristic of our olden-time fairs, and there will be few who will say that we are not more prudent (in the matter of pleasures) than our forefathers.[63]

Not that the fairground had become universally acceptable; the Nonconformist campaign against Accrington's August fair in 1890, for example, spoke of a 'carnival of vice' and a 'horrid nuisance'.[64] But there was widespread agreement by this time that the worst excesses of the fairs and wakes had been moderated. This was, however, a fairly recent development, and it coincided with the rise of a new element in wakes observance which was to do more than any other single influence to transform the festival in Lancashire: the rise of the working-class seaside holiday.

Day trips to the seaside were already well established at the wakes in the late 1840s, but it was not until the 1860s and early 1870s, when trips lasting several days were becoming commonplace, that the railways seriously affected the popularity of local wakes fairs. The wakes holidays themselves were lengthening slightly by the mid-nineteenth century, having contracted over the previous generation. This allowed people to take excursions as well as to offer hospitality on the Sunday and attend the fair. Indeed, many of the earlier excursions arrived back around tea-time, so the trippers could spend the evening at the fair. If anything, the short-term effect of the railways was to boost the local wakes fairs by bringing in crowds of friends, relatives and pleasure seekers.[65] It was only during the late-Victorian price fall that the seaside holiday, as opposed to the day excursion, really became a mass experience in the cotton towns. By the 1870s the attractions of

Blackpool and its rivals, which offered fairgrounds on the beach as well as more sophisticated and spectacular entertainments on dry land, were beginning to outweigh the homelier pleasures of the wakes in the inland towns. August bank holiday was irrelevant in Lancashire,[66] where the nation's first working-class holiday industry came to centre on the traditional wakes, with the variations in timing from town to town ensuring a season of adequate length.[67] During the 1890s approved summer holidays were officially extended to a week by industrial agreement in most of the cotton towns, and the exodus to the seaside could often be counted in tens of thousands. The local press featured descriptions of such places as Burnley and Nelson under headlines reading 'A deserted town', with shops closed and chapels having to join forces to provide a choir for Sunday services. Falling attendances had led Burnley's Sunday-school procession to be switched from the July fair to Whitsuntide in 1890.[68]

These changes were apparent throughout textile Lancashire. The most prosperous and best organised of the working class were likely to be tempted to the coast, and local festivities suffered. Most fairs, like that at Accrington, probably reached their peak in the prosperous early 1870s, declining steadily but not always spectacularly thereafter. Towns with a densely populated area of surrounding villages, such as Oldham and even Burnley, saw their fairs survive more strongly despite the exodus of their own townspeople.[69] But the rise of the seaside, especially from the 1870s onwards, clearly contributed significantly to the decline of the old-style wakes.

The seaside visit itself, however, could become an expression of urban and neighbourhood identity as streets, pubs and religious organisations figured prominently among excursion-promoting bodies, and neighbours joined forces to stay at boarding-houses kept by people from their own home town, at resorts where their local newspaper could be bought at wakes time. It was quite possible to transport local pride and community identity to the seaside, although the excursion was a less potent and more abstracted form of it than the rushcart.[70] Even so, it was the seaside excursion, and especially the rise of the working-class seaside holiday, that brought the greatest disruption to the old ways of observing Lancashire's wakes and summer fairs. Until the mid-Victorian period the changes are a matter of emphasis and nuance, and the continuities predominate. If this is the case, it remains for us to examine the earlier pressures on the Lancashire wakes, and to explain their limited impact.

III

Threats to the wakes from external forces probably reached a peak in the tense and conflict-ridden second quarter of the nineteenth century, when the new industrialist magistrates and the new police forces were mounting a direct assault on popular recreations.[71] Where there was a strong attachment to wakes and fairs, however, the authorities often lacked the means to impose their will. Even where the sense of community and tradition which reinforced the wakes themselves was not present, coercion was sometimes ineffective. By the mid-1830s, for instance, the Bolton authorities were beginning to worry about the unofficial Whitsuntide fair on nearby Rivington Pike, which drew particularly large crowds on the Sunday. 'Orgies' were denounced in 1835, when two traders were fined for 'neglect of divine service'; but the fair continued to flourish, attracting 'humanity in its worst form . . . the concentrated terror of a mighty district harmonising only in their most dangerous proclivities'. In 1883 a local historian unsympathetic to the fair admitted that 'Only within the last few years, when railway companies have proved successful competitors, has it declined.'[72]

Up to mid-century, coercion through legal restraint and labour discipline might shorten the wakes, and change their pattern of observance by restricting activities on the Sunday, but this was usually the limit of its achievement. Even in the cotton factories more holidays than were required by the factory acts were being given in 1840, owing, it was thought, to the power of tradition rather than the master's generosity. In Oldham, for example, the earliest references to cotton mills in this context show them allowing free time at the wakes. In good times it was impossible to prevent absenteeism, and this was reinforced by the general observance of the wakes in other trades.[73] Even attempts merely to channel wakes observance into different days were capable of provoking violent resistance. An attempt in 1829 to ban rushcarts in Oldham on the wakes Saturday, on the grounds that the town was too crowded on that day, was successfully defied by the Greenacres rushcart after 'a terrible conflict . . . in which . . . the authoritys and their assistances were totally defeated [sic]'.[74] For decades, indeed, the police were particularly unpopular at wakes time. Drunken men and women, outraged at being arrested, would attack the police, sometimes with the active assistance of friends and bystanders. In 1864 an editorial in the *Oldham Chronicle* subjected the police to a derisive attack for interfering in the pleasures of the wakes with a string of petty arrests.[75]

This should remind us that the leading citizens of the textile towns were far from unanimous in their attitude to wakes. Admittedly, many did see them as a barbaric survival inappropriate to an age of progress and enlightenment, making people unfit for manual work and imperilling their immortal souls; others saw them as originating in innocent rural diversion, but corrupted by the artificial environment of the factory town and by the evil machinations of the beerseller; while some radicals regarded them as dangerous diversions, distracting people from the self-improvement and political agitation which alone could bring real betterment.[76] These last suspicions, aimed for example at the Tory-inspired revival of the 'nudger sports' at Rochdale Wakes in the 1840s, constituted an angry response to the more tolerant and easy-going side of what may loosely be termed 'middle-class attitudes'. From this latter perspective, the wakes were regarded as a legitimate expression of the working-man's right to spend his limited free time as he chose. Drink, gambling and even blood sports could be be seen as traditional outlets for pent-up energies, to be protected against moralistic intervention from those in authority. Attitudes of this kind were not confined to Tories, although they can rarely have been expressed in nonconformist circles, but sympathy for the working-man's pleasures extended much more readily to the familial and 'respectable' side of the wakes (house-cleaning, hospitality, new clothes and family visits) than to those aspects which shaded over into drunkenness, violence and the frivolous spending of hard-earned income. Even so, the lack of agreement in the attitudes of leading citizens suggests that a concerted assault on the wakes in many towns would have been politically difficult, even if it had been physically possible.[77]

Coercion had a limited impact on the wakes, blood sports apart, and labour discipline, sometimes coupled with the pressures of bad trade, reduced the length of the festivities in the short run without suppressing them altogether. The provision of counter-attractions to lure the young and impressionable away from the temptations of the fairground and the singing saloon was even less successful. When the Bolton Methodists attempted to evangelise the handloom-weaving hamlet of Gate Pike, known locally as 'Hell's Mouth', in the 1840s, they achieved some success with a tea party to keep their scholars away from the nearby Deane Wakes, aided by the novel attraction of real tea as opposed to the concoctions of mint and herbs that prevailed for the rest of the year; but they had no control over where the scholars went when this was over.[78] 'As an antidote these parties are very weak,' it was said in 1877, 'seeing that they are no sooner over about nine o'clock at night than a large majority of those who have been present at them hie themselves off to the fairgrounds.' Temperance groups tried to remedy this by staging meetings lasting several hours and marked by dozens of speeches; their effect as a counter-attraction need only be guessed.[79] The railway excursion was particularly welcome under these conditions as a more thorough-going antidote to temptation than the field day or the tea meeting; but even the Sunday school or temperance trip only took its passengers away for a single day of the wakes.[80] There remained plenty of scope for the working man and his family to don or remove the cap of respectability (a word with many shades of meaning) at will.[81]

The most potent threat to the wakes in the first half of the nineteenth century came not from the machinations of factory masters, magistrates and moral reformers, but from economic stringency. Evidence from Oldham suggests that the prevailing attitude to the wakes among the working classes was one of 'eat, drink and be merry'. People celebrated to the limit of their means, and beyond that if they could. Generosity and indulgence prevailed over thrift. In 1831 the Oldham diarist, Edwin Butterworth, complained that people were 'fond of drinking themselves into the midst of distress, for the sole purpose of supporting the disgraceful, useless wake'.[82] Despite the determination to celebrate at all costs, times were so hard in some years during the French Wars and their aftermath that the wakes almost disappeared and the streets filled with people who came simply to look, and to be there. As late as 1842 there were no rushcarts, amusements were 'extremely scanty', and the mills worked right through the wakes in the aftermath of the great strike.[83] More generally, the plight of the handloom weavers steadily reduced the participation of an occupational group which in Bamford's time had been well placed to support the celebrations. But the wakes survived the worst slumps of the 1830s and 1840s, despite middle-class expectations of their final demise, to continue into the more prosperous mid-Victorian years.

As the trade cycle bit less deeply during the second half of the nineteenth century, the pressures on the wakes became more subtle. Attempts at outright suppression of fairs persisted, usually spearheaded by militant evangelicals and Nonconformists. Such pressures reached a peak in the late 1870s. Eccles Wakes Fair was suppressed in 1877, as were the street fairs at Church and Oswaldtwistle and the most famous casualty of all, Manchester's Knott Mill Fair at Easter. In the latter case, unavailing support for the fair came from antiquarians and local councillors who were concerned to defend working-class amusements; but they were powerless against a memorial from the local clergy, endorsed by Mr Harwood's confident belief that 'the intelligence of the citizens desired the discontinuance of Knott Mill Fair, and therefore the Council had only one course to pursue'.[84] The view that the opinion of 'the intelligence of the citizens' on the wakes outweighed that of the masses who actually celebrated the holiday, and who could therefore scarcely be trusted to reason objectively, was a common one among the opponents of popular recreations. 'A Tradesman', who supported the abortive attempt to change the date of Cheadle Wakes in 1884-5, countered the evidence of overwhelming votes in factories in favour of the old wakes by asserting that of eleven people he had interviewed in a political club, only one — who worked in a brewery — had opposed the change. 'Such', he concluded triumphantly, 'is the opinion of representative working men.'[85] The Eccles and Manchester Fairs were suppressed under an enabling act of 1871 which simplified the legal procedure of abolition. Nearly three hundred fairs were listed as being abolished between 1871 and 1898, but only a handful were in Lancashire. The vast majority were in the rural south, and nearly half in the East Anglian counties of Essex, Suffolk and Norfolk.[86] In practice, this legislation could only be used against fairs held on open public spaces.

Another occasional tactic was for employers and local authorities to change the date at which they gave the annual wakes holiday. In Oldham, for example, the School Board spearheaded a campaign in 1878 to consolidate the area's wakes into a single week in order to prevent repeated absenteeism by pupils and employees observing several different holidays. They won the support of the Town Council, reformers and some employers to establish a new wakes in early August, but it proved impossible to stop people observing the old one. Rather than support two annual holidays for the town, the experiment was abandoned in 1882.[87] Stockport had a similar experience in 1884-6.[88]

Many wakes acquired powerful local defenders. At Stockport the Edgeley Fair at Cheadle Wakes was successfully defended for twenty years after 1865 by publicans and local tradesmen as the Corporation, against the wishes of the local workpeople, responded to pressure to abolish street stalls and alter the timing of the wakes. Here, commercial interests could successfully exploit the rhetoric of community and conviviality against external interference. Publicans and tradesmen also cleverly used the link in the popular mind between a good wakes and economic well-being by implicitly identifying their own profits from the wakes with local prosperity. Reformers point to the self-interest of such arguments, and to the hypocrisy of the 'Mr. Spend-your-money-with-your-neeburs' men who spent their wakes profits on holidays as far away as America. They insisted passionately that the wakes was a time of dissipation and impoverishment, but such killjoy logic was quite foreign to the bulk of the population.[89]

As in London, no doubt, a mellowing of middle-class attitudes (already divided and uncertain) towards popular leisure activities was combined with the growing confidence of a maturing police service in its ability to control festive crowds, whose behaviour was itself becoming less violent and unreasonable.[90] The local wakes were becoming more tolerable to the propertied classes as the holiday crowds headed increasingly for the seaside rather than the fairground. The wakes changed their character over our period, but they did so far more in response to social and economic change than to reform from above.

IV

The Lancashire wakes, especially in the area around Manchester where rushbearing flourished, were more than just well-established fairs. They remained for most, if not all, of the nineteenth century affirmations of community identity, both past and present, in which people expressed themselves through uninhibited pleasure-seeking. Significantly, though, the holiday was being approached in an increasingly calculative manner by the 1870s and 1880s as people were obliged to prepare for unpaid seaside holidays by steady saving throughout the year, although it often remained a point of honour that what had been saved should be spent to the last penny.[91]

We have argued more generally that pressure from above was not an important influence on the evolution of the wakes. What counted was economic change, as the decline of the handloom weavers undermined the wakes during the first half of the nineteenth century, while the trade cycle almost extinguished celebrations in some years. During the second half of the nineteenth century the railway excursion, the rise of the seaside holiday and improving living standards generally played important roles, as did the cumulative impact of urbanisation. Responses to economic change were themselves affected by changes in working-class attitudes, of course, and here one can point to a growing prosperity for thrift, calculation and what contemporaries saw as 'rationality'. We have not been able to identify a culture of improvement and 'rationality' with the emergence of a new kind of labour aristocracy in the textile towns; and in this respect our findings incline towards Joyce's interpretation of Lancashire society and politics rather than Foster's.[92] Our evidence suggests that attitudes to wakes cut across status barriers within the working class; at any rate, such barriers do not seem to have been an important influence on the evolution of the wakes.

The considerable measure of continuity in the Lancashire wakes may seem surprising, but it accords with much recent scholarship which has tended to stress the underlying stability of the textile district, in spite of short-term disruption.[93] Evidence from other industrial areas suggests that they, too, cleaved strongly to traditional holidays and modes of enjoyment. In the Potteries, the Black Country and the West Riding the wakes, feasts and similar festivals may well have survived for an even longer period in a form which would have been recognisable to Samuel Bamford.[94] In Lancashire, as in the nation at large, the wakes and fairs of the rural, rather than of the industrial, areas appear to have been the main casualties.[95] This paper is only a start, but it suggests that many popular customs in Lancashire survived not only in spite of, but also because of, industrialisation.

Notes

1. S. Bamford, *Early Days* (Cass reprint, London, 1967), pp.134-60.

2. R.W. Malcolmson, *Popular Recreations in English Society 1700-1850* (Cambridge, 1973), pp.16-19; F.W. Hackwood, *Staffordshire Customs, Superstitions and Folklore* (Lichfield, 1924; reprinted Wakefield, 1974), pp.104-7 (we owe this reference to Doug Reid); N. McKendrick, 'Joseph Wedgewood and Factory Discipline', *Historical Journal*, vol.4 (1961); John Sykes, *Slawit in the 'Sixties* (Huddersfield, n.d.), p.63; J.K. Walton, 'The Demand for Working-Class Seaside Holidays in Victorian England', *Economic History Review* (May 1981).

3. Manchester and Bolton had no wakes of their own, although they flourished in the surrounding villages and smaller towns. Whitsuntide long remained the main holiday of the spring and summer in these centres, and also at Blackburn and Preston.

4. Bamford, *Early Days*, pp.146-56.

5. D. Bythell,*The Hand-Loom Weavers* (London, 1969), *passim;* see also J.G. Timmins, *Hand-loom Weavers' cottages in Central Lancashire* (Lancaster, 1977), p.59.

6. S. Pollard, *The Genesis of Modern Management* (London, 1965), Ch.5.

7. See especially T.R. Tholfsen, *Working-Class Radicalism in Mid-Victorian England* (London, 1976), Ch.2.

8. R.D. Storch, 'The Plague of the Blue Locusts: Police Reform and Popular Resistance in Northern England 1840-57', *International Review of Social History*, 20 (1975), pp.61-90; idem, 'The Policeman as Domestic Missionary: Urban Discipline and Popular Culture in Northern England, 1850-80' *J. of Social History*, vol.9. (1975-6), pp.481-509; D. Foster, 'The Changing Social and Political Composition of the Lancashire Magistracy 1821-51', unpublished thesis, Unviersity of Lancaster, 1971, Ch.3.

9. Storch, 'The Blue Locusts', *passim*. P. Bailey, *Leisure and Class in Victorian England* (London and Toronto, 1978), Ch.1.

10. Bamford, *Early Days*, p.132.

11. P. Joyce, *Work, Society and Politics; the Factory North of England 1860-90* (Brighton, 1980), especially Ch.4.

12. V.A.C. Gatrell, 'The Commercial Middle Class in Manchester, c. 1820-57', unpublished PhD thesis, University of Cambridge, 1974, p.81; idem., 'Labour, Power and the Size of Firms in the Cotton Industry in the Second Quarter of the Nineteenth Century', *Economic History Review*, vol.30 (1977), pp.95-139; R. Lloyd-Jones and A.A. Le Roux, 'The Size of Firms in the Cotton Industry: Manchester 1815-41', *Ec.H.R.*, vol.33 (1980), pp.72-82; M. Anderson, *Family Structure in Nineteenth-Century Lancashire* (Cambridge, paperback ed., 1974), pp.22-9, 121-2.

13. A. Redford, *Labour Migration in England 1800-50* (Manchester, 1926); Anderson, *Family Structure*, pp.34-41; J.D. Marshall, 'Colonisation as a Factor in the Planting of Towns in North-West England', in H.J. Dyos (ed.), *The Study of Urban History* (London, 1968), pp.215-30; Joyce, *Work, Society and Politics, passim*.

14. Walton, *Working-class Seaside Holidays, passim*.

15. Storch, 'Blue Locusts', p.86; idem, 'Policeman as Domestic Missionary', p.489.

16. Joyce, *Work, Society and Politics*, pp.286, 338; on the themes of this paragraph, see H. Cunningham, *Leisure in the Industrial Revolution* (London, 1980), Ch.2.

17. Cunningham is now the most conspicuous exception.

18. B. Harrison, *Drink and the Victorians* (London, 1970), p.330.

19. Malcolmson, *Popular Recreations*, p.151; E.P. Thompson, 'Time, Work-Discipline and Industrial Capitalism', *Past and Present*, no.38 (1967), p.76.

20. H. Cunningham, 'The Metropolitan Fairs: a Case Study in the Social Control of Leisure', in A.P. Donajgrodzki (ed.), *Social Control in Nineteenth-Century Britain* (London, 1977), pp.163-84: D. Reid, 'The Decline of Saint Monday 1766-1876', *Past and Present*, no.71 (1976), pp.76-101.

21. Bailey, *Leisure and Class, passim*.

22. *STA*, 27 Aug. 1824, 6 Aug. 1828, 3 Aug. 1829, 29 Aug. 1839, 26 July 1867.

23. Robert Poole's forthcoming thesis will have more to say about this.

24. Malcolmson, *Popular Recreations*, pp.125-6.

25. T. Swindells, *Old Eccles* (Pendleton, 1914), pp.28-30; J.T. Slugg, *Reminiscences of Manchester Fifty Years Ago* (Manchester, 1881), p.310.

26. J. Dyson, *Rural Congregationalism* (Manchester, 1881), pp.81-3; W. Nicholls, *The History and Traditions of Radcliffe* (Manchester, n.d.), p.208; C.E. Warrington, *The History of a Parish* (Rochdale, 2nd ed., 1970), pp.30-1. The difference between 'wakes' and 'fairs' becomes increasingly confused over the nineteenth century. A 'wakes' proper was in origin a festival commemorating the patron saint of a church. A 'fair' proper was in origin a chartered trade fair. By

the mid-nineteenth century, many trade fairs had become predominantly pleasure fairs (such as Blackburn's Easter Fair), and many unchartered pleasure fairs had sprung up, particularly at local wakes. The annual holidays of northern Lancashire were known as 'fairs' and 'feasts' rather than as 'wakes'. From the late nineteenth century, the term 'wakes' came to be applied to all the Lancashire cotton holidays, regardless of whether they originated from wakes or fairs. In addition, some 'wakes' and 'fairs' were the creations of publicans. For example, 'Cross Keys Fair' was instituted by the landlord of the Cross Keys Inn, Howcroft, to commemorate the siege of Gibraltar in 1792; 'Halshaw Moor Wakes' was created by a Farnworth publican in 1827. Such unofficial celebrations were not in themselves holidays, although some were timed to coincide with existing holidays, while others, such as Cross Keys Fair, came to be observed as such locally. To complicate matters still further, the term 'rushbearing', denoting a wakes custom, was current as far north as Cumberland.

27. T. Middleton, *History of Hyde and its Neighbourhood* (Hyde, 1932), pp. 516-18.

28. Malcolmson, *Popular Recreations*, pp.125-6. The last bull-bait at Lydgate, an Oldham out-township, occurred as late as 1849: W. Bates, *The Handy Book of Oldham* (Oldham, 1877).

29. House of Commons Select Committee on Public Houses and Places of Entertainment. *PP* (1852-3), 6273 ff.; *Preston Chronicle*, 18 June 1859; T.H. Hayhurst, *The Conquest of Gentleness* (Bury, 1910), pp.124-7.

30. See Cunningham, *Leisure in the Industrial Revolution*, p.10, for some perceptive comments on the difficulty of evaluating apparent 'survivals' of this kind.

31. Dyson, *Rural Congregationalism*, pp.81-3; Nicholls, *Radcliffe*, p.208; Jesse Blakey, *Annals and Stories of Barrowford* (Nelson, 1929), p.358.

32. Large-scale fighting was still a common and expected feature at some wakes in the 1870s and 1880s: *RO* 16 Sept. 1876 (Whitworth Wakes); *BC*, 10 Sept. 1870 (Turton Fair); *OC*, 11 Aug. 1877 (Saddleworth and Delph). It was more general and probably more brutal at mid-century; see, for instance, Lord George Sanger, *Seventy Years a Showman* (London, 1926), p.62.

33. Rushcarts were not as old as wakes, but by the late eighteenth century they had become the centre of wakes activity in many places.

34. A. Burton, *Rushbearing* (Manchester, 1891), Ch.3 and 4.

35. Bamford, *Early Days*, pp.149-50.

36. *Manchester Examiner*, 31 Aug. 1847, 2 Sept. 1848; *OC*, 1 Sept. 1860.

37. Illustrative comments and examples can be found in: *BC*, 8 Sept. 1877, 4 Sept. 1880; *RO*, 24 Aug. 1878; *OC*, 7 Sept. 1861, 2 Sept. 1865, 8 Sept. 1877. Apart from the intolerant *Rochdale Observer*, newspapers in the 1850s and 1860s generally refer to rowdy elements rather than a rowdy population, but actual details are obscured by vague phrases such as 'much rowdiness, as usual, prevailed'.

38. Bamford, *Early Days*, pp.147-9; T. Middleton, 'Rushbearing and Morris-Dancing in North Cheshire', *Lancashire and Cheshire Antiquarian Society Transactions*, 60 (1948), pp.47-55; A. Helm, 'Rushcarts of North-West England', *Folk Life* (1970), pp.22-31.

39. Rushcarts appeared in the 1880s in Saddleworth, Delph, Middleton, Milnrow, Royton, Lees, Newton Heath, Shaw and Oldham. At Uppermill rushcarts were occasionally appearing around 1909, and at Hyde the Godley Hill rushcart continued until the First World War (Middleton, 'Rushbearing', pp. 51-3). See also Burton, *Rushbearing*, pp.64, 79-88; and *OC*, 25 Aug. 1883, 30 Aug. 1884, 6 Sept. 1884.

40. *RO*, 21 Aug. 1869.

41. Oldham Local Interest Centre, Butterworth Mss., Sept. 1834.
42. *OC*, 1 Sept. 1860.
43. For illustrations, see Burton, *Rushbearing*, pp.69, 87.
44. *OC*, 3 Sept. 1864. The man killed was an obstreperous drunk who tried to join the rushcart and fell under the wheels.
45. Burton, *Rushbearing*, pp.53, 81-4; J. Bradbury, *Saddleworth Sketches* (Oldham, 1871), p.253; *OC*, 24 Aug. 1878 (rushgathering), 31 Aug. 1861 (sale of rushcart to publican).
46. *OS*, 16 Sept. 1879.
47. W. Bowman, *England in Ashton-Under-Lyne* (Altrincham, 1960), p.302.
48. *OS*, 26 Aug. 1865 (Middleton); Burton, *Rushbearing*, p. 88 (Uppermill); *STA*, 13 Aug. 1886 (Withington).
49. Burton, *Rushbearing*, p.61.
50. *OC*, 5 Sept. 1863 (grove carts, Adam and Eve carts, dirt cart); Butterworth Mss., Sept. 1835, Sept. 1836 (first coal carts); *OC*, 6 Sept. 1856; *RO*, 21 Aug. 1880 (falling standards).
51. Burton, *Rushbearing*, p. 73; Bradbury, *Saddleworth Sketches*, p.258.
52. S. Hill, *Bygone Staleybridge* (Stalybridge, 1907), pp.145-6.
53. *STA*, 29 Aug. 1851; *OC*, 31 Aug. 1861; *OC*, 3 Sept. 1864; Burton, *Rushbearing*, p.81.
54. *OC*, 24 Aug. 1878.
55. Bamford, *Early Days*, pp.154-5.
56. Blakey, *Barrowford*, p.357.
57. Sykes, *Slawit*, pp.63-5; *Huddersfield Examiner*, 14 Aug. 1875.
58. *Huddersfield Examiner*, 14 Aug. 1880; cf. Joyce, *Work, Society and Politics, passim.*
59. *BC*, 30 Aug. 1879.
60. For examples, see *STA*, 18 July 1873, 30 July 1876.
61. *OC*, 26 Aug. 1854, 11 Aug. 1860.
62. Sykes, *Slawit*, pp. 65-8; *Oldham Evening Chronicle*, 4 Sept. 1897; Sanger, *Seventy Years a Showman, passim.*
63. *Burnley Express*, 14 July 1888.
64. *AT*, 9 Aug. 1890.
65. By the 1850s, one day of the wakes was usually set aside for excursions.
66. Pace Joyce, *Work, Society and Politics*, p.338.
67. J.K. Walton, *The Blackpool Landlady: a Social History* (Manchester, 1978), p.39, and 'Working-class Seaside Holidays', *passim.*
68. *Burnley Express*, 18 July 1888, 20 May 1890, 19 July 1899, 16 Aug. 1899.
69. *Oldham Evening Chronicle*, 4 Sept. 1897: *AT*, 3 Aug. 1872; *Preston Guardian*, 11 July 1877, 20 July 1881.
70. Walton, *The Blackpool Landlady*, pp.31-40.
71. Storch, 'Blue Locusts', p.84. Pressure on fairs and wakes also mounted in the 1870s, as local government gained in power and self-confidence in the cotton towns.
72. T. Hampson, *Horwich: its History, Legends and Church* (Wigan, 1883), pp.237-8.
73. House of Commons Select Committee on Factories and Mills, *PP* (1840), vol.10, pp.384-9, 1335-8.
74. Samuel Andrew (ed.), *Annals of Oldham*, p.149 (volume of cuttings from *Oldham Standard*, 1887-9, in Oldham Local Interest Centre).
75. *OC*, 3 Sept. 1864.
76. Butterworth Mss., Aug. 1831, Sept. 1833, Sept. 1834, Aug. 1835; *The Spectator: a Rochdale Miscellany*, 19 (September 1845), pp.147-9.
77. For tolerant attitudes to wakes, *STA*, 5 Aug. 1825, 6 Oct. 1837. For

divisions among elites, Gatrell, 'Commercial Middle Class', pp.211-14, and Joyce, *Work, Society and Politics, passim.*

78. H. Cottrell, *Gate Pike, the Story of Eighty Years' Methodism* (Bolton, 1923), pp.10-61; for length of holidays, J.K. Walton, 'The Social Development of Blackpool 1788-1914', unpublished PhD thesis, University of Lancaster, 1974, pp.269-72.

79. *Farnworth Journal,* 22 Sept. 1877; see *OC,* 5 Sept. 1863, for a wakes Sunday temperance 'love feast' with 36 speeches.

80. Walton, thesis, pp.283-4.

81. Cf. P. Bailey, 'Will the real Bill Banks Please Stand Up? Towards a Role Analysis of Mid-Victorian Working-class Respectability', *J. of Social History,* vol.12 (1979), pp.336-53.

82. Butterworth Mss., Aug. 1831.

83. Butterworth Mss., Sept. 1842; Andrew, *Annals,* Sept. 1793, Aug. 1799, Aug. 1811, Aug. 1816. Such short-term declines resulting from the trade cycle should not be confused with long-term declines from other causes. For examples of such confusion see M. Hodgson, 'The working day and the working week in Victorian Britain', unpublished thesis, University of London, 1974, pp.222 and 242 n.4.

84. Swindells, *Eccles,* p.34; *AT,* 18 Aug. 1877; *Manchester Guardian,* 13 Apr. 1877.

85. *STA,* 18 Sept. 1885.

86. Public Record Office, HO45/9807/B6343.

87. *OC,* 6 Sept. 1879, 4 Sept. 1880, 3 June 1882.

88. *STA,* 11 Apr. 1884, 30 May 1884, 15 Aug. 1884, 14 Aug. 1885, 30 July 1886, 27 Aug. 1886, 30 Aug. 1877.

89. *STA,* 11, 18 & 25 Sept. 1885. Cheadle Wakes was celebrated as Stockport's wakes as well, even though the two towns were in different parishes. By the 1870s, the festivities had almost completely moved to Stockport (*STA,* 25 Aug. 1874). The fair at Edgeley, an area of Stockport, was part of the Stockport side of the celebrations.

90. Cunningham, 'Metropolitan fairs', pp.178-81.

91. Such attitudes were still much in evidence in 1911, when an August rail strike left thousands of holidaymakers stranded, having spent all their savings: *Blackpool Gazette,* 22 Aug. 1911. Some observers, particularly outsiders, regarded the 'going-off clubs' as agencies for dissipation rather than for saving. 'Thrift of a sort, but hardly of the right sort', was how one London newspaper put it: *OC,* 30 Aug. 1890.

92. J. Foster, *Class Struggle and the Industrial Revolution* (London, 1974), pp.223-4; Joyce, *Work, Society and Politics, passim.*

93. Especially the work of Gatrell and Joyce, cited above.

94. Walton, 'Working-class Seaside Holidays', *passim.*

95. Cunningham, *Leisure in the Industrial Revolution,* pp.62-3; cf. e.g. F. Cookson, *Goosnargh Past and Present* (Preston, 1887), p.16, for the suppression of Inglewhite pleasure fair. More work on rural Lancashire needs to be done.

6 INTERPRETING THE FESTIVAL CALENDAR: WAKES AND FAIRS AS CARNIVALS*

Douglas A. Reid

This essay will reconstruct the experience of the wakes and fairs of eighteenth- and nineteenth-century Birmingham in the light of the concept of the 'carnivalesque'. It will contend that much that is seemingly unconnected or bizarre falls into place if we make the 'carnivalesque' the central organising concept of our efforts to categorise the content and social functions of these popular festivals. The essay analyses the causes of the 'taming' of the wakes and the gradual decline of both the wakes and fairs. Precisely because the wakes were 'carnivalesque' they came under early attack from both without and within the plebeian culture, though, ultimately, the forces arrayed against the wakes were similar to those which attacked the fairs: industrial capitalism, urbanisation, and, perhaps most important, the hostile culture − strongly associated with evangelicalism − of sobriety, orderliness, 'rationality' and the pursuit of progress.

I

The classic locations of carnivals in early modern times were in Southern Europe.[1] Though England lacked the festival of carnival proper it had other festivals which shared its characteristics. What were they? The dominant *motif* is suggested by the etymology of the word carnival: *carnem levare*, 'the putting away of flesh' before Lent, encouraged a valedictory indulgence in the sins of the flesh, in gluttony, intemperance and lechery. Hence the *motifs* of licentiousness, of abandonment of restraint, of liberation. Carnival, then, was a period of indulgence in food and drink, enhanced sexuality, singing and dancing in the streets, familiarity between strangers, the acting out of aggressiveness, the acceptance of folly and carnival 'madness'. Its *leitmotif* was the inversion of the normal rules of culture.

The relaxation of inhibition and the acceptance of folly were encouraged by the adoption of costume and masking by the participants; the blackening of faces or the fully fledged masquerade disguised the normal self and excused lack of responsibility. In addition

125

there were ritual spectacles – processions, effigies, floats, plays, pageants – which travestied and symbolically inverted the normal order of things. Carnival was also characterised by sporting competition – foot-races, horse-races, jousts, football matches (although the latter were often ritual battles rather than true sport). What is the essence of the excitement offered by competition in sport? It is the possibility of the over-turning of the odds, and established reputations, of the reversal of 'normality'; hence the uncertainty of sporting competitions was eminently appropriate at a carnival. Carnival was 'a time of institutionalised disorder, a set of rituals of reversal', in which nothing was sacred, including ecclesiastical and temporal authority, for the ultimate symbolic inversion was the inversion of the social hierarchy.[2]

Peter Burke cites many examples of the carnivalesque in the observation of the English festival calendar: for instance, at Christmas (*vide* the personification of Yule and his wife in procession at York, and the Feast of Fools on 28 December), and May Day (with its elaborate May Games organised under the authority of temporary 'Kings' and 'Queens' and its associated sexual licence). However, these festivals were severely curtailed at the Reformation, and so eighteenth-century English festival activities substantially lacked the mock games and ritual spectacles which persisted in Catholic Europe.[3]

Nevertheless, once we begin to look at the English popular holiday calendar in our period in terms of the carnivalesque, the concept offers a key to the meaning of the cluster of customs attached to many popular holidays. The editor of this volume himself demonstrates its applicability in his discussion of Guy Fawkes Day.[4] Much evidence presented in R.W. Malcolmson's *Popular Recreations in English Society 1700-1850* may also be read in this light, adding a new, integrative dimension to his otherwise valuable account.[5] The following analysis of wakes presents a case-study in this approach[6] in an important provincial town.[7]

Wakes were annual feasts commemorating the dedication of a parish church. William Hutton gave a colourful account of their origins, together with his impression of their status in 1781:

When a church was erected, it was immediately called after a saint . . . and the day belonging to that saint [was] kept as an high festival. In the evening preceding the day, the inhabitants, with lights, approached the church, and kept a continual devotion during the whole night; hence the name *wake*: After which they entered into festivity. But now the devotional part is forgot, the church is deserted, and the festivity turned into riot, drunkenness and mischief.

The oldest Birmingham wake took place in the hamlet of Deritend where a chapel was erected in 1382[8] Birmingham had two fairs by this time, their charters granted in 1250 and 1251. The first lasted four days, beginning on the eve of Ascension Day; the second lasted three days, pivoted on Midsummer Day, but was later transferred to Michaelmas (28 September), perhaps during the Reformation. The Spring Fair was transferred from Ascension Day to Whit week at the introduction of the New Style calendar in 1752[9] Both were trading occasions with ancillary pleasure functions, in contrast to the wake, which was confined to pleasure, although townspeople erected stalls and tents for the sale of small consumables.[10]

By the early nineteenth century the religious significance of the wake was greatly diminished. Bulrushes were still carried to the chapel, but it was largely a secular festival under publicans' patronage.[11] This was also the case with the two new wakes begun in 1750 and 1751. Chapel Wake took its name from the newly built St Bartholomew's Chapel, but — according to Hutton — it was 'hatched and fostered by the publicans, for the benefit of the spiggot'. Bell Wake originated 'from the same cause, in 1751, in consequence of ten bells being hung up in St Philip's steeple'.[12] Bell Wake was held in the Navigation Street area, and Chapel Wake at the opposite, north-eastern, side of the town. The three wakes began on the Sundays closest to 25 July, 7 August, 24 August, and a 'good wake often lasted for three or four days . . . Monday was, however, the principal holiday'.[13]

For several decades after 1750 then the wakes were holidays — great days of high spirits, sport, folly and release. There was eating and drinking on a great scale. Publicans held ox-roastings at which unlimited quantities could be eaten for threepence.[14] Throughout the wakes 'the ale houses and taverns . . . were the chief resort'.[15] Hutton noted:

> In the evening the passenger cannot proceed without danger; in the morning he may discover which houses are public, without other intelligence than the copious streams that have issued from the wall. The blind may distinguish the same thing, by the strong scent of the tap.[16]

A nineteenth-century observer recalled that 'a crowd of persons round a drunken man lying insensible on the streets during the afternoon was not uncommon'.[17]

Wakes were occasions for many sports and competitions, some involving brutality to animals: 'Chapel Wake was the best for sports . . . and an unusual amount of bull-baiting, cock-fighting, badger-baiting . . . was there indulged in '.[18] Another contest was found only at wakes. A live goose was tied by its legs upon a string stretching from one side of the street to the other, and 'men on horseback struggled to gain the bird, whose neck had been soaped, by pulling it from the rope as they rode underneath'.[19]

The wakes therefore were festivals of cruelty. No doubt they were crudely functional here, funnelling violent feelings and displacing aggression from men to animals.[20] However, the nature of the sports also indicates the more immediate influence of the eighteenth-century gambling mania and its encouragement by publicans. A particular 'yard in Coleshill-Street' was mentioned in connection with bear-baiting and pugilism; it was doubtless an inn yard, and doubtless this inn which gave Chapel Wake its especial sporting reputation.[21] Horse and donkey racing was also promoted. 'What singular genius introduced the horse race into a crowded street'. Hutton knew not, but — in an indication of the pressure on space which increasingly dogged these wakes — someone was killed one year, which 'rather slackened the entertainment'.[22] Nevertheless, the wakes remained occasions when the labouring poor took over the streets, when they were important, at least in their own eyes, and to that extent 'the world was turned upside down'.[23]

The games and competitions which involved people characteristically offered a distorted image of normality and conventional social behaviour. 'There was grinning through collars . . . and leaping in sacks', 'bobbing at treacle rolls, [and] climbing up poles for legs of mutton'. 'Full grown men', said the disapproving reporter, 'had their hands tied behind them, and standing in rows round public house tables strove who would first eat their platters of hot hasty pudding'.[24] this might not be Carnival madness, but it was certainly not everyday behaviour, the normal rules of culture had been suspended.

Wakes also represented a period of sexual release. 'Boys in a nude state, and females almost in a similar condition, ran for caps and gowns . . . unseemly races in the public thoroughfare'.[25] Women ran 'smock races' (in their underwear) for gowns and pounds of tea.[26] Men, 'nude, bedaubed with treacle, and sometimes feathered, were seen competing for prizes in the principal streets of the town'.[27] In the evening 'music and dancing' were carried on in 'almost every public house', stimulating amorous relationships.[28] A later music-hall comic singer alluded to the wakes as times when 'the big boys and girls/With crinoline and curls/Get kissing each other/Like sisters and brothers/And at lots of other games about which I'll not speak'.[29] The scandals which arose were grist to the mill of the broadside press, which chaffed Kate Billy, a 'wire bodger', for neglecting her sick mother to 'ramble about the Wake with your fancy chaps', and a 'bouncing bedstead-maker' from the same street, who 'made love to fourteen gals in one night at Deritend Wake'.[30]

Wakes were glorious annual flings, festivals of cruelty and sensuality. They stood for the ancient tradition of carnival, and even for that of Saturnalia, 'the few days in the year when the barriers erected by the conscious mind were dropped and people abandoned themselves to the irresponsible . . . [impulses] which lay in their unconscious'.[31] It is of course possible that, to some of the participants, drinking feats, fighting,[32] cruel sport with animals, and bawdy behaviour, were simply *intensifications* of their normal pursuits rather than the inversion of 'normality' — in which case doubts might be raised about the application of the concept of the carnivalesque to the participants *vis-à-vis* the spectators.[33] However, 'goose-riding', horse-racing, foot-racing in *déshabillé*, all through the main streets of the town, bizarre competitions and great feasting, were certainly reversals of everyday norms, even for the chief participants. To most of the crowd the extraordinary concentration of unfamiliar amusements and familiar activities taken to excess must have constituted wakes as 'rituals of disorder'.

Recent scholarly speculation has concluded that such events probably served (sometimes were intended to serve[34]) as safety-valves for the release of tensions which build up in vastly unequal, strictly hierarchical societies.[35] Such an analysis cannot be fully applied to Birmingham by the mid-eighteenth century, for the social hierarchy could not seem fixed and immutable in such an economically progressive town; therefore a 'safety-valve' was hardly so necessary.[36] It is a mark of this that local elites were beginning to query the utility of wakes rather than encouraging or, at least, tolerating them, and secondly that a noticeable cultural differentiation occurred within the ranks of the labouring poor leading an unquantifiable but important section to reject the carnivalesque. Nevertheless, wakes were more than just declining survivals from a more hierarchical age; they certainly remained functionally relevant to the most over-worked, least privileged sections of the working population, to those who were not able to take 'Saint Monday' holidays, to those such as labourers or domestic servants perhaps whose pent-up energies and accumulated tensions may well have given the wakes some of their zest.[37] Inequality remained even if the social hierarchy was less rigid.

Evidence that the wakes were tolerated or encouraged by local elites is not easy to come by; it is interesting, however, that in 1745 the company of players at Moor Street Theatre announced that they would not perform that night 'on account of Deritend Wake'.[38] There were certainly genteel supporters of bull-baiting and cock-fighting in the late eighteenth and early nineteenth centuries and a nude runner was protected from prosecution 'by a powerful interest' in 1809.[39] By this time, however, hostility was much the most prominent reaction to wakes from local elites. In 1773 the Street Commissioners procured an Improvement Act which banned bonfires and fireworks from 'any of the streets ... or ... publick places' but made bull-baiting a fineable offence 'in *any part* of the town'.[40] Shortly afterwards the following notice appeared:

> There having been great Disturbances ... in or near this Town, occasioned by Bull-baiting, [*inter alia*] ... to the great Annoyance of the Publick Peace; Therefore this is to forwarn all Publicans and others from having Bulls baited, Races, or any other Methods usually practised at Wakes, as the Magistrates are determined to punish all such People to the utmost of their Power.[41]

There was concern that baiting bulls in urban streets was dangerous to life and limb,[42] but apprehension about disorder was the dominant theme.[43]

The 1790s also saw protests because of cruelty to animals at wakes:

> A Correspondent laments ... that, in this neighbourhood ... a custom so barbarous as bull-baiting should still have continuance among the common people. A few days ago he beheld a scene ... that deeply affected his feelings ... the relentless mob were leading the mangled object of their outrage ... Its nose and lips (lacerated by dogs) seemed strings of bleeding flesh![44]

Such tender feelings were new in Europe in the eighteenth century, and were perhaps a symptom of the Enlightenment, though this particular example was late enough in the century to be influenced by English evangelicalism.[45]

Evangelicalism was certainly instrumental in raising the threshold of tolerance; three prosecutions in 1809 seem to have permanently halted the participation of adults in the nude races through the streets.[46] By 1849 fear of disorderliness, disgust at drunkenness, antipathy to cruelty and intolerance of 'indecency' had come together in a general condemnation of 'dissipation and folly'.[47]

This is not altogether surprising given what is known about the appreciating concern for labour discipline by employers in this period.[48] The themes of this chapter cannot be reduced to simple reflections of the process of disciplining the labour force, but they were, of course, highly congruent with it, and we often find them together. Bull-baiting was condemned both as 'a barbarous and brutal sport' and as a hindrance of business'.[49] In 1829 Henry Hughes, charged under the Master and Servant Laws 'with neglecting the service of . . . his master, by absenting himself at . . . [a] Wake, for the best part of a week, . . . was committed to . . . jail for one month's hard labour'.[50] In 1843 twelve children and young people, from a range of trades, were questioned about their holidays; all but two of them had holidays at the fairs, but none at the wakes.[51]

By 1851 contemporaries had begun tolling the funeral bell for the wakes, 'For about twenty years', said one, 'the wakes have been gradually falling off in importance, and are likely to become almost extinct in a few years'.[52] To consider the decline of the wakes is to consider the wane of a particular phase of popular culture. Their falling-off cannot be explained solely in terms of exterior pressures however; account must be taken of changes *within* popular culture.

The advanced division of labour which characterised Birmingham workshop manufactures (which was the partial cause of the discouragement of the wakes by employers) was also a cause of increased social differentiation within the ranks of the poor. Thus by the 1780s a graphic contrast could be drawn between 'japanners' and pin-makers, 'which may be considered as the extremes of high and low' with 'manners and morals . . . as different as the employments'. Such contrasts were decided fundamentally by skill, and related earning power, but were most strikingly displayed in leisure time.

The . . . japanners, rarely associated, in their hours of relaxation, with the workers of copper, brass, iron, &c., the latter frequent the common pot-house, the former get into the third and fourth inns and club rooms, with the little tradesmen, considering themselves rather as artists than artisans.[53]

These tendencies to differentiation were reinforced by the growth of a 'popular articulacy'. Some artisans now shared in the self-consciously literate culture of newspaper reading, book clubs and tavern debating societies,[54] cutting themselves off from a wider popular culture which was primarily oral and traditional. They became more receptive to the ethic of industriousness, sobriety and moral improvement, and perhaps to evangelical theology. Thus we find the 'apprentices' and 'mechanics' of the Free Debating Society at the *Red Lion,* Digbeth, in 1774, deciding that 'Prayer to God for the Renewal of the Heart is the most likely Means to prevent . . . the Increase of Criminal Offences'[55] Superior artisans could now emphasise their separateness and superiority by shunning those aspects of plebeian culture already rejected by 'the respectable inhabitants'.[56] Thus we now find artisans debating whether 'Holidays' were 'of Bad consequence either to Servants or Masters'![57]

A new artisan sub-culture was evolving, characterised in varying measure by rationalism, evangelicalism and political radicalism, and deeply hostile to the licentious release associated with the wakes. Its characteristic recreational institutions were to be the temperance societies of the 1830s, the Christian Chartist Church, the Hall of Science and the Athenic Society of the 1840s, the Public Recreation Society and St Martin's Working Men's Association of the 1850s; and its chief achievements in the field of recreation were the encouragement of excursions, the Saturday half-holiday, and the public park movement.[58] It is in this light that we should assess statements that 'decent artisans' now avoided the wakes 'as scenes of debauchery and drunkenness'.[59] Popular culture thus became polarised between two hostile blocs, with much of the 'natural leadership' of the working class fiercely opposed to the carnivalesque.

It was, however, undoubtedly possible for working people to be influenced by those developments without becoming enthusiastic advocates of change themselves. The emergence of new types of recreation could set a seal on the rejection of much of the most objectionable content of the old culture. This is clearly shown in the case of the working-class excursionist. Whether they went by railway or by a works' trip, workers tended to be affected by the novelty and the variety of the experience, and these trips assumed a large place in the recreational calendar even as early as the 1840s. As such they provided recreational foci which competed for their summer time and many of 'the men save[d] up their spare cash to be spent, rather than spend it as they used to do, in bull-baiting and cock-fighting . . . at the wakes'.[60]

Wakes did not die away easily or quickly, however. In fact, additional wakes were established in the nineteenth century in response to the growing population and to the pressures of both authority and diminishing spaces on the existing wakes; but the institution of an effective police after 1840 led to the taming of their most egregious features and the curtailing of their extent. There was a distinct revival of Deritend Wake in the 1850s on temporarily vacant land. Its ultimate demise was only postponed, however, for presently the land was withdrawn, the market once more proving the effective arbiter of choice about the direction of urban development.[61]

The fact that the population of Birmingham more than doubled in the first thirty years of the nineteenth century helps to account for the establishment of additional wakes.[62] Most of these new wakes had no convincing ecclesiastical connections. Ashted and St George's Wake were in northern and eastern suburbs, Erdington, Smethwick and Moseley in nearby villages.[63] 'We used to have a "wake" . . . in every parish of the town once a year', reminisced an aged buckle-maker in 1851, 'and [together] with . . . the neighbouring wakes there used to be one nearly every month',[64] Newspaper evidence shows that he exaggerated the calendar distribution, though not the actual number of wakes: Deritend began the season on 25 July, three more followed early and two late in August, one came early in September, and then there was a gap until the first and second Sundays in October.[65] The distinct hiatus in mid-August, and then again in mid- and late September, is suggestive of a traditional, harvest-orientated pattern.[66] The two most prominent 'new' wakes were held in fact in ancient parishes: Handsworth and Edgbaston. Both probably developed in conjunction with the decline under pressure of the three 'old' town wakes. Of Handsworth, more anon; as for Edgbaston, it had 'by degrees left its proper domain, and enlivens the suburban streets of Birmingham, which abut upon Edgbaston parish'.[67] Races were held off fashionable Bath Row, and in 1828 more than a thousand people viewed a bull-bait behind Islington glass-house.[68]

Tradition and vested interests thus had great tenacity. As the authorities applied pressure to the most visible and vulnerable aspects of the wakes, there was a centrifugal movement of bull-baiting from inner Birmingham to Edgbaston and, especially, towards Handsworth. The latter is better documented than most of the 'new' wakes, and its history provides a good illustration of the way in which they could be built up from very slim origins into substantial festivals.[69] The coming of the Soho Manufactory in 1759-65 transformed what had been a minor wake.[70] It was first held near the *Waggon and Horses,* the chief resort of the workmen employed at Matthew Boulton's famous works.[71] The first Sunday in October was Wake Sunday, and on Tuesday 3 October 1780 we find a frustrated James Watt complaining that many of the men had gone 'a-holiday making'.[72]

In 1798 when the Birmingham Volunteers mobilised to capture a bull baited at Chapel Wake, the 'bullards' headed out to Birmingham Heath adjacent to the Soho district of Handsworth. 'The bull was captured on the Heath' and 'guards . . . with fixed bayonets, reconducted the poor animal in triumph into the town, a vast crowd . . . "assisting"'. The bull was safely lodged in the old prison yard though during the night an abortive rescue-attempt was made. For years afterwards the street boys revenged themselves by vilifying the volunteers:

> They spoiled the waake,
> And pulled up the staake,
> And put the bull i' the dungill.[73]

After the enclosure of the Heath in 1799 the shift to Handsworth was logical. Located in a separate parish and another county, it was outside the reach of the Birmingham constables and the Warwickshire magistrates. A favourite spot was the junction of three roads: 'if the Birmingham "Peelers" interfered, all we had to do was to step over the boundary into Staffordshire'.[74] This arena was conveniently near the *Old Engine Tavern,* but the immediate beneficiary was the occupier of a small cottage which stood at the junction. A 'stately tree' stood in his garden, from which 'people watched the sport at a charge of a penny each'.[75]

In 1820 West Bromwich Wesleyans began a mission to this 'Nineveh'.[76] They attracted some of the Soho men and held tea meetings as a counter-attraction, but they could not be effective against the thousands of non-local people who flocked to Handsworth. Nevertheless, such defiance of authority (especially after the Cruelty to Animals Act in 1835) could not proceed indefinitely after the introduction of efficient police forces.[77] In the 1820s there had still been some traditionalists among the wealthier sections of the population who had paid the fines of arrested bullards,[78] but in 1840 a police force was established in Handsworth and, aided by the Animals' Friend Society, it finally suppressed bull-baiting at the

Birmingham Wakes.[79] The new Borough police were equally effective in repressing the nearly-nude races, which children still ran in 1836.[80]

It is not easy to discern the exact downward course of the Birmingham Wakes, nor is it necessary.[81] They were indubitably in a slow decline. The town was pressing on them too much to enable them to mount a distinctive challenge to the alternative attractions. In the 1850s the commercial acumen of the landlord of the *Forge Tavern*, Deritend Pool, temporarily delayed this process, thereby illustrating the significance of location in the survival or decline of these festivals. In 1853 the old mill pool was levelled, affording an excellent field for 'the usual sports' and the revival of horse races. 'Wombwell's menagerie, and . . . shows of all kinds, crowded the ground'[82] and thousands turned out. Here, apparently, was the basis of a transformed festival which would survive many years. It was well organised; there was an entrance fee of ten shillings for the races, and 'no kind of gambling [was] allowed'.[83] It was 'a very big thing, and the whole of the community . . . seemed to turn out'.[84] It was true that any institution so un-utilitarian was liable to produce many 'drunk and disorderly' charges and summonses for assault,[85] yet the old plebeian culture was now sufficiently tamed, and the counter-culture of 'respectability' so widespread, that no real threat was posed by such occasional binges. In fact a section of progressive middle-class opinion in Birmingham in the 1850s was ready to accept this wake, and even saw some merit in it as being 'calculated to keep what have been termed "the dangerous classes" from indulging in amusements of a less innocent tendency'. Indeed a section of middle-class opinion was developing a frank acceptance of leisure for itself: 'A large number of the more respectable visitors say, "I want amusement, and am not very particular what it is. I enjoy those opportunities for pleasure . . . that are afforded me, and I don't care to analyse them very deeply"'. Their presence had the added advantage of 'strengthening that bond of union among all classes that was never more needed' after the alarums of the 1840s.[86]

Deritend Wake became a victim of the continuing process of urbanisation. Steeplechases — which gave the wake its *cachet* at this stage — could not be run without space; in 1857 it was withdrawn. It seems clear that Deritend Mill Pool had been all along intended for industrial development and had been only used for racing while the site of the old pool was settling. It did not make economic sense to keep a central urban site free for use just once a year. By 1858 some of the land was being leased for industrial purposes. By 1861 the site of the mill pool was covered by a new street, court housing and several metal works.[87] By 1889 Deritend Wake was 'now not noticeable outside two or three of the lowest public houses'.[88]

At this stage it is useful to draw together the threads of our analysis of the wakes' decline. Clearly it is necessary to make a distinction between the taming of their full carnivalesque vigour on the one hand, and their actual demise on the other. In the taming of their cruel animal sports, nude racing and fighting we have to recognise the influence of the steadily appreciating concern for public order felt by the JPs and the emergent *bourgeoisie*. The *definition* of what was acceptable public behaviour was vitally shaped by the evangelical movement; and as a counterpart to that there was the insistent, if underlying, theme of concern for labour discipline. The physical context of the growing industrial town also made the carnivalesque features of the wakes increasingly objectionable to the local elites. The coming of the new police in the 1840s was important in finally extirpating bull-baiting from the local area, but determined political will had already been sufficient to drive it from the town itself with the aid of only the parish constables and the Birmingham Volunteers. Repression seems to have been the keynote of the first phase, of the *taming* of the wakes, but it occurred in a political context in which much of the 'natural leadership' of the working class had little wish to protest or resist.

This gradual emergence of a hostile artisan sub-culture provides a link with the second phase in the decline of the wakes, in which the latter became less and less central to popular culture. It would be an exaggeration to dwell on the influence of the artisan sub-culture because its influence must be considered with others of a more general nature, such as employer preference for the fairs as holidays, and the emergence of attractive alternatives, particularly summer excursions. The second major factor in the decline of the wakes in their latter phase was the pressure of urban development on their space, a theme which is particularly clear for Deritend Wake.[89] Without space for sports and games, tables and stalls, wakes dwindled just to drinking and dancing, lost their distinctive traditions, and something more of their claims to centrality in popular culture.

II

At about the same time as urban development was leading to the retraction of the new venue of Deritend Wake and thus to its demise, a similar cause was instrumental in summoning up the first attack on the Birmingham Fairs. In July 1860 Councillor Arthur Ryland complained to the Borough Council that show booths and stalls in the streets were an 'annoyance and inconvenience'.[90] Ryland represented St Peter's Ward, wherein lay the premises of most of the influential shopkeepers and from whence came a memorial supporting the discontinuance of the shows and stalls.[91] But Ryland's opposition to the fairs had a deeper spring than mere shopkeeper interest; he saw the question in moral terms. For Ryland, and for the Quaker Charles Sturge, the fairs were 'not attended by any advantage at all commensurate with the evil'.[92]

However, they met opposition. The Market and Fairs Committee worked out a compromise involving the removal of the fairs from the sensitive streets to the Smithfield open-market area. Here travelling shows and theatrical booths were confined, while stalls were allowed in the Bull Ring and the upper parts of Digbeth.[93] Perceptive observers saw this as 'the thin end of the abolition wedge', and many rejoiced that the fairs had 'been obliged to give way before the march of better manners as savages have . . . to give way to the anglo-saxon and other civilised races'.[94] Hostile reporters registered the cultural disjunction which Birmingham's fairs increasingly represented: 'twice a year our intensely modern town is invaded by a picturesque army of Bohemians'; to get rid of the fairs 'would compel masses of people who now lead a nomadic life to comport themselves according to the social usages of modern society, and seek a steadier and more respectable mode of existence'.[95]

Yet the fairs had chartered status, and they continued to possess economic functions into the mid-nineteenth century. In 1756 'hardware' was noted as a staple commodity of the Birmingham fairs; they probably provided an important outlet for metal buckles, brooches and other 'Brummagem ware',[96] as well as for cattle, sheep, horses and 'agricultural produce generally'. At the Michaelmas Fair 'such a quantity of onions' were sold — 56 waggon loads in 1782 — that it gained the name of the Onion Fair.[97]

'Fair week was one of the greatest events in the town in the old days', reminisced William Downing in 1908. Above all, he remembered, 'there was a procession'.[98] After breakfast at the Royal Hotel the governors of local society assembled, and at noon, amid the clamour of church bells and the flutter of flags, Jacob Wilson, Town Crier, proclaimed' 'Oyez! Oyez! Oyez! . . . this day a Fair is held in the right of Christopher Musgrave, Esquire, Lord of the Manor . . .God save the

King, the Lord of the Manor, and all the inhabitants of the town'. Constables cleared the way, and three insurance-company firemen carrying axes made up the vanguard, followed by a band, the Crier, the 'Headborough', and the 'Collector'. Next came the High and Low Bailiffs, and the Jurymen to the Court Leet, two by two, carrying wands, all flanked by firemen; then the High and Low Tasters, and the Beadles carrying javelins.[99] Their duty done, the gentlemen repaired to a hostelry for dinner. In 1822 the company comprised 'the heads of most of the principal families of the town of all parties, clergy and laity'.[100] 'Immense throngs' stood to watch this display of authority.[101]

The fairs were thus accepted holidays in the town. At Michaelmas 1789 a Methodist button-maker 'ordered the [work-] shops to be shut up . . . at noon [on the Thursday] for the remainder of this and the following day'.[102] Even James James, brother of the noted evangelical John Angell James, himself a proponent of 'rational recreation', gave a fair holiday to his men. So important were the fairs that Whit Monday was not a recognised popular holiday in Birmingham in the mid-nineteenth century: 'The first three days of Whitsun week in Birmingham . . . are generally spent in hard work and preparation for the holiday of the last three, for the Fair has always been regarded as the feature of the week'.[103]

The fairs were increasingly differentiated from the wakes by their ability to attract 'some of the first people in this town and neighbourhood'.[104] Middle-class representation at the fairs in the mid-nineteenth century was mainly juvenile, yet references crop up to 'quiet, respectable people' there and in 1857 a reporter met a member of the Board of Guardians at the rifle stalls![105] Nevertheless by this period the staunch bourgeois was unlikely to be a fair-goer, for religious reasons (it was not coincidental that Sunday schools held tea meetings or trips to the country on Whit Fair days)[106] and because of unpleasant encounters with 'noisy, vulgar, excited crowds from the rural and mining districts, whose rude pushing, foul language, and uncultivated habits and manners made the thoroughfares impassable to decent people'.[107] Great numbers of agricultural workers and Black Country miners attended the Birmingham Fairs by a 'fly-boat' service on the Birmingham Canal and by railway.[108] In the 1860s and 1870s railway companies ran excursions from London and parts of the Midlands, especially to the Onion Fair.[109]

To what extent were these fairs also carnivalesque occasions? According to Mikhail Bakhtin, 'even if there was no carnival, strictly speaking, its atmosphere reigned at every fair'.[110] There was an unusual consumption of food and drink, and a kind of fair-time folly involving the flinging of rice, yet these features were greatly outweighed by the commercial entertainment which was the hallmark of the fairs in their pleasure aspects. The fairs had no salacious reputation (except in the minds of a few of their later opponents), no competitions and they were well-supervised by authority. Neither in their nature nor in their atmosphere were they strikingly carnivalesque. This would suggest that where wakes and chartered fairs existed side by side the wakes were the carnivalesque, the fairs the conventional festivals.[111] Even by the 1850s and 1860s when the wakes had been tamed, the races and the separate traditions of the wakes continued to differentiate them from the fairs. Nevertheless, the fairs were sufficiently different from the ideal image of respectable 'elevating' working-class leisure which had developed from the 1830s onwards in the minds of much of the middle class that they caused increasing outrage and dismay.[112]

The fairs were certainly a time for indulgence, a time for people not to count the cost: ginger beer, ice cream, oranges, nuts, fried fish, whelks, 'and other creatures from the briny deep'.[113] Hot sausages, a prominent feature of London's Bartholomew Fair (abolished in 1855), were to be had at the Onion Fair; but the great staple item, of course, was tripe and onions. Tripe shops were 'as common as penny pie shops' were in London. In Digbeth in particular there were several, each one claiming to be the 'real original'. And in the evenings the 'keepers of the beerhouses were happy, for somehow a fair is always associated with ale more or less nut-brown'.[114] Fairs preserved 'entire the true characteristics of the country assemblage, with all its excitement and qualification; — mixed, it must be confessed, with the more boisterous mirth and vicious indulgence which are apt to prevail at such times'[115] Dancing booths catered for the amorous and Terpsichorean tendencies of young and old and excitement was created by people throwing rice. But the carnivalesque acting-out of an otherwise-suppressed aggressiveness was not an outstanding feature.[116] Perhaps the fairs would have had more of the character of wakes in this respect had they not been under fairly tight supervision by the authorities. It was one of the prime duties of the High Bailiff that 'if he sees any Persons . . . using Unlawful Games . . . he may seize them and commit them to Custody, to be taken before a proper Magistrate'.[117] This did not protect petty traders, who used their stalls as sleeping places, from 'the young bucks' who overturned their stalls in the middle of the night.[118]

This diversion of the 'bucks' had no essential connection with the fair *qua* fair; the 'bucks' were undoubtedly known as such because of similar behaviour on other occasions in the year. It was the easy target of the stalls rather than any feeling that fairs were times of licensed disorder which attracted the 'bucks'. There were other examples of outbreaks of disorderly collective action, but they were extrinsically rather than intrinsically connected with the fairs. Thus 'disorderly persons' assembled in the town at the 1766 Onion Fair to 'regulat[e] ... the price of provisions', but other attempts at *taxation populaire* had already taken place on market days a month or so earlier; if there were crowds available to support illicit action it made little difference whether it was a market-day or a fair-day.[119] Similarly, it was the dense crowds at the fairs which encouraged that later-nineteenth-century social phenomenon, the 'rough', to engage in deviant behaviour.[120]

It is more accurate to consider the fairs simply as festivals. They fulfilled the essential precondition of such events: they were opposed to the everyday. This was recognised and encouraged by the special selection of comestibles, and by the people wearing their choicest clothes.[121] In 1874 'the earlier and bountiful' harvest resulted in a greater influx of country people to the fair, equipped with 'tolerably well-lined pockets'.[122] But even when, as in 1837-8 and 1843 depression had kept down the numbers of townsfolk at the fairs, those who did go were observed to be 'gay and sprightly', for one of the functions of the fair was to take people out of themselves, to banish discontent, if only for a day.[123]

Festivals are marked off from the everyday by ceremonial. The Birmingham Fairs had their proclamation, and even though that was abolished in 1852 it seems to have been replaced by a kind of unofficial opening ceremony:

> The streets were lined with spectators, awaiting the entrance into the town of the huge procession. It was usually timed for the parade to take place at ... [the dinner hour] when the working men could leave the factories and workshops to see the great sight. The gorgeous band-carriages, the gay uniforms of the musicians, the elaborate trappings of the horses [were] splendidly spectacular.[124]

The fairs brought fascinating freaks, undemanding drama, gory waxworks, scientific marvels and Mr Punch. The variety offered at Birmingham differed little from that offered at any other fair, for most of these shows and menageries were on giant circuits throughout England.[125] Together they straddled the boundaries of theatre, early music hall, circuses and menageries, and comprised 'a vigorous popular culture of entertainment', highly developed by commercialisation since the mid-eighteenth century, and capable of greatly bolstering the variety and appeal of a local fair or a reformed wake.[126]

Three general points can be made about this. First, the theatrical and other large shows of the fairs gradually became less and less essential for Birmingham popular leisure, if not to that of the rural and Black Country visitors, as regular theatre-going developed in the town, and as the music hall emerged. In 1823 the Theatre Royal felt it necessary to engage 'Mr Davis and his stud of Horses' in order to 'provide for the gratification of the holiday people during the Fair.' By the 1850s the Theatre Royal ignored the fairs.[127] Secondly, fairs were beginning to act as a half-way house in introducing the populace to scientific wonders in a way no Mechanics Institute could match: model steam-engines, microscopes, weighing machines, galvanic batteries, telescopes and ornithology.[128] Pig-faced ladies still appeared, but the credulity upon which they depended was being diminished by a town-bred sophistication, a process to which the fairs were themselves contributing.[129] Finally, the impact of the fairs as entertainment has to be considered in the light of the fact that they attracted 'thousands of people revelling in easily provoked mirth'.[130] They went partly from tradition, because it was a holiday occasion, and because the showman's world had a collective magic which lifted them out of themselves. Only the fairs packed in such an array of easy knowledge and marvellous curiosities. They entered into the fair with a 'willing suspension of disbelief', recognising that they might be cheated but prepared to take the chance.

III

To the *Birmingham Post* in 1872 fairs were just an 'annual nuisance'.[131] As traffic grew with the expansion of the town, so did the congestion and sense of cultural dissonance caused by the fairs. The road to the fair was in a state of perpetual bustle and noise, the dust flew in clouds, ginger-beer corks went off in volleys, and every public house was crowded with people. The Bull Ring and Smithfield were cacophonous with noise as showmen contrived to draw customers.[132] In the 1870s a London reporter described

> The . . . almost bygone rough-and-tumble sawdusty, naptha-flaring carnival that our fathers recollect, with a merry crowd elbowing its

way through long avenues of gingerbread booths, or responding loyally to the bewildering invitation to 'Walk up, walk up', accompanied by the clash of cymbals and the bang of gongs. Bartlemy is not dead.[133]

Thus the reporter brought together the idea of a fair as a festival of entertainment and the word 'carnival', stripping the latter of its layers of meaning in the process, taming the word itself. But to many members of the Town Council even a festival of entertainment was an affront. It asserted the pleasure principle in the main thoroughfare of a town whose governing body (inspired by evangelicalism) was attempting to 'improve' it.

Inconvenience to traffic was seized upon by Councillor James Whateley, one of the artisans who had agitated for public parks, now a small employer. In 1874 he introduced a motion worded similarly to that concerned with traffic congestion in 1861. This time Whateley stated frankly that 'his great objection to the Fairs was on account of the immorality to which they tended'.[134] The question was referred to the Market and Fairs Committee, as in 1860, but, as then, 'mindful of the revenue (in relief of the Rates) derived from the Tolls', it merely suggested a redisposition of the shows and stalls.[135] Only Whateley and two others continued to object.[136] Superficially the 'anti-fair' councillors suffered a resounding defeat, but the changing composition of the Council gave the abolitionists grounds for future confidence. From 1868 onwards a new type of councillor was appearing, drawn from large-business backgrounds, and influenced by the 'Civic Gospel' preached by George Dawson and R.W. Dale and practised by Joseph Chamberlain. As E.P. Hennock has shown, the shared background of these particular variants of dissent made the tide of civic improvement so influential.[137]

Birmingham municipal politics in the 1850s and 1860s were largely dominated by the 'Economist' councillors (known as the *Woodman* group, after their favourite hostelry), the political representatives of the small-property ratepayers.[138] The triumph, in the 1870s, of the adherents of the 'Civic Gospel' meant the doom of the Birmingham Fairs, for what the 'Economists' tolerated (for the sake of tolls, stall rents and business for some of their constituents) the civic improvers saw as an affront to the dignity of a modern and 'improving' town and to the evangelical conscience. In July 1875 Alderman E.C. Osborne successfully proposed that the fairs be denied the use of Corporation land or of the public streets. Twenty-four of the abolitionists had entered the Council since 1868.[139]

In the abolition of the fairs we see the repressive underside of the 'Civic Gospel'. The gospellers could not bear the thought of anachronistic fairs in the middle of Birmingham when they had been abolished elsewhere, considering them 'out of harmony with the improving spirit',[140] but behind this lay the verities of evangelical nonconformity, The abolition debate revealed a multiplicity of moral (and social) objections to the fairs. Of the thirty-two abolitionists, twenty can be traced in their religious affiliation: seven were Congregationalists or Baptists; five were Quakers; three were influenced by the Quaker Severn-Street First-Day School for adults; another three were Unitarians.[141] At least ten of the thirty-two were also either members of temperance organisations or spoke against the evils of drink.[142]

Osborne opened the debate.[143] Fairs were anachronisms in the age of retail shopping and railways. Manton agreed. To Marris, 'exhibitions of fat women, shooting galleries, and such things [were] an insult to the common sense of the 19th century'. Osborne complained about the freedom of the thoroughfares, despite the rearrangement of shows and stalls in 1874. Fairs formed 'a great hindrance to business'. White agreed: 'to stop up the streets for three days . . . was not a . . . trifling matter, but a serious injury to legitimate trade and the larger ratepayers'.[144] Osborne pointed out that fairs 'had been entirely abolished' elsewhere.[145] He then conjured up the spectre of an invasion of domesticity.[146] Fairs were 'a great nuisance to families residing in the district, especially if they chance to have sickness in the home'. He slipped easily into the 'labour' question: 'it was said that the Fairs offered opportunities for the holiday enjoyment of the people, but . . . they had been affording . . . to the working classes, holidays rather more than enough for them'.[147] William White reverted to the older Birmingham tradition of talking about respectable 'industrious artisans' rather than labour as if it were just a factor of production:

> look at it in the interest of the working classes, when a large amount of wages was every fair time lost to many industrious men who would pursue their calling but who were locked out in consequence of some drunken few . . . having chosen to idle away the time and stop the machinery.[148]

At the root of the abolitionist case, however, was evangelical dismay at open 'sin' and an appeal for moral improvement.[149] On the whole the fairs were 'helpful to demoralisation and social degradation'. The 'vulgar taste' encouraged by the amusements was bad, but worse were intemperance, card sharpers, men with loaded dice, pickpockets and, worst of all, 'more illegitimate births at the workhouse . . . about the month of March, pointing . . . to what took place at the Whitsuntide Fair'. Fairs should be replaced by holidays of 'a higher and more elevating character'.

This appeal was especially effective when linked to the ideology of the Civic Gospel with its stress on the moral responsibility of the Council as a public body.[150] Did fairs afford 'the sort of pleasure which the gentlemen of the Council would like to endorse'? And behind this argument lay that highly developed sense of personal responsibility for eliminating sin which characterised the evangelical conscience. Would they, as individuals, approve 'of the pleasure . . . provided at the Fairs'? Would they like their children and friends to witness such exhibitions? Their duty was to *'improve the tastes* of the inhabitants' by substituting 'healthy amusement . . . such as would . . . elevate them and lift them up'.[151] Fears were expressed that fairs did more harm during six days than the good done by free libraries, schools and Sunday schools in a year. Underlying many of the arguments was the sentiment: 'The Fair is not a necessity, it is merely a question of pleasure.'

IV

The fairs were defended by a coalition of less-evangelical Civic Gospellers — including Joseph Chamberlain — and 'Economists'. Their case was grounded on scepticism about the supposed immorality of the fairs and on the Economists' solicitude for the small ratepayers,[152] Significantly, most of these councillors either had no strong religious identification, or belonged to the tradition of heterodox, non-evangelical dissent.[153]

The radical liberal, Henry Hawkes, maintained that fairs were not trading anachronisms, and that 'large commercial transactions still took place'. Since no statistics existed to prove that fairs increased crime, and the assertions of immorality were unprovable, why should commerce and 'the innocent diversion . . . of the common people' be meddled with?[154] Chamberlain agreed. The accusation of increased illegitimacy upset his civic pride: 'some people . . . put on magnifying glasses when anything is going on in the shape of amusement'; interference would only be justified by 'something exceptional in its character', otherwise those with intellectual tastes had no licence to put down 'the amusements of the people'.

The old-style liberal William Brinsley thought it odd that those who wanted to provide 'free water, free gas, free libraries and free everything' wished to stop 'the free enjoyments of the people'. Another 'Economist', Henry Heyden, denounced those 'who were always harping on the needs of the working man as though they understood . . . [him] better than anyone else'. But the Economists' chief concern was that the abolition of tolls and stall rents would put up the rates. Such views were swept aside, however, by Osborne's pronouncement that 'social [effectively, moral] considerations . . . were paramount to all financial questions'.

The views of the *Woodman* group were bound to carry little weight with the anti-drink evangelicals,[155] but the defence of the fairs by the leading Civic Gospellers, Chamberlain and Collings, was a different matter altogether. Sceptics though they were, however, they did share a fundamental outlook with the abolitionists, they equated literary and intellectual culture with moral elevation. They thus found it difficult to escape the converse that fairs and fairgoing indicated moral inferiority. Thus Chamberlain only disagreed with the abolitionists' procedure. 'Let them . . . improve the morality of the people, but he was sure they would not do it by any vulgar intolerance or puritanic interference.' The defenders of the fairs were not so much for them as opponents of the attempt to suppress them. Only Heyden positively asserted 'there was a vast amount of enjoyment in the Fair', but added the qualification 'to the working classes'. This was no answer to the abolitionist challenge to show 'what good it did'. The defenders' case was thus essentially negative and appeared weak when set against the powerfully affirmative nature of evangelical moralism in full cry.

The triumph of the Civic Gospel then led ineluctably to the expulsion of the pleasure functions of the fairs, at once because of its ideology of civic improvement and because it was carried out by the standard-bearers of the evangelical tradition. What might have saved the fairs was the kind of working-class support which once saved Fairlop and Barnet Fairs,[156] but in Birmingham the abolitionists organised petitions from mutual-improvement societies and other working-class groups under their influence. A particularly telling point was that the teachers at Severn-Street First-Day School — 'the aristocracy of the working men' according to White — were 'altogether against the Fair'.[157] Such opinion counted more with the Council majority than a much-more numerous counter-petition from the Bull Ring area.[158]

Opposition was expressed in the press by working men offended at the moral paternalism displayed by the Council – 'the fairs should have been left to us', they said – but it was a small and ineffective response.[159]

Why was it so? The answer has three strands: first, most working men who could have been politically effective probably were part of the respectable artisan sub-culture described above, and sympathetic to abolition. Secondly, indifference; the fairs must undoubtedly have been losing much of the cultural centrality they formerly held. This process was discussed above with respect to entertainment, it must also have been assisted in 1852 when the Council took over responsibility for the Fairs and dropped the Proclamation ceremony.[160] Thirdly, Whit Fairs had been losing ground in Birmingham since the 1871 Bank Holiday Act. In the words of the anti-abolitionist Brinsley: 'things were changing . . . Look . . . at the effect on the Fair of the general holiday, last Whit Monday, and every succeeding Whit Monday it would be the same, . . . if left alone the Fairs would die out themselves'.[161]

The evangelicals succeeded in banishing the pleasure fairs from the town, but those who hoped for the entire extirpation of this source of moral contamination were disappointed. Certain 'persons interested to keep the pleasure fair in life' invited the showmen to pitch their tents on a site in the adjoining borough of Aston, and 'several thousand persons visited the ground' on the Thursday after Michaelmas in 1875. To the hostile reporter it was 'nothing better than a low-class wake'.[162] By 1880, both at Whit and Michaelmas, fairs were held on 'as large a scale as ever', complete with new-fangled stream roundabouts.[163] The centre of Birmingham still 'filled with excursionists', for the railway companies ran special trains into the town until the First World War; unhidden by toy and cake stalls the wreaths of onions 'now formed the leading object'.[164] By the 1930s the Whit Fair had gone, finished off, no doubt, by the War; yet the Onion Fair, with no close competition from a Bank Holiday, still thrived.[165] As a small pleasure fair it even lasted into the post-war period, before succumbing to the hand of Progress.[166]

At the beginning of this essay I could write about a plebeian popular culture in which carnivalesque elements, spontaneity, disorderliness and hedonism were strongly marked. But even in the eighteenth century there was no unanimity within popular culture: the emergence of an artisan sub-culture which accepted and aspired to material and moral progress and 'improvement' opened an important cultural rift.

Although it remained a minority culture it may well have played a role in changing the whole by example, and it certainly lowered the level of potential resistance to the direct attacks on the old values and festivals from magistrates, police, employers, and the powerful fusion in Birmingham of evangelicalism and the ideology of civic improvement. Moreover all of this was reinforced by impersonal forces: the industrial structure of the town, pressures on urban space and the power of the land and property market. Faced with this opposition, the force of custom which, above all, gave plebeian popular culture its legitimacy, was bound to diminish, for it was, by definition, unsuited to rapid change. That it did so relatively painlessly must also owe much to the development of alternative recreational attractions, which, in the case of the railway excursion, itself represented the diffusion of the benefits of technological and material progress. By 1900 something of the old holiday calendar survived, but its content and its context had changed radically.

Notes

*I should like to thank Bob Storch, Bob Poole and John Walton for helpful comments on this essay.

1. Mikhail Bakhtin, *Rabelais and His World* (Cambridge Mass., 1968), pp. 218-9; Peter Burke, *Popular Culture in Early Modern Europe* (London, 1979), p.192.
2. Burke, *Popular Culture*, pp.199-204; Bakhtin, *Rabelais*, pp.5-11, 244-56; E. le Roy Ladurie, *Carnival in Romans* (Harmondsworth, 1981), Ch.12.
3. Burke, *Popular Culture*, pp.192-6, 199.
4. This volume, Ch.4. See also Hugh Cunningham, *Leisure in the Industrial Revolution* (London, 1980), pp.77-9, 124; and Peter Bailey, *Leisure and Class in Victorian England* (London, 1978), p.22.
5. (Cambridge, 1973); see pp.76-84 and quotations on pp.21, 28, 60, 62, 111, 165. Malcolmson calls wakes 'a community's own petty carnival' (p.19), but there is no explication of the concept in his book.
6. Apart from Malcolmson the only other recent historical discussion of wakes is E.P. Thompson, 'Patrician society: plebeian culture', *J. of Social History*, vol.7 (1974), pp.392-4.
7. In general see C.W. Chalkin, *The Provincial Towns of Georgian England* (London, 1974); C. Gill and A. Briggs, *History of Birmingham* (Oxford, 1952), vol.1 and 2; VCH, *A History of the County of Warwick*, vol.7, W.B. Stephens (ed.), *The City of Birmingham*, (London, 1964).
8. William Hutton, *An History of Birmingham* (Birmingham, 1781), pp.132-3.
9. Walter Barrow, 'Birmingham Markets and Fairs', *Birmingham Archaeological Society, Transactions*, vol.38 (1912), p.13; for calendar reform see W.A. Speck, *Stability and Strife. England 1714-1760* (London 1977, reprint 1980), pp.254-5.
10. *M. Chron.*, 3 Mar. 1851. For distinctions between wakes and fairs elsewhere see Malcolmson, *Popular Recreations*, pp.16-24 esp. pp.21, 22-3,

although Walton and Poole have more difficulty in distinguishing Lancashire wakes and unchartered fairs by the mid-nineteenth century (above, Ch.5). By 1893 a Birmingham journalist was unclear about the distinction, see *Mail*, 7 Oct. 1893.

11. W. Showell, *Dictionary of Birmingham* (Birmingham, 1885), p.264.

12. Hutton, *History of Birmingham*, pp.134-5.

13. *M. Chron.*, 3 Mar. 1851.

14. *BJ*, 24 July 1847; *Mail*, 3 Oct. 1903.

15. [J. Jaffray], 'Hints for a History of Birmingham', Ch.16 (BRL 174534).

16. Hutton, *History of Birmingham*, p.134.

17. Jaffray, 'History of Birmingham', Ch.16.

18. *M. Chron.*, 3 Mar. 1851.

19. Jaffray, 'History of Birmingham', Ch.16.

20. Burke, *Popular Culture*, p.183.

21. *M. Chron.*, 3 Mar. 1851; *B. Chron.*, 11 Sept. 1823. I am indebted to Clive Behagg for this reference.

22. Hutton, *History of Birmingham*, p.134.

23. Burke, *Popular Culture*, pp.189-90. See also Barbara A. Babcock (ed.), *The Reversible World: Symbolic Inversion in Art and Society* (Cornell, 1978).

24. Jaffray, 'History of Birmingham', Ch.16; Hutton, *History of Birmingham* p.133.

25. Jaffray, 'History of Birmingham, Ch.16, cf. Hutton, *History of Birmingham*, p.135.

26. For 'smock races' see Dennis Brailsford, *Sport and Society. Elizabeth to Anne* (London, 1969), pp.239-40.

27. Jaffray, 'History of Birmingham', Ch.34.

28. *M. Chron.*, 3 Mar. 1851.

29. Geo. Ware, *A New and Original Historical, Graphical and Comical History of Birmingham as sung nightly by him at Holders Grand Music Hall, with Immense Success* (Birmingham, ? 1860).

30. *Sam Sly's Birmingham Budget*, no.24, 3 Aug. 1850.

31. Derek Jarrett, *England in the Age of Hogarth* (London, 1974), p.181. Jarrett's comment is on Hogarth's print *Southwark Fair* (1733). See also pp.182-4.

32. *M. Chron.*, 27 Jan, 1851; Jaffray, 'History of Birmingham', Ch.16.

33. On the distinction between participants and spectators in carnival see Roger D. Abraham and Richard Bauman, 'Ranges of Festival Behaviour', in Babcock, *Reversible World*, pp.193-208

34. N.Z. Davis, 'The Reasons of Misrule: Youth Groups and Charivaris in Sixteenth-century France', *Past and Present*, no.50 (Feb. 1971), p.41.

35. This type of anthropological analysis is most closely associated with Max Gluckman's work; for a critical discussion see Babcock, *Reversible World*, pp.21-9.

36. See VCH, *County of Warwick*, pp.81-125, 209; John Money, *Experience and Identity, Birmingham and the West Midlands 1760–1800* (Manchester, 1977), pp.259-60.

37. D.A. Reid, 'The Decline of Saint Monday', *Past and Present*, no.71 (May 1976), esp. pp.77-9.

38. *ABG*, 29 July 1745.

39. Jaffray, 'History of Birmingham', Ch.34; *ABG*, 28 Aug. 1809; *M. Chron.*, 3 Mar. 1851; see also note 78 below.

40. 13 *Geo*. III, c. 36 [1773] – my emphasis.

41. *ABG*, 10 July 1777. Deritend and Bordesley were granted Street Commissioners in 1791. For the Birmingham Commissioners versus bull-baiting see Commissioners of the Birmingham Street Acts, Mss. Minutes, vol.2, 7 Sept. 1976 (BRL).

42. See *ABG*, 6 Sept. 1790, 2 Sept. 1811, for breakaway bulls.

43. [George Yates], *Picture of Birmingham* (Birmingham, 1830), p.92; *A Pictorial Guide to Birmingham* (Birmingham, 1849), pp.28-9.

44. *ABG*, 8 Oct. 1792.

45. See Malcolmson, *Popular Recreations*, pp.100-4, 123-5.

46. *ABG*, 28 Aug., 4 Sept., 9 & 30 Oct. 1809. See also the comment in Jaffray, 'History of Birmingham', Ch.34 and the letter in *The Philanthropist*, 1 Sept. 1836.

47. *BJ*, 22 Sept. 1849; cf. Malcolmson, *Popular Recreations*, pp.146, 148-9.

48. Reid, 'Decline of Saint Monday' esp. refs. 2-7.

49. *ABG*, 4 Feb. 1811. See also *B. Chron.*, 11 Sept. 1823.

50. *BJ*, 19 Sept. 1829. The wake in question was at Oldbury, for which see note 65 below. On the question of the small use made of the Master and Servant Laws against absenteeism from work, see Reid, 'Decline of Saint Monday', p.81, n.30.

51. CEC (Trade and Manufactures), *Appendix to the Second Report of the Commissioners*, pt. I, *Reports and Evidence from Sub-Commissioners*, PP (1843), 432, xv, pp.f122, f123, f133, f138, f139, f144, f148, f154, f161, f162, f165.

52. *M. Chron.*, 3 Mar. 1851.

53. S.J. Pratt, *Harvest Home* (3 vols., London, 1805), vol.1, p.385n.

54. Money, *Experience and Identity*, Ch.5.

55. Ibid., pp.114-15. For the local religious picture see VCH, *County of Warwick*, pp.416-18; for an example of informal evangelicalism see Reid, 'Decline of Saint Monday', p.94.

56. The phrase comes from an account of the suppression of a bull-bait in 1798, quoted in J.A. Langford, *A Century of Birmingham Life* (2 vol., Birmingham, 2nd edn. 1870-71), vol.2, p.137.

57. Money, *Experience and Identity*, p.114. The split within the 'natural leadership' of the working class is discussed in Reid, 'Decline of Saint Monday', pp.86-7, 93-9. The theme of 'confrontation *within* working-class culture' also appears in Victor Bailey, 'Salvation Army Riots, the "Skeleton Army" and Legal Authority in the Provincial Town', in A.P. Donajgrodzki (ed.), *Social Control in Nineteenth Century Britain* (London, 1977), p.241. See also Storch, this volume, Ch.4 and Brian Harrison, *Drink and the Victorians* (London, 1971), pp.23-7.

58. See my forthcoming University of Birmingham PhD thesis on 'Popular Culture and Popular Leisure: Birmingham 1750-1875'.

59. Jaffray, 'History of Birmingham', Ch.16; see also *BJ*, 22 Sept. 1849.

60. *M. Chron.*, 3 Mar. 1851. There is some irony in the fact that some of the Birmingham excursionists were travelling to St Giles's Fair at Oxford! See Sally Alexander, *St. Giles's Fair, 1830-1914: Popular Culture and the Industrial Revolution in 19th Century Oxford* (Oxford, 1970), p.38.

61. A conclusion paralleled by David Cannadine, in 'Urban Development in England and America in the Nineteenth Century: Some Comparisons and Contrasts', *Economic History Review*, 2nd ser., vol.33 (1980), pp.321-2.

62. VCH, *County of Warwick*, pp.14, 109.

63. This can be seen by comparing wake and church consecration dates. For wake dates see *BJ*, 30 Aug. 1845, 5 Aug. & 14 Oct. 1848, 9 Aug. 1851; *M. Chron.*, 3 Mar. 1851. For consecration dates see VCH, *County of Warwick*, pp.362, 364, 369, 373, 379, 381, 385, 387. F.W. Hackwood, in *Some Records of Smethwick* (Smethwick, 1896), wrote that Smethwick Wake was 'quite a modern institution' (p.67).

64. *M. Chron.*, 27 Jan. 1851.

65. Other village wakes at Oldbury and Harborne, and in the Black country at

Tipton, Darlaston, Wednesbury, Willenhall and Walsall, show a similar pattern. See F.W. Hackwood, *Staffordshire Customs, Superstitions and Folklore* (Lichfield 1924; Wakefield, E.P. edn, 1974), pp.106-7; idem, *Oldbury and Round About in the Worcestershire Corner of the Black Country* (Wolverhampton & Birmingham, 1915), p.309; Newspaper Cuttings (BRL 302129), p.52.

66. Cf. Malcolmson, *Popular Recreations,* pp.16-18, 24-5, and Thompson, 'Patrician Society: Plebeian Culture' p.342.

67. [J. Drake] , *The Picture of Birmingham* (Birmingham, 1825), p.22.

68. *Birmingham Weekly Post,* 15 July 1905; *BJ,* 13 Sept. 1828; *ABG,* 15 Sept. 1928.

69. For another example see Alexander, *St. Giles's Fair,* pp.4 & 8.

70. For Soho see Paul Mantoux, *The Industrial Revolution in the Eighteenth Century* (London, 1961 edn), pp.324-7.

71. *Mail,* 3 Oct. 1903, 4 Oct. 1904.

72. Watt to Boulton, 3 Oct. 1780 (Assay Office Mss., BRL). I am indebted to Professor S. Pollard for this reference.

73. Langford, *Birmingham Life,* pp.137-8.

74. *Handsworth Herald,* 3 Oct. 1903.

75. *Mail,* 4 Oct. 1903.

76. *Ibid.,* 29 Dec. 1896; *Handsworth Herald,* 3 Oct. 1903.

77. Malcolmson, *Popular Recreations,* p.124.

78. *ABG,* 10 Jan. 1825; *BJ,* 11 Oct. 1828. It was presumably some of these traditionalists who celebrated Erdington Wake with an annual dinner at the Green Man Inn, *BJ,* 5 Aug. 1848, 2 Aug. 1856.

79. Malcolmson, *Popular Recreations,* pp.125-6; David Philips, 'Riots and Public Order in the Black Country, 1835-1860', in R. Quinault and J. Stevenson (eds.), *Popular Protest and Public Order. Six Studies in British History 1790-1920* (London, 1974), pp.148, 167, 175 n.17, 180 n.82 & n.84. Showell, *Dictionary,* p.27; CEC, *Second Report* (1843), p.f195.

80. *Birmingham Faces and Places,* vol.2 (1 Sept. 1889), p.75; see also *The Philanthropist,* 1 Sept. 1836.

81. See *BJ,* 2 Aug. 1845, 24 July 1847, 19 July, 9 & 23 Aug. 1851, 12 Nov. 1853: *Post,* 10 Sept. 1873. Only Bell Wake was remembered with Deritend towards the end of the nineteenth century: *Birmingham Faces and Places,* vol.2 (1 Sept. 1889), p.75; also see *Mail,* 22 June 1909.

82. *BJ,* 6 Aug. 1853.

83. *Ibid.,* 15 July 1854; for a gambling prosecution at St George's Wake see *BJ,* 9 Aug. 1851.

84. *Mail,* 22 June 1909.

85. *BJ,* 6 Aug. 1853.

86. *B.D. Press,* 31 July 1855. This paper had a close association with George Dawson, the heterodox nonconformist. On the frank pursuit of leisure see Bailey, *Leisure and Class,* Ch.3.

87. Compare the survey of the Borough of Birmingham of 1852-61 (BRL: sheets 128, 147 & 147's Supplementary Sheet no.1, plan no.2) with the 1st edition OS 1:500 series (1889), sheets XIV, 5, 14 & 19. See also the leases contained in the Lee Crowder deposits 1263, 1264, 1266 & 1308 (BRL).

88. *Birmingham Faces and Places,* vol.2 (1 Sept. 1889), p.75.

89. Handsworth Wake seems to have survived longest of all the wakes in the immediate district; however, speculative builders eventually struck and took the fields on which the races were held. See *Mail,* 7 Oct. 1893; *Handsworth Herald,* 12 Oct. 1895, 3 Oct. 1903.

90. *Procs.* 1859-60, p.253.

91. *Ibid.,* pp.318-19.

92. *Ibid.*, p.253.

93. *ABG*, 16 Feb. 1861; *Procs.*, 1860-1, pp.139, 141.

94. *ABG*, 25 May 1861, 28 Sept. 1865.

95. *Ibid.*, 25 May 1866, 25 May 1861.

96. W. Owen, *An authentic account published by the King's authority of all the fairs in England* (London, 1756), p.89.

97. *Ibid.*: Robert Rawlinson, *Report to the General Board of Health on ... the Sanitary Condition ... of ... Birmingham* (London, 1849), p.12; Showell, *Dictionary*, p.72.

98. *Birmingham Gazette and Express*, 5 Dec. 1908.

99. This account is based on 'Jacob Wilson and the Birmingham Fairs', *Mail*, 25 Feb. 1880.

100. *ABG*, 3 June 1822; see also 6 Oct. 1794, or *BJ*, 9 June 1838.

101. *BJ*, 28 Sept. 1850. Perhaps the theatricality of these proceedings was part of the means by which the local elites sought to impose a cultural hegemony during the eighteenth century, see Thompson, 'Patrician Society: Plebeian Culture', pp.388-9. By the 1850s there were other means, and the ceremony was dropped.

102. 'The Diary of Julius Hardy, Button-maker of Birmingham (1788-1793)', transcribed and annotated by A.M. Banks (1973, BRL 669002); Entry for 29 Sept. 1789. See also 30 May 1789: 'The Fair commencing on Thursday next, at the request of my men I put off reckoning tonight on that account until Wednesday night'.

103. *B.D. Press*, 5 June 1857. For the rest of England see Malcolmson, *Popular Recreations*, pp.31-3. Of course, Saint Monday may well have been celebrated with special vigour at Whitsuntide; the festival (rather than the fair) was one of the occasions for bull-baiting (*M. Chron.*, 3 Mar. 1851).

104. *M. Chron.*, 5 Oct. 1807.

105. See speeches of Collings and Chamberlain in *BDG*, 9 June 1875, and Arthur L. Matthison, *Art, Paint and Variety* (London, 1934), p.42; *BDG*, 21 May 1874; *B.D. Press*, 25 Sept. 1857.

106. *Birmingham Gazette & Express*, 26 Feb. 1909; *B.D. Press*, 6 June 1856. At every fair stalls were erected in the bull ring for the sale of Bibles and the holding of services: *BDG*, 9 June 1875.

107. *Mail*, 25 Feb. 1880.

108. *BJ*, 20 May 1837, 14 June 1851, 21 May 1853.

109. *Birmingham Morning News*, 2 Oct. 1871; *BDG*, 25 Sept. 1874; *Mail*, 22 Sept. 1874.

110. Bakhtin, *Rabelais*, p.154.

111. Cf. King's Norton Mop or October Statute Fair for the hiring of servants and labourers. The village was five miles south-west of Birmingham, in Worcestershire, and here 'the Lord of Misrule' held sway, according to Showell, *Dictionary*, p.117. On statute fairs generally see Malcolmson, *Popular Recreations*, pp.23-4.

112. For the general evolution of the ideal see Bailey, *Leisure and Class*, Chs.2 & 4, and R.D. Storch, 'The Problem of Working-class Leisure. Some Roots of Middle-class Moral Reform in the Industrial North: 1825-50', in Donajgrodzki, *Social Control*, Ch.5.

113. *ABG*, 25 May 1861, 9 June 1865; *Post*, 24 May 1872.

114. *Birmingham Morning News*, 2 Oct. 1871 – 'written by a Special Correspondent of the *Daily Telegraph*'; H.J. Jennings, *Chestnuts and Small Beer* (London, 1920), p.125.

115. Drake, *Picture of Birmingham*, p.20.

116. *ABG*, 25 May 1861, 9 June 1865; *Mail*, 29 May 1880; cf. Alexander, *St. Giles's Fair*, p.33; *M. Chron*, 3 Mar. 1851; Jennings, *Chestnuts*, p.125.

117. J.T. Bunce, *History of the Corporation of Birmingham* (Birmingham, 1878), vol.1, p.6, quoting 'The Duty of the Respective Officers appointed by the Court Leet, in the Manor of Birmingham', which was drawn up in 1779.

118. *Birmingham Gazette & Express,* 12 June 1908.

119. *ABG,* 6 Oct. 1766, cf. D.E. Williams, 'Midland Hunger Riots in 1766', *Midland History,* vol.3, no.4 (Autumn 1976), pp.260-1, 267.

120. *BDG* 21 May 1875.

121. *BJ,* 14 June 1851. For festivals see Burke, *Popular Culture,* pp.178-9.

122. *BDG,* 25 Sept. 1874.

123. *BJ,* 20 May & 30 Sept. 1837, 9 June 1838, 10 June 1843.

124. *Birmingham Gazette & Express,* 26 Feb. 1909.

125. For an excellent synthesis see Cunningham, *Leisure in the Industrial Revolution,* pp.28-38.

126. Ibid., p.37.

127. *ABG,* 22 Sept. 1823. See in general D.A. Reid, 'Popular Theatre in Victorian Birmingham', in David Bradby, Louis James and Bernard Sharatt (eds.) *Performance and Politics in Popular Drama* (Cambridge, 1980), pp.65-89.

128. *BJ,* 28 Sept. 1850.

129. Cf. Bailey, *Leisure and Class,* p.86.

130. *ABG,* 25 May 1861.

131. *Post,* 24 May 1872.

132. Mail, 25 Feb. 1880.

133. *Birmingham Morning News,* 2 Oct. 1871. Naptha lamps dated only from 1851 in fact: Alexander, *St. Giles's Fair,* p.42.

134. *BDM,* 22 Apr. 1874.

135. 1873-4 *Procs.,* pp.334, 501. The Council had received rival memorials from ratepayers in the streets directly affected by the fairs; 59 signatories were for abolishing the fairs, 564 wanted to retain them. Ibid., pp.342, 386, 499.

136. Ibid., p.503. The others were Osborne and Kenrick. Manton abstained.

137. E.P. Hennock, *Fit and Proper Persons. Ideal and Reality in Nineteenth Century Urban Government* (London, 1973), pp.64, 70, 76-7, 80, 82, 92-9, 101, 140-53.

138. Gill, *History of Birmingham,* vol.1, pp.409-24; Asa Briggs, *Victorian Cities,* (Harmondsworth, 1968), pp.206-19.

139. Twenty of the abolitionists had entered since 1870, and eight since 1873: *Procs., passim;* information on councillors from Hennock, *Fit and Proper Persons,* and BRL biographical newspaper-cuttings collection.

140. Quotation from *Mail* editorial, 23 Apr. 1874.

141. The seven were Manton, Derrington, Wheateley, Arculus, Wright, Edwards, S. and Marris; the five — Sturge, C., Lloyd, Baker, G., Barrow and White; The three — Downing, Baker, J.E. and Cook; the three Unitarians were Smith, Kenrick and Martineau. Kneebone was an unidentified Nonconformist. Osborne was the only abolitionist member of George Dawson's flock; his attitudes to the fairs are therefore interesting.

142. White, Derrington and Morley were Band-of-Hope or United-Kingdom-Alliance men. The others all revealed a measure of antipathy to drink: Ellaway, Arculus, Baker, G., Barker, J.E., Sturge and Wright. See also Harrison, *Drink and the Victorians,* pp.328-9.

143. This account is based on the full account in *BDG,* 9 June 1875.

144. Information in Hennock, *Fit and Proper Persons,* and in occupational declarations in the *Procs.* allows the following occupational analysis of the abolitionists: small master = 6; working class = 2; professional = 4; comfortably-off merchants, manufacturers and 'gentlemen' = 20.

145. For the only other serious investigation of the abolition of fairs see Hugh

Cunningham, 'The Metropolitan Fairs: a Case Study in the Social Control of Leisure', in Donajgrodzki, *Social Control,* Ch.6. Concerned with police and Home Office attitudes towards fairs, Cunningham concludes that by the late nineteenth century fairs were 'a relatively routine ingredient in an accepted world of leisure' (p.164). Perhaps London was ahead of the rest of the country, as it was ruled by a Home Office sceptical of Quaker enthusiasms against fairs. Where 'authority' was a strongly Nonconformist town council, however, it is possible that fairs continued to be in danger up until World War I. Walton and Poole have discovered that several Lancashire Fairs were suppressed in 1877 (this volume, Ch.5).

146. Cf. Ian Bradley, *The Call to Seriousness, The Evangelical Impact on the Victorians* (London, 1976), Ch.10.

147. Cf. Bailey, *Leisure and Class,* pp.103-4, quoting *The Times* and *Saturday Review, inter alia.*

148. He was referring to self-employed workers who hired steampower to operate lathes, grindstones and the like – less prominent in 1875 than in 1835, but an element to conjure with: see Reid, 'Decline of Saint Monday', pp.95-6.

149. Cf. T.R. Tholfsen, *Working Class Radicalism in Mid-Victorian England* (London, 1976), pp.61-72.

150. Hennock, *Fit and Proper Persons,* pp.92-3, 141-2.

151. My emphasis.

152. It must be noted that two *Woodman* supporters – Thomason and Morley – voted with the abolitionists.

153. Collings with Dawson, Joe and Richard Chamberlain with Crosskey; Avery a Congregationalist, Biggs and Sadler Unitarians, Davis a Jew, and rest unknown.

154. A police report comparing drunkenness, misdemeanours, felonies and vagrancy in fair weeks and the immediately preceding and succeeding weeks from 1871 to 1874 gave little support to the idea that fairs were accompanied by crime waves. See 1874-5 *Procs.,* pp.500-1.

155. Cf. text at n.139 above, and Hennock, *Fit and Proper Persons,* pp.149-153.

156. Cunningham, 'The Metropolitan Fairs', pp.168, 176-7.

157. Hennock, *Fit and Proper Persons,* pp.147-8 ff.

158. *BDG,* 12 & 26 May, 9 June 1875.

159. Ibid., 11 June 1875.

160. *BJ,* 12 June 1852; Market and Fairs Committee of the Council, Mss. Minutes, no.244 (BRL). See also Bailey, *Leisure and Class,* pp.20, 26 and 50.

161. *BDG,* 9 June 1875. For the 1871 Act see J.A.R. Pimlott, *The Englishman's Holiday: A Social History* (London, 1947; Hassocks, 1976 reprint), pp.144-9; and Cunningham, *Leisure in the Industrial Revolution,* p.143.

162. *Post,* 1 Oct. 1875.

163. *Mail,* 8 May, 18 Sept, & 2 Oct. 1880.

164. Barrow, 'Birmingham Market and Fairs', p.22; *Post,* 1 Oct. 1875; Francis Perrot, *Reporter* (London, 1938), pp.267-9.

165. R.D. Smith (ed.), 'A Tram Ride to the Bull Ring' (a BBC Television film; first transmitted on BBC 1 on 18 June 1974); *Birmingham Evening Dispatch,* 25 Sept. 1935.

166. *Sunday Mercury* (Birmingham), 2 Oct. 1949; *Mail,* 28 Feb. 1964.

7 SECRECY, RITUAL AND FOLK VIOLENCE: THE OPACITY OF THE WORKPLACE IN THE FIRST HALF OF THE NINETEENTH CENTURY

Clive Behagg

A good deal has been written on the culture of the workplace in the second half of the nineteenth century. Patrick Joyce's recent research, for example, has demonstrated that the work experience of this period can be retrieved and imaginatively recreated from a plethora of available documentation.[1] The interventionist role which the state increasingly claimed, has provided a wealth of detail from which to begin the process of understanding the authority structures of the factory. The concentration of trade-union historiography on developments post-1850 reflects, in itself, the increased formalism of industrial relations in this period, and the gradual ascription of an accredited role to the trade union as the century passed. The historian who chooses to operate on similar themes for the earlier part of the century, however, is likely to encounter a number of difficulties. There is, in short, an apparent openness to the later-nineteenth-century workplace that is absent earlier in the period.

Nevertheless, the relative opacity of workplace culture in the first half of the nineteenth century cannot be explained simply by reference to those difficulties of available documentation that confront, say, the historian of eighteenth-century plebeian life. There are certain aspects of the early-nineteenth-century working-class experience that are fairly well documented and therefore eminently retrievable. This is particularly true of the 1830s and the 1840s, the two decades that form a focus of study in this essay. The many social histories of radical politics that have emerged since Edward Thompson's pioneering work in 1963 furnish examples of those aspects of its affairs that the working class of the time chose to conduct in full view of the public gaze.[2] The predominantly constitutional nature of Chartism, for example, demanded that a large proportion of the movement's business be overtly visible. The same cannot be said of many aspects of workplace culture in the same period. Here the relationship between what was made public and what was held secret was of crucial importance for what has been called, by Richard Price in his excellent study of the building trades, the 'autonomous regulation' of work by the workforce.[3]

This is not to suggest a contradiction or a disjunction between the Chartist political consciousness and the way the working community sought to control its immediate working environment.[4] The line between the covert and the overt was drawn, in both cases, according to strategic considerations. Historians have, for obvious reasons, been constrained to analyse only that which was made public. This essay attempts to explore the significance of what was held secret and mysterious by the trades. It also examines the way in which the opacity of the workplace was extended and reinforced through the wider culture of the working community. Most of the analysis relates to my own work on Birmingham in the period, but the focus will be thematic rather than geographical. The set of workplace relationships under scrutiny here is essentially that which characterised the workshop and the early factory, where the work group concerned attempted to cling to a perceived 'traditional' status by adopting a variety of devices. Secrecy, ritual and folk violence were all elements within a highly integrated culture that found itself on the defensive in these years. In this sense the experience of workers in small and large units of production, and the way they evaluated that experience, was far closer than has sometimes been appreciated.[5]

It was only with great trepidation that the middle-class outsider ventured into the early-nineteenth-century workplace. This did not always reflect a concern for the privacy of the working community. The domestic urban missionaries, for example, who in Birmingham would happily enter the working-class home uninvited and unannounced to deliver their moral strictures, only rarely appear to have penetrated the workplace. This was not because they considered it unimportant in terms of its influence upon the moral condition of the individual. The reverse was the case; the workplace was seen as the repository of every value that was calculated to undermine the missionaries' efforts. Edward Derrington drew attention, in 1839, to the independence that the experience of work afforded otherwise pliable Sunday school scholars: 'the youths have at a very early age', he complained, 'been their own or nearly their own masters'.[6] Such independence threatened to undo the work of the rational recreationalists for, as Derrington added, 'they are the fighters — the pigeon flyers — dog fighters and gamblers'.[7] Another missionary, Peter Sibree, recorded with some concern the case of a widow in his district who had supervised the running of a manufactory since the recent death of her husband. The woman explained 'that her children had been brought under the teaching of the Gospel among the Wesleyans, but now they were unhappily infidel having imbibed the notions from some of the workmen'.[8] This interesting case of employees inculcating their employers with their values may be a reversal of the flow of that particular traffic that we have come to expect, but it does serve to emphasise the powerful, and obvious concentration of those values within the workplace.

Despite this, the missionaries directed their attentions toward the working-class home, only rarely setting foot in the workplace. Obviously employers were themselves often less than enthusiastic about outsiders observing their operations. The foreign visitor particularly was discouraged. As one manufacturer put it in 1823, 'It is a well known fact that when they have spent the day inspecting our most curious manufactories they devote the evening to making drawings and writing descriptions of the mode of working.'[9] Even later in the century, when large firms were happier about making their operations public, the exposure that this entailed was always likely to be less than total. In 1852 Harriet Martineau visited a number of Birmingham's larger factories to gather information for 'a full but picturesque account of manufacture and other productive processes'.[10] The results of her researches later appeared as a series of articles in *Household Words*. But after visiting Chance's glass manufactory (of special interest since it produced the glass for the Crystal Palace), she was asked 'not to notice the circumstances of women being employed instead of men' in one particular process. As Follet Osler, himself a glass manufacturer, put it to Martineau, 'in London it may perhaps create some unpleasantness and there may be those who might suppose that women not being so strong as men might not do their work so well though this is really not the case'.[11]

There was, however, rather more than this to the trepidation of the urban missionary. William Jackson, a missionary in Birmingham from 1842 until 1847, congratulated himself upon having entered and preached in a fire-iron workshop in 1846: 'I this day engaged in an effort from which some four years ago at the start of my missionary labours I should probably have shrunk'.[12] Jackson's obvious reticence to enter the workplace had not been assuaged by an experience only five months earlier. 'While urging the importance of divine things' in a nailer's shop, he was stopped and challenged to open debate by an 'infidel' workman.[13] On those few occasions when he preached to the navigators digging a canal through his district, Jackson thought it wise to take along Edward Derrington for support. Jackson subsequently professed himself to be impressed by 'the willingness with which these apparently repulsive characters listened to our serious remarks'.[14] Derrington's abiding memory of one such visit, however, was of 'an hour's close argument' with an 'infidel' navigator who 'eulogised Robert Owen as a most benevolent man'.[15]

To these harbingers of the evangelical ethic the workplace and its reflected image, the public house, represented an unknown culture at its strongest points. Here were twin streams feeding the same collective values and beliefs, enabling the working community to add a frustratingly complex dimension to the missionaries' essentially straightforward message of sin and repentence. A button-shank maker in Staniforth Street, for example, felt that his absence from church required no explanation 'while the clergy in the town were all Tories'.[16] Commenting on a similar case in his district, Derrington lamented:

> there is much of this kind of skepticism among the lower orders of mankind, the men are instructed in it at the public house and then they bring it home to their wives and spend the Sabbath in conference on these subjects aided by some of the low publications of the present day.[17]

A dying workman in Digbeth ignored Sibree's exhortations to repent at his last, asking the anxious priest 'Do you think the present ministers will go out?' There was more than a little of the smug in Sibree's journal comment: 'He died soon after, a sad warning to all working men who, like him, spend their Sabbath in the alehouse'.[18]

This kind of observation was far more than a simple equation between drink and immorality. When the workplace was reinforced by an active relationship with the public house, working-class culture appeared at its most impenetrable. Eschewing both, the missionaries aimed their best endeavours toward the home and haunted the working-class wife while her husband was at work. Derrington, in 1843, was dismayed, however, to find that regular missionary visits to one woman in his district did little to influence her husband's pattern of behaviour: 'he goes out and spends his evenings at the public house', she explained, 'I talk with him when he tells me that he had heard as good as I have at the Lodge'.[19] The same priest despaired when he discovered the existence of a network of 'Female lodges where mothers and single females go to drink ale till twelve or one o'clock'.[20]

The symbiosis of the workplace and the public house represented, to the outsider, a culture that embraced not only drunkenness, violence and sensuality, but also radical politics, Owenite infidelity and, at times, an almost puritanical concept of moral justice. Once within either institution the intruders were confronted by an alternative set of values and beliefs that would intimidate them both physically and intellectually. It is argued here that in the first half of the nineteenth century the working class deliberately emphasised the distinct nature of their own culture, particularly the separateness of the workplace and their autonomous role within it, in an attempt to retain some control over a work process that was undergoing structural change.

Ritual and Secrecy: the Anonymous Traditions of the Workplace

The activities of organised labour in this period was neither highly formalised nor continuous in a structural sense. But there is enough evidence to demonstrate a critical conflict for authority within the workplace from the 1820s onwards, escalating dramatically in the 1830s and 1840s.[21] The trade societies that did emerge in this period clearly placed an enormous premium upon secrecy. Many, following the example of the United Order of Smiths formed in 1839, fined heavily 'any member divulging any of the transactions of the Order to any person not a member'.[22] Such provisions were often reinforced by oaths taken at elaborate initiation ceremonies. In November 1833 William Boultbee, a member of the Political Council of the Birmingham Political Union, warned the local trades against following the advice 'of men who were leading them to take oaths which were unlawful and to enter into secret combinations . . . for however secret they might imagine their plans were kept the government would have spies among them and . . . they would be betrayed'.[23] The detailed accounts that we have of these ceremonies would suggest that Boultbee was substantially correct in his judgement. The initiation rites of the Leeds wool-combers, the London tailors, the West County weavers and the Operative Stone Masons are sufficiently similar in style to suggest a universal format with only minor local variations.[24] The blindfold initiate calling for admittance to the Lodge room, the chanted liturgy of Psalms and Old Testament extracts, and the oath of secrecy administered by a surpliced official are recurring elements in all of these ceremonies.[25] John Doherty's claim, to the 1838 Select Committee on Combination of Workmen, that secret oaths had not been taken by the spinners since the repeal of the Combination Acts was, in all probability, a piece of post-Dorchester back-pedalling.[26] James Morrison's denials of the extensive use of such forms, in March 1834, can also be accounted for in much the same way.[27] In September 1833 he had written to Owen urging him to include provision for initiation rituals in the rules of the GNCTU: 'I know you consider these ceremonies as so many relics of barbarism. But the spirit of the times requires some concessions to popular prejudice and by conceeding a little we may gain much.'[28]

It is possible to see these kinds of rituals as 'traditional' in that they linked the working community with an apparently tangible past. Nevertheless, it is likely that such forms were, during the 1820s and 1830s, far more elaborately developed than at any point in the past. In condemning initiation ceremonies Richard Carlile commented, 'The Trades Unions have made a wrong start. They must purge themselves; begin better, or be broken up.' His advice to the unions in this respect was clear,'Let them be wise and do without secrets: and then they will be approaching a more respectable situation'.[29]

The kind of ceremoney to which Carlile was so opposed appears to have represented an extension of the theatre inherent in the culture of the workplace rather than a continuation of specific forms. Thus there are echoes here of the apprenticeship initiation as well as the collective activity of the 'foot ale' or the 'marriage ale'.[30] In their reorganisation of 1833 the Birmingham carpenters found it necessary to introduce the paraphernalia of tylers and passwords for the first time to ensure the secrecy of Lodge night. Their rules were adamant on this point: 'That should either of the tylers admit any member without the password, or otherwise give any member the password without obtaining the consent of the President they shall be fined threepence each'.[31]

In the trade societies of the 1830s extravagant theatre existed alongside the 'solid and quiet work of the benefit society and burial society'.[32] When the President of the Leamington Lodge of the Irish Labourers Conjunction Union was arrested in Birmingham on suspicion of murder, he was carrying a letter from the Birmingham President which emphasised this particular combination of features:

> Mr. Boulton we are sorry that it was Not in our power to answer your parcel dated Feby the 25th concerning the signs and passwords we could not send we had not got them we had a little dispute with the Grand Lodge. Mr. Boulton you are requested to attend the Delegate Meeting Personally all Presidents in the Kingdom must attend by Monday morning By 9 o'clock or he be fined ten shillings you must be in full uniform you must bring your white surplice and cap with you there is to be presidents in attendance All belonging to

our Society all to join our conjunctive bond to pledge themselves to secure the Society you are to take a balance an account of the tramps you have relieved and a certificate from the Siety and you must make this declaration on oath that the above contents are true . . .[33]

There is, of course, no need to search too far for the origins of a tradition of secrecy within organisations that were explicitly illegal from 1800 to 1824 and of rather dubious legal status thereafter. Nevertheless, the emphasis upon secrecy through association cannot be entirely accounted for by pointing to the quasi-legal status of trade societies throughout the period. The tradition of organisation within the workplace was never an entirely anonymous one. Even during the period when the Combination Acts were at their most effective wage demands were often accompanied by the signatures of workplace representatives. In Birmingham in 1810, despite the successful prosecution only two years earlier of five shoemakers and four brass-candlestick makers under the Combination Acts, the local press carried demands for price increases from 27 trades. These were, in all cases, accompanied by the signatures of representatives. The demand of the heavy-steel-toy makers (forgers and filers) in May 1810 was fairly typical of this approach. Their advertisement in *Aris's Gazette* called 'for an advance on the price of our work, as there has been no advance for 50 years'. Speaking 'on behalf of our brother journeymen', the ten signatories added, 'We trust the masters will fairly consider this and not hesitate to comply with our reasonable request.'[34] Where it suited them to do so, workplace organisers were perfectly prepared to make public their activities in restraint of trade.

The theatre of trade secrecy, in fact, faced two ways, both into the working community and out from it.[35] Morrison stressed this bifurcation in March 1834 while answering Carlile's case against lodge initiation. 'Their ceremony', he claimed, 'is a public etiquette to keep each lodge in order'.[36] Much of the *Pioneer* was directed at the 'initiated bees', but Morrison was adamant that the ceremonies to which he referred involved an 'affirmation' of loyalty rather than a secret oath. In his respect we should be careful not to confuse secret oaths with oaths of secrecy (although the judgement upon the Dorchester labourers indicated that the law made no such distinction). If the London tailors had wished their rituals to be completely covert they would presumably not have carried out initiations in batches of two hundred men, and would also have found somewhere a little less public than the Rotunda for the ceremony. Likewise in 1834 the Birmingham lodge of the Operative Stone Masons actually published their Initiating Parts, in printed form, complete with oath of secrecy.[37]

The same public use of 'secret' (or at least mysterious) ceremonial can be seen in the funeral processions that were increasingly a feature of trade activities in the early 1830s; The *Pioneer* reported in 1834 the case of a Nottingham workman followed to his grave by 'forty two presidents and vice presidents in their robes or white gowns'. [38] In the same month, at Derby, a carpenter was accompanied to his last resting place by a hundred women in white robes and hoods and the officers of more than eleven trade societies, similarly attired.[39] At Hinckley in Leicestershire, in March, the coffin of Joseph Timpson was preceded by a hundred women in black robes with white hoods, and followed by five hundred fellow trade unionists each carrying a branch of ivy.[40] Three months later in Birmingham James Preston's funeral procession included the officers and full membership of his own woodsawyers' society and representatives of the other branches of the building trades. Each man carried a small bunch of thyme. After lowering the coffin and singing the dexology 'the trades came two by two to the grave, dividing at the foot, one on each side, shook hands and dropped the thyme on the coffin, and returned in procession to the deceased's house.'[41]

The initiation and funeral ceremonies should be seen as part of the same matrix of 'mysterious' brotherliness. In March 1834 the *Pioneer* reported to its readership:

> our correspondent from Tunbridge informs us that before the procession they only initiated about four or five members a week; but since the procession they have initiated in two nights twenty-two, and expect a dozen or fifteen more next week. They have nearly trebled their numbers by means of the ceremonial.[42]

The trade funeral emphasised the life-long commitment undertaken by society members at the point of initiation. Both this and the initiation ceremony expressed visually the separate and distinct nature of the values that characterised the working community. They were, in this way, a formal declaration of what was recognised informally in every aspect of working-class culture. The clear message of the trade funeral, irrespective of the way the actual detail of the mummery varied from area to area, or between village and town, was that the individual who respected collective values was, in turn, deserving of collective respect. The motto of the Birmingham carpenters, 'May carpenters be men, and nought but men carpenters',[43] made the same point by indicating that an individual's adherence to the collective code could be made the measure of all things.

The ceremonial, with its obscure forms, also served notice upon the wider public that the visible manifestations of workplace organisation were simply the tip of a much larger iceberg, most of which was hidden from view. Thus the implicit secrecy of the initiation ceremony and the 'mysteries' of the trade funeral were ably complemented by the occasional rather-more-straightforward display of strength. In taking to the streets of Birmingham in August 1832, for example, the United Trades were achieving more than the celebration of the Reform Bill's passing which was the ostensible purpose of the procession. They were also demonstrating the existence of 16 unions able to parade their members under their respective flags and banners behind a workingmen's committee headed by Morrison'[44] In a similar kind of public statement the building trades, late in 1833, began work on their own Guildhall. This was to be a magnificent classical edifice, designed as the physical embodiment of the objectives behind workplace organisation. In the words of the United Trades committee it would 'give permanency and efficiency to the efforts of the working-builders to obtain and secure sufficient wages and full employment for every member of their body'.[45] The planned provision, within the Guildhall, of schools for both children and adults represents an attempt to construct facilities that served the specific and distinct needs of the working community. The ceremony of laying the foundation stone was a celebration of these aspirations. Accompanied by two bands of music the lodges of the eight branches of the building trades marched through the main streets of the town alongside the coopers, silk hatters, pearl-button makers, heavy-steel-toy makers, tailors, comb-makers, shoemakers and locksmiths. The *Pioneer* noted that it was 'a procession of an entirely new and important character'.[46]

It was clearly the operations of the trade society, or where this did not exist the work group, within the workplace that were to be cloaked and hidden rather than the ceremonial itself. The actual rules of behaviour by which the workforce governed their own activities and attitudes at the place of work were largely unwritten and it is these rather than the elaborate initiation ritual that constitute the anonymous tradition of early English industrial relations. In order to control the work process, or rather to reorganise it, in a period of structural economic change, so that it answered the needs of capital rather than those of labour, the manufacturer had first to penetrate the collective culture of the workplace. This was a culture based upon assumptions which he did not share, transmitted through face-to-face relationships in which he had no part. Penetration was made doubly difficult where collectivity was underpinned by mystification and, as we shall see later, folk violence. Even as an apprentice rule-maker in Birmingham during the 1840s, Dyke Wilkinson felt fully justified in deciding upon his own working rhythms. While he worked he kept a volume of literature open on his bench. He explained in his autobiography, 'Burns, Byron, Oliver Goldsmith and Pope were my saints: Shakespeare was my God'.[47] To avoid detection from his employer he constructed a false tool rack within which the volume could be secreted in case '"Mr. John" paid one of his flying visits'. Wilkinson recalls:

> I never scrupled about using it . . . because I was at this time a sort of piece worker — that is my day's work was set me, and it had to be done before I could leave the place. So while I filed and chiselled and drilled I had ever the beloved little volume before me, and was committing its choicest bits to memory.[48]

'Mr. John's' authority was hardly stamped efficiently upon the workshop as a whole. In order to facilitate fuller surveillance of work in progress he, at one point, took to approaching the shop wearing carpet slippers to soften his footsteps. 'This so exasperated the lads', Wilkinson remembered, 'they took to shying at him rotten potatoes, stale bread, and, I am ashamed to say, on occasions things of a worse description'.[49] This was rather more than the conflict of paternal authority with the spirit of youth, for Wilkinson (who was not apparently a member of any trade society) argued firmly from the premises of the working community. 'You are no master of mine', he informed his employer at one point, 'but only a man who buys my labour for a good deal less than it's worth'.[50]

Few attempts were made by the workforce to fully systematise the 'mysteries' of the workplace into formally-agreed working conditions. The brass-cock founders in Birmingham, for example, exerted an organisational pressure, albeit of a highly 'spasmodic' nature, from the late 1820s onwards. An observer in 1851 found 'so much jealousy between masters and men that it is extremely difficult to procure information from either of them on any point connected with the trade'.[51] Even he, however, was able to establish that 'by a rule of the union no journeyman can have more than one boy to work under him.'[52] Despite this very clear understanding within the work group, the brass-cock founders had no written rules until 1885.[53] This did not prevent them from referring to 'legitimate practice' as a yardstick by which to measure the imposition of change in the workplace during their frequent disputes with their masters. Similarly the Birmingham lodge of the Britannia metal workers, established in the late 1830s, operated a rigorous closed-shop policy, yet as one member admitted:

> There is no rule of the union which forbids a master to employ other workmen than members of the union, but in an establishment where unionists are employed they do not and will not associate with others except members of their own body which is pretty much the same as forbidding them to work in that establishment.[54]

In 1838 a button burnisher, Joseph Corbett, found himself expelled from his trade lodge for defying their 'long established laws and practices'.[55] Corbett had contested the regulation of apprenticeship exercised by the lodge. They had banned the taking of apprentices for a year but Corbett had accepted a boy to accomodate his employer. This focused sharply a critical issue regarding the exercise of authority in the workplace and Corbett clearly appreciated this, explaining 'I would not be a party in telling a master that he should not put a boy into his own workshop'.[56] For their part the trade lodge refused to retain a member who had declared, by his actions, 'that we had no right to judge for ourselves'.[57] The fact that Corbett could point out in mitigation that 'we have no written regulations . . . there being none to refer to',[58] did nothing to reduce the heinous nature of his offence in the eyes of his workmates. Anybody who was part of the face-to-face relationship of the workgroup could be expected to know the correct way to act.

Within this context 'custom' and 'tradition' were necessarily omnibus terms. They could be used to cover agreements or modes of working that were of actual longevity. Alternatively they could be used to give legitimacy to rather-more-flexible strategies, designed to meet the varying needs of labour in a workplace undergoing accelerated structural change. This was a way of shifting the debate from the context of market considerations, where the employer inevitably held *carte blanche* to institute whatever changes made his business more competitive, to ground held rather more firmly by the workforce. To systematise too formally what 'customary practice' actually was could only serve to weaken its force as a universal argument and severely hinder its adaptability.

Folk Violence: the Cultural Constraints of the Working Community

The exact dimensions of customary usage may have been imprecisely formulated, but, as Corbett found out, the obligations that this imposed upon individual members of the workforce were both explicit and exact. The culture of the wider working community functioned in a way that emphasised the essential mutuality of the work group, thus legitimising the nature of these obligations. This was particularly important where they involved behaviour that was clearly outside the law and it was at this point that workplace organisation was at its most 'informal'. As William Broadhead pointed out to the Royal Commission on the Sheffield Outrages in 1867, rattening among the saw grinders had not been carried out under the rules of the trade society. 'It has', Broadhead asserted, 'simply been an understanding'.[59] John Doherty was able to claim in all truthfullness, to the 1838 Select Committee on Combinations of Workmen, that intimidation was not sanctioned by any of the cotton spinners' rules.[60] The strikes of 1829 and 1837 in both Manchester and Glasgow had involved a good deal of intimidation, however, and clearly a similar 'understanding' over such matters existed amongst the spinners.[61] As Tufnell pointed out in 1834, in connection with the 'Yorkshire Union', 'a perusal of the rules by which this and other unions profess to be guided will give a very faint and inaccurate idea of their operations'.[62]

Violence in one form or another remained the ultimate sanction of the work group, or the wider community, against the individuals who refused to accept the obligations of their role. The actual violence was often minimal, greater importance being attached to ritual humiliation than to bodily harm. In Birmingham the deviant was likely to be pelted with mud or thrown into a canal, elsewhere long-staffing or donkeying served a similar purpose.[63] It was, of course, at this point that the worker was most vulnerable to prosecution for trade-based activity. This was partly because intimidation became the focus of the 1825 Combination Act, and partly because of the ease with which the common law of assault could be applied in petty sessions. By the same token it was at this point that the organisations of the workplace were most vulnerable to the condemnation of contemporaries and, as it has proved, the subsequent condescension of historians.

This kind of violence has invariably been seen, by historians, as a 'primitive' form of expression, particularly when assessed alongside the emergence in the third quarter of the century of 'modern' trade unions which achieved a continuous, and eventually accredited, role within a more formal workplace relationship with the employer. But to depict trade-based organisations in the first half of the century as simply 'in transition' is to miss the way in which the formal and the informal, the public and the secret, the non-violent and the violent, were deliberately combined in this period to produce an effective form of organisation directed at the control of work by the workforce.[64]

In all of this the role of the fundamental institutions of working-class culture, outside the workplace, was crucial for what went on within it. The public house, for example, provided far more than just a meeting place for the working-class club or trade society. As a central focus of leisure within the working community it was, if anything, more impenetrable to the social outsider than the workplace itself. During the tense fortnight that followed the disturbances in the Bull Ring on the evening of 4 July 1839, the streets were patrolled regularly by a combination of police, army and special constables. But while these forces clearly commanded the streets, they were under strict instructions not to enter the public houses.[65] This followed an incident in which an off-duty soldier had been beaten senseless by angry locals.[66]

Drinking patterns within the working community were traditionally defined in occupational terms. An observer in 1805 noted that 'for instance, the first rank namely the japanners rarely associated in their hours of relaxation with the workers of copper, brass, iron etc. the latter frequent common pot-houses, the former get into the third and fourth inns and club rooms'.[67] Certainly trade clubs, and less formal associations of workers, focused on specific houses and although any extension of such territorial imperatives could be interpreted as representing a deeply sectional consciousness within the working community as a whole, in fact this was a critical device enabling the work group to internalise and enforce consensus values. By the 1830s there was a widespresd and growing acceptance that the problems facing individual trades were actually universal.[68] Nevertheless the form taken by infringement necessarily varied in particular detail from trade to trade, and control of work therefore required a firm grasp upon the immediate environment of the workplace itself. While the workplace and the public house were firmly integrated, the distinctiveness of the line between work and leisure was by no means apparent.[69] The unwritten lore of the shop could therefore be reflected and reinforced outside of the workplace.

When Thomas Parrish, a carpenter, arrived from Coventry in November 1833 to take up work he found himself making the unsought acquaintance of a number of society men. The contractor that Parrish had agreed to work for was in dispute with the men. The society had passed a resolution agreeing that 'Old Barnett shall be put upon the shelf and shall not have a man to work for him'.[70] Parrish was now 'persuaded' to leave his new found employment and for this purpose was taken to 'Falstaff' in Holland Street, where the carpenters met. Here he was invited into an upstairs room to undergo a ceremony of initiation including the swearing of an oath. When he refused he was attacked by Josiah Knight, the landlord of the 'Falstaff', armed with a red hot poker. By now Parrish was convinced that the professions of 'brotherly love and friendship'[71] offered by his hosts were likely to prove hollow and he bolted, pursued from the district by a group of twenty men. Such cases of intimidation were a prominent feature of most trade disputes at this time and could be multiplied countless times for each industrial centre. But two points are perhaps worth noting. First, that as in so many of these cases it was within the public house itself that the violence took place. Secondly, the role of the landlord in this particular case is significant, since he was clearly deeply involved with the carpenters trade organisations. An ex-carpenter himself, Knight was described by Barnett at his subsequent trial as 'the organ of this society'. In his own defence Knight explained that 'the object of the society was to keep men just and honest together and it would take something to frighten him from doing that which he considered for the general good of mankind'.[72]

Knight's typicality as a landlord is, of course, impossible to estimate. Certainly the prevalence of exclusive dealing directed at publicans, particularly at election time, would seem to suggest that many landlords were themselves at odds with the values of the wider community.[73] Nevertheless, within a certain stratum of public house it is likely that the integration of work and leisure was almost total and that the nexus between the two provided a barrier to those self-destructive elements with which the working community was imbued by a free-market economy in a state of high competition.

For the manufacturer seeking to reorganise work through a new labour discipline the problem of 'drink' was rather more than simply the problem of drunkennness and its attendant irregularity within the workplace. The employer was far more likely to extend his workplace authority where the cultural controls built into the working community were undermined or rejected from within. Thus the worker who was inclined to accept the subordinate role of labour within the workplace had also to reject certain aspects of the wider culture of his own community. Joseph Corbett suggested in 1838 that his dispute with his fellow button-burnishers stemmed directly from his own acceptance of temperance: 'I had declined visiting the lodge so long objecting to its being held at a public house, having adopted the temperance principle'.[74] The Loyal Albion's reply was perhaps predictable: 'His first leaving the Lodge was not from temperance principles as he states'. Instead, according to the Albions, this was a fundamental dispute over workplace authority: 'There has not existed a good understanding for the last three or four years in consequence of his overbearing conduct towards his shopmates'.[75]

The workman who rejected from within represented a chink in the armour with which the working community surrounded itself. Such men became the heroes of the establishment press. The *Birmingham Chronicle,* for example, decided to drop its usual euphemistic niceties of description in relating the action of Sampson Webb in July 1825, when confronted by a crowd of two hundred fellow workers whose strike he refused to join. The evidence of James Rogers, a member of the crowd on this occasion but not himself a member of any trade society, was related in full detail to *Chronicle* readers following the trial of three men for riot and assault:

> In a few minutes Webb came out when Jones said to him 'Ah Sam, I did not think you had been a man of this kind; I thought you would have stood up for the good of the trade.' Webb turned round, said he was independent of them and they might kiss his —; as he said this he pulled up his coat and applied his hand to the part in a very insulting way. The hissing and groaning began now.[76]

Webb and workmen like him who stood out against the interests of 'the trade' were invariably portrayed as champions of the freedom of the individual by the middle-class press. To those unfamiliar or unsympathetic to its allusive norms the workplace appeared to represent an alien and violent culture within which the organiser wielded enormous power. Charles Mackay in 1850 noted and deplored 'the control exercised over women by tool-makers and others who have management of workshops and give out work to them'. This he claimed 'very often leads to improper intercourse or to early marriage to atone for past evil'.[77] When in February 1834 the shoemakers adopted a common strike tactic of placing a single workman outside a suspect shop to take the names of employees reporting for work, the *Birmingham Advertiser* announced : 'Here is an enemy secretly and silently at work undermining the dearest right of the whole community and bending our best interests to suit the convenience of a set of democratical tyrants'.[78]

The workplace organiser as a 'democratical tyrant' is the key anti-union image of the period.[79] During the trial of striking glass-workers in 1848 the Birmingham magistrate and manufacturer Charles Geach condemned trade societies in exactly these terms: 'It was not even in many cases the tyranny of the many over the few', he explained to a courtroom packed with union members, 'it was, from their peculiar organisation, the tyranny of the few over the many'.[80] Whilst carrying out research into trade-union organisation on behalf of his aunt Harriet, Robert Martineau interviewed a victim of trade-union intimidation who apparently confirmed this kind of impression. The tin platers were on strike in 1854 and this man alone went into work at the firm of Griffith and Blewitt. On the first day he was drenched with 'dirty water' thrown over him as he passed beneath the apprentices' shop. The next day the water was replaced with 'brickbats' and on the third day, still stubbornly holding out, he was waylaid on his way home and soundly beaten. Martineau recounted the interview to his aunt as follows:

> 'Ah, said the man, 'it's all comfortable for the committee, living at a public house all the while as they do, and while we can hardly keep ourselves and children alive on five shillings a week they are fattening on salmon and green peas.' The committee have the management of the money, the accounts are most leniently audited and the strike therefore suits admirably the agitators who got it up. – I asked do not the men see this? Why do the majority surrender their welfare to the minority? Because the minority are the clever, active, scheming men, who know how by clap trap speeches and appealing to the lowest feelings of their fellow workmen to gain some power over them.[81]

Harriet Martineau's article based on this research appeared in the *Edinburgh Review* in 1859 under the title, 'The Secret Organisations of Trades'. It was, above all, the opacity of the workplace to the outsider that enabled the image of the 'democratical tyrant' to be so assiduously cultivated. The image itself was at once a misconception and a divisive strategy on the part of employers. 'We prefer employing any man to the ringleaders in these movements', announced W.B. Smith in 1867.[82] But if this was the image, the reality was that within the workshops a highly active form of popular democracy was being operated. Corbett was given the opportunity to account for his transgression before a meeting of the trade held at the Royal Oak in Little Charles Street.[83] James Clare, a gunstocker working under price in 1842, was given the same chance at a meeting held at the Marquis Cornwallis in Weaman Street, where 'the charge was made loudly and publicaly'.[84] In both cases the trade court presented the transgressors with the opportunity to recant before more extreme measures were adopted. In the event Corbett was expelled from his society and Clare's workshop was mobbed by two hundred fellow gunstockers. Much has been made in the past about the way in which William Lovett was intimidated by his fellow workers when, as an unskilled man, he took up work in a London cabinet-making shop. But, as John Rule has recently pointed out, he was able to explain his case and win over his critics by exercising an acknowledged right to call a 'shop meeting'.[85]

Within the societies that periodically grew up and disappeared at this time the emphasis was clearly upon active participation by all members. The Birmingham carpenters, like the Sheffield saw-grinders, fined members who did not attend meetings, while the wire workers specified that 3d be provided for beer by all members on lodge nights, whether they attended the meeting or not.[86] Such rules that have survived suggest the regular rotation of executive posts throughout the membership, with fines imposed where eligible members refused to fill these posts. In each lodge of the smiths in the 1830s the posts of President, Vice-President and Junior and Senior Stewards were balloted twice a year. A fine of 2s 6d was imposed on any member refusing office and no officer was eligible for re-election until a full six months had elapsed.[87]

H.A. Turner, in his study of the cotton unions, has suggested that these procedures reflected a conscious attempt on the part of the workforce to prevent the emergence of an elite of leaders who might be distanced from both the realities of the workplace and the feelings of the membership.[88] This is obviously a compelling analysis for any historian writing from the context of a highly formalised twentieth-century trade-union movement facing exactly this problem. However, to suggest that the workforce foresaw the problem of remoteness, and took steps to avoid it through their procedures, makes their acquiescence to the development of a professional union leadership in the second half of the century rather mystifying. The full-time, paid, union official emerged as a result of a changed emphasis in the workplace relationship between masters and men in this later period, and the difficulties that this involved only became really clear as the system operated. The collective leadership of the earlier, less formal structures reflected the considerations of groups of workers who were rather more concerned with controlling the total work process than entering into a continuous dialogue with the employer. Thus the opacity of the workplace was exemplified in the comparative anonymity of the workplace organiser. This was clearly perplexing to the outsider, like Tufnell, who found it difficult to determine in the case of trade societies whether it was the committee that controlled the members or vice versa.[89] In effect the active democracy of the trade society was a characteristic present in most forms of workplace organisation in this period, whether formal or informal.

It was only by adopting these kinds of procedure (whether established by formal rules or not) that 'the trade' could present itself as a consensus. Within this lay the justification for violence against the individual rejecting that consensus. Folk violence was often only the last element in a sequence of events determining by an accepted process that was demonstrably equitable and fair to all members of the group. It was legitimated by a strict view of morality which placed its emphasis less upon the freedom of the individual and more upon the obligations and responsibilities owed to the wider group. It was this concept of democratic form, described by Tufnell as 'the worst of democracies',[90] that was projected in the working-class political movement. Behind the six points of the 'People's Charter' lay the experience of the workplace with its emphasis upon total participation and collective responsibility.[91]

The Opening up of the Workplace

From about the 1860s onwards there appears to be less about the workplace that is inaccessible and covert and this is partly explicable in terms of the new role which evolved for the trade union. Writing of the Lancashire cotton industry in this period, Patrick Joyce has referred to a '*de facto* acknowledgement, at first grudging and then more open minded, that the unions were essential for the successful running of the industry'.[92] The emergence of modes of arbitration and conciliation in the third quarter of the century has been a commonly recognised aspect of trade-union history,[93] but Richard Price has rightly warned against seeing this very gradual acceptance of 'formal' unions as an unqualified triumph for labour.[94] Their newly accredited role was part of a wider and more effective form of labour discipline than it had been possible for employers to impose earlier in the century.[95] The work of Douglas Reid on the decline of 'St Monday' by the early 1860s locates fairly precisely the point at which this new discipline began to take effect in Birmingham under the pressure of increased scale and mechanisation within its industry.[96] Here the structural shift in the nature of the local economy was accompanied by fundamental changes in the cultural patterns of the working community. Reid's chapter in this volume particularly stresses the growth of a section of the skilled working class in the 1850s and 1860s who shared the rational recreationalists view that 'thinking and drinking' were mutually exclusive activities.[97]

For the 'new model' employers[98] drawing the unions into the open, the advantage was that the trade union was always rather more narrowly representative than 'the trade'.[99] The informality of the latter distinction always carried the potential to draw in the wider workforce. After the defeat of the Chartist political initiative and the apparent failure of autonomous regulation to substantially alter the nature or pace of structural economic change, the tacit acceptance of trade unions by employers at least held the possibility of 'official' recognition in a workplace relationship between manufacturer and employer which was increasingly being defined in specifically legal terms.[100] The double blind was, of course, that legal recognition presupposed a greater adherence to operating within the law than had previously characterised the organisations of the workplace. Although the 'new' unions led the move into the territory of legal justification, the old habits of association died hard. In 1834 James Morrison, at that time one of the most visionary of labour leaders, explained to one middle-class observer that unions would have to defend their members in acts of violence since 'it was necessary to hold the Unions together to befriend members however imprudent or wrong doing'.[101] The outright condemnation of the 'Sheffield Outrages' in 1867 by the 'Junta' suggests the distance covered in the intervening three decades.[102]

There was, perhaps, an even more critical shift taking place within the mode of explanation surrounding trade-union activity. Justification through 'custom' was being replaced by justification through the market. Trade organisations had, of course, always played the market by regrouping for strikes when demand was high and labour short, but the explanation which they set upon their own actions had previously lacked the immediate pragmatism of political economy. 'Trades' Unions: Are They Consistent with the Laws of Political Economy?' asked Charles Hibbs, a member of the Operative Gunmakers Society, in a lecture to the Birmingham Society of Artisans in 1869. His resoundingly affirmative answer, while it was far from compliant, undoubtedly softened the combative element that earlier workplace organisers had drawn from a case argued on the basis of a separate and definable moral code:

> I can well understand that the labourer should content himself with such a moderate share of his labour, that the residue should be sufficient to replace the capital that was used in giving him the employment with the addition of a profit sufficient to induce the capitalist to venture again. If he demanded more than this the capitalist would have no inducement to go on. But I cannot understand that it is the duty of the labourer to accept an inadequate recompense for himself in order that his employer may get rich and retire from trade.[103]

Thus, if the overall pattern was one of subordination, this did not in itself obviate the possibility of continuing resistance on the part of a labour force that was rapidly learning the 'rules of the game'.[104] It did, however, restrict the context within which the game itself was to be played. This point was demonstrated by Martineau's Birmingham researches in 1859. In one interview with the tinplate-manufacturer Blewitt, he uncovered the kind of contest over control so characteristic of the workplace in the first half of the century. The firm had a long history of industrial conflict and it is quite clear that the employer had the utmost difficulty in making direct workplace contact with his employees' organisation:

> I asked him if he would get me a copy of the laws of the union; he said he would try but thought they would not be much use if he did, as they would be sure to show nothing but the most innocent objects, such as the relief of men out of work, the giving them money to get from a town where work was slack to another where it was good and so forth. But he said he would try; though he must do it through his foreman, for just now he is rather afraid of a coming strike.[105]

On the other hand, Martineau also interviewed Dr George Lloyd of Lloyd and Summerfield, an extensive glassmaking concern. Here rather a different situation existed. The trade had been shaken the previous year by a decisive confrontation in which the Flint Glassmakers Society found themselves locked out and defeated by a powerful employers association. Rather than abolishing the union, however, the employers took the opportunity to refashion it:

> In answer to my question as to why when the masters appeared to have it in their power ... they did not break up the union altogether, he said they could have done so if all the masters had acted together but that as some would not, it made it difficult, besides, if the men abide by the laws of the union the masters have drawn up the latter will have nothing to complain of.[106]

In conclusion it must be said that the future for the trade-union movement was not always as bleak as Summerfield's comment might suggest. Peter Bailey's recent work has delivered a timely warning against too direct an equation between bourgeois norms and the 'respectability' of the mid-Victorian working class.[107] Trade unions in the third quarter of the nineteenth century still represented working-class values and interests even if the focus of attention was more narrowly the wage bargain rather than the question of work control. By the mid-century accelerating industrial change made it clear that the attempt by the workforce to control the labour process, by emphasising the separateness of workplace culture and their own autonomous position within it, was at best a holding operation. Workplace organisation with these objects in mind was always a delicate balance between public display and covert activity. The strategy of the new labour discipline, where it accepted a role for the trade union, was to place more emphasis on the former than the latter. But if the historian must struggle to reach and to understand the intricacies of workplace organisation in the 1830s and 1840s, it is precisely because the workforce itself intended that all outsiders be placed in that position and thus be reminded of their alien status. As long as the workplace retained its enigmatic quality it could be controlled by those whose position within its broadly integrated culture made them privy to its internal complexity.

Notes

1. P. Joyce, *Work, Society and Politics. The Culture of the Factory in Later Victorian England* (Brighton, 1980).

2. E.P. Thompson, *The Making of the English Working Class* (London, 1963). See, for example, F.J. Kaijage, *Labouring Barnsley 1816-1856*, unpublished PhD thesis, University of Warwick, 1975; J.C. Belchem, *Radicalism as a 'Platform' Agitation in the Periods 1816-1821 and 1848-1851 with Special Reference to the Leadership of Henry Hunt and Feargus O'Connor*, unpublished DPhil thesis, University of Sussex, 1975; J.A. Epstein, 'Fergus O'Connor and the English Working Class Radical Movement 1832-1841; a Study in National Chartist Leadership', unpublished PhD thesis, University of Birmingham, 1975.

3. R. Price, *Masters, Unions and Men. Work Control in Building and the Rise of Labour, 1830-1914* (Cambridge, 1980).

4. For the inter-relationship of the political response and workplace organisation in Birmingham at this time see C. Behagg, 'Custom, Class and Change: the Trade Societies of Birmingham', *Social History*, vol.4, no.3 (October 1979).

5. G. Stedman-Jones has reminded us that 'the mental world of the cotton spinner was still much closer to that of the radical artisan than the modern factory proletarian', 'Class Struggle and the Industrial Revolution', *New Left Review*, vol.90 (1975), p.60.

6. Journal of E. Derrington, 14 July 1839, Carrs Lane Town Mission. The same point about the pernicious influence of work on Sunday school pupils was made by town missionaries in Leeds: R.D. Storch, 'The Problem of Working Class Leisure. Some Roots of Middle Class Moral Reform in the Industrial North: 1825-1850', in A.P. Donajgrodzki (ed.), *Social Control in Nineteenth Century Britain* (London, 1977), p.154.

7. Derrington, Journal, 12 Dec. 1839.

8. Journal of P. Sibree, 12 Dec. 1838, Carrs Lane Town Mission. In the Town Mission Journals the term 'infidel' is usually another term for 'Owenite'.

9. *B. Chron.,* 20 Mar. 1823.

10. H. Martineau, *Autobiography* (London, 1877), vol.2, p.385.

11. Follet Osler to Harriet Martineau, 10 Feb. 1852. Martineau Papers, 713, University of Birmingham.

12. Journal of William Jackson, 11 Dec. 1846, Carrs Lane Town Mission.

13. Ibid., 26 Aug. 1846.

14. Ibid., 21 Aug. 1843.

15. Derrington, Journal, 11 Sept. 1843.

16. Sibree, Journal, 6 July 1838.

17. Derrington, Journal, 20 Apr. 1838. On this occasion the missionary was told by a woman 'that there could not be much in religion since . . . Bishops and parsons made a trade of it'.

18. Sibree, Journal, 8 Apr. 1839.

19. Derrington, Journal, 19 Oct. 1843.

20. Ibid., 23 Feb. 1843.

21. Behagg, 'Custom, Class and Change', pp.462-3. For a full analysis of the importance of 'spasmodic' activity, see Price, *Masters, Union and Men*, pp.19-93.

22. *Rules to be Observed by the Members of the United Order of Smiths* (Derby, 1839). Reprinted in *Rebirth of the Trade Union Movement* (New York, 1972).

23. *Pioneer*, 9 Nov. 1833.

24. G.D.H. Cole, *Attempts at a General Union 1818-1834* (London, 1953), pp.70-5; Thompson, *English Working Class*, (1968 edn), pp.557-61; T.N.

Parssinen and I. Prothero, 'The London Tailors Strike of 1834 and the Collapse of the G.N.C.T.U.: a Police Spy's Report', *International Review of Social History*, vol.27 (1977), pp.81-3; R. Postgate, *The Builders History* (London, 1923) pp. 63-7; A.J. Randall, 'Labour and the Industrial Revolution in the West of England Woolen Industry 1756–1840', unpublished PhD thesis, University of Birmingham, 1979. Randall traces the activities of the secret societies of Gloucestershire, Wiltshire and Somerset, formed in late 1828, and notes that 'The ceremonial facet of the secret society was far more elaborate than that of previous unions . . .' (p.584).

25. As late as 1843 Edward Derrington reported from his district in Birmingham that 'The case is thus, at some of these iniqitous places where such societies are held they have what they call a lecture delivered – the lecturer stands behind the form of a coffin on which is placed a skullbone – the lecture is delivered in a kind of theatrical style, the lecturer occasionally exhibiting the skull and illustrating part of what he advances'. Derrington, Journal, 19 Oct. 1843.

26. Doherty was consistently opposed to much ceremonial forms. Despite his statement in 1838 to the effect that the spinners union had taken no oaths since the repeal of the Combination Acts, such ceremonies did form part of the spinners organisation in the 1830s. *First and Second Reports from the Select Committee on Combinations of Workmen*, PP, (1837-8), vol.8, q.3359. R.G. Kirby and A.E. Musson, *Voice of the People. John Doherty 1798-1854* (Manchester, 1975), pp.36-7, 88, 111, 176, 191, 291-2, 310.

27. For the debate between Morrison and Carlile over ceremonial see *Gauntlet*, 9, 16, 23 & 30 Mar. 1834; *Pioneer*, 15 Mar. 1834.

28. Morrison to Owen, 2 Sept. 1833, Owen Documents (Holyoake House, Manchester). Owen took Morrison's advice to heart. Rule 31 of the GNCTU made provision for an initiation ceremony; *Rules and Regulations of the G.N.C.T.U. of Great Britain and Ireland* (London, 1834), Webb Trade Union Collection, Section C, vol.109 (British Library of Political and Economic Science).

29. *Gauntlet*, 23 Mar. 1834.

30. On the nature of these forms see J. Rule, *The Experience of Labour in Eighteenth Century Industry* (London, 1981), pp.198-201.

31. *Bye Laws for the Government of the Operative Carpenters and Joiners Society of Birmingham* (Birmingham, 1833).

32. Thompson, *English Working Class*, p.561.

33. *BA*, 20 Mar. 1834.

34. *ABG*, 14 May 1810.

35. For the importance of 'theatre' in popular culture see E.P. Thompson, 'Patrician Society: Plebeian Culture', *J. of Social History*, vol.7, no.4 (Summer 1974), pp.400-5.

36. *Pioneer*, 15 Mar. 1834.

37. Parssinen and Prothero, 'London Tailors Strike', p.81; *The Initiating Parts of the Friendly Society of Operative Stone Masons* (Birmingham, 1834), Modern Records Centre, University of Warwick.

38. *Pioneer*, 1 Feb. 1834.

39. Ibid.

40. *Pioneer*, 29 Mar. 1834.

41. *Pioneer*, 7 June 1834. For similar ceremonies among Northampton shoemakers see M.J. Haynes, 'Class and Class Conflict in the Early Nineteenth Century: Northampton Shoemakers and the G.N.C.T.U.', *Literature and History*, 5 (Spring, 1977), pp.85-8.

42. *Pioneer*, 1 Mar. 1834.

43. Ibid., 7 Dec. 1834.

44. *BJ.* 25 Aug. 1832.
45. *Pioneer,* 7 Dec. 1833.
46. Ibid.
47. D. Wilkinson, *Rough Roads. Reminiscences of a Wasted Life* (London, 1912), p.30.
48. Ibid.
49. Ibid., p.18.
50. Ibid., p.19.
51. *M.Chron,* 13 Jan. 1851.
52. Ibid.
53. Webb Trade Union Collection, Section A, f.70-1. On unwritten rules, see also Price, *Masters, Unions and Men,* pp.73-9.
54. *M.Chron.* 5 Feb. 1851.
55. *BJ,* 17 Mar. 1838.
56. Ibid., 10 Mar. 1838.
57. Ibid., 17 Mar. 1838.
58. Ibid., 24 Mar. 1838; Corbett referred to the rules of the society as 'traditionary laws'.
59. S. Pollard, *The Sheffield Outrages* (Bath, 1971). p.xxii.
60. *S.C. on Combinations of Workmen,* q.3363.
61. Ibid., qq 483-7. 1936-41, 3214-42, 3299-302, 3331-5.
62. E.C. Tufnell, *Character, Objects and Effects of Trades Unions: With Some Remarks on the Law Concerning Them* (London, 1834), p.63.
63. *Rule Experience of Labour,* pp.187-8. Although rare in Birmingham, donkeying of small masters appears to have been a characteristic of nearby Coventry; see P. Searby, 'Weavers and Freemen in Coventry 1820-1861: Social and Political Traditionalism in an Early Victorian Town', unpublished PhD thesis, University of Warwick, 1972, pp.51-6.
64. See Rule, *Experience of Labour,* pp.184-7 on this particular blend on activities.
65. 'Statement of Mr May respecting the riot at Birmingham on Monday evening, 15 July 1839': Metropolitan Police Papers 2/61.
66. *BJ,* 13 July 1839.
67. S.J. Pratt, *Harvest Home,* (London, 1805) pp.i, 385n.
68. Behagg, 'Custom, Class and Change', p.456.
69. Payment of wages in public houses reflected this integration. One woman informed town-missionary Thomas Finigan in 1837, 'Jem brought me home sixteen shillings clear last night and all he had was one pint of ale at the house where he was paid his money'. Finigan, Journal, 13 Aug. 1837.
70. *BJ,* 24 Nov. 1833.
71. Ibid.
72. Ibid.
73. Evidence of John Gilbert, *Report from Select Committee on Bribery at Elections,* PP, (1835), vol.8, qq. 4101-25.
74. *BJ,* 10 Mar. 1838. In 1843 Corbett recommended the replacement, through government intervention, of public houses with 'other recreative resources, as for instance gymnastic exercises, quoits, cricket, etc; public gardens, walks, baths, reading rooms, etc.' *Childrens Employment Commission, Appendix to the Second Report of the Commissioners,* PP, pt. I (1843) (432), xv, f.132.
75. *BJ,* 17 Mar. 1838.
76. *B.Chron.* 21 July 1825.
77. *M.Chron.* 25 Nov. 1850.
78. *BA,* 20 Feb. 1834.
79. Alternatively the union committees were 'leeches which suck the very

hearts' blood of the operatives'. *Nottingham Journal*, 14 Mar. 1834, quoted in M.I. Thomis, *Politics and Society in Nottingham 1785-1835* (Oxford, 1969), p.73.
    80. *BJ*, 24 June 1848.
    81. R.F. to H. Martineau, 7 Aug. 1859. *Martineau Papers.*
    82. *Royal Commission on Trades Unions 1867-9, 10th Report* (3952), PP, vol.32.
    83. *BJ*, 17 Mar. 1838.
    84. Ibid., 8 Aug. 1840.
    85. Rule, p.200.
    86. *Articles to be observed by the members of the carpenters society who have agreed to meet at the house of Mr. R. Colman, the sign of the George and Crown, John St.* (Birmingham, 1822), BRL; Pollard, xii; *Rules and Orders to be observed by a society called the United Brethren of Wire Workers and Weavers* (Birmingham, 1833), BRL.
    87. *Rules . . . United Order of Smiths* (1839).
    88. H.A. Turner, *Trade Union Growth, Structure and Policy. A Comparative Study of the Cotton Unions* (London, 1962), pp.87-9; Rule, p.150.
    89. Tufnell suggests that 'The committee of the Spinners Union in Manchester seem invested with absolute power'. But at another point he comments of the 'Yorkshire Union' that 'the constitution of the body is essentially democratic: the authority of the committee is little more than nominal, and they are perpetually controlled by the clamours and violence of the constituency.' The ambivalence is that of the outsider distanced from the mores of working-class culture rather than real organisational differences between the two unions. Tufnell, *Trades Unions*, pp.23, 59.
    90. Ibid., p.125.
    91. On the nature of active participation within the working-class concept of the democratic political form, see C. Behagg, 'An Alliance with the Middle Class: the Birmingham Political Union and Early Chartism', in D. Thompson and J. Epstein (eds.), *The Chartist Experience* (forthcoming).
    92. Joyce, *Work, Society and Politics*, p.71.
    93. V.L. Allen, 'The Origins of Industrial Conciliation and Arbitration', *International Review of Social History*, vol.9 (1964); W. Hamish Fraser, *Trade Unions and Society. The Struggle for Acceptance 1850-1880* (London, 1974), pp.98-119; A.E. Musson, *British Trade Unions 1800-1875* (London, 1972).
    94. Price, *Masters, Unions and Men*, pp.94-163.
    95. K. Burgess, *The Challenge of Labour* (London, 1980), pp.21-39.
    96. D.A. Reid, 'The Decline of Saint Monday 1766-1876', *Past and Present*, no.71 (May 1976).
    97. See above, Ch.7.
    98. R. Harrison, *Before the Socialists* (London, 1965), pp.33-9. For the importance of 'new model' employers in Birmingham in the 1860s and 1870s see A. Hooper, 'Mid-Victorian Radicalism: Community and Class in Birmingham 1850-1880', unpublished PhD thesis, University of London, 1978, pp.74-164.
    99. Price, *Masters, Unions and Men*, pp.64-5, 71.
    100. In 1867, for example, Birmingham industries were drawn into line with the textile factories by the Factory and Workshops Extension Acts.
    101. The interview was with Joseph Parkes: Parkes to Abercromby, 12 Jan. 1834, Papers of 2nd Earl Grey (University of Durham, Department of Palaeograpy and Diplomatic).
    102. S. Pollard, 'The Ethics of the Sheffield Outrages', *Transactions of the Hunger Archaeological Society*, vol.7, no.3 (1954) pp.118-9.
    103. C. Hibbs, *Trades Unions: Are They Consistent With the Laws of Political Economy?* (Birmingham, 1869), p.13.

104. E.J. Hobsbawm, *Labouring Men* (London, 1968), pp.344-70; Joyce, *Work, Society and Politics*, p.62. On continued opposition in the workplace despite what 'trade union leaders were to say about the need for the joint partnership of Capital and Labour', see J. Saville, 'The Ideology of Labourism', in R. Benewick, R.N. Berki and B. Parekli, *Knowledge, Belief and Politics, the Problem of Ideology* (London, 1973), p.217; see also N. Kirk, 'Class and Fragmentation. Some Aspects of Working Class Life in South East Lancashire and North East Cheshire 1850-1870', unpublished PhD thesis, University of Pittsburgh, 1974.

105. R.F. to H. Martineau, 7 Aug. 1859, Martineau Papers.

106. Ibid., 15 Aug. 1859. Summerfield explained the origins of the lockout in the following terms: 'The masters had been troubled for a long time by the usages of the union; they found they were not the rulers in their own shops'.

107. P. Bailey, '"Will the Real Bill Banks Please Stand Up?" Towards a Role Analysis of Mid-Victorian Respectability', *J. of Social History*, vol.12, no.3 (Spring 1979).

8 CUSTOM, CAPITAL AND CULTURE IN THE VICTORIAN MUSIC HALL

Peter Bailey

The British music hall is conventionally regarded as one of the success stories of nineteenth-century popular culture, yet the most commonly received images of the halls seldom reach back to their Victorian prime, for today's television and theatre reconstructions remain fixated on the whiskers and waistcoats of some effete Edwardian wonderland. Thus our historical perspective has been abruptly foreshortened for, though such representations provide evidence (twice over) of the incorporation of the music hall into the world of modern show business, they ignore its previous efflorescence as an autonomous formation of popular culture with a durable traditional inheritance that was often at odds with new modes of cultural production. The transformation of the Victorian halls was a process of negotiation and conflict within a complex of social relationships whose specific configuration anticipated but hardly guaranteed the emergence of a modern entertainment industry. This essay, which falls somewhere between a survey and an agenda for future research, examines the changing pattern of these relationships and the consequences for the content of music-hall culture.

I

Although the entertainment provided by the halls has a complex inheritance, the music hall as an institution is more simply explained as a hybrid of the public house and the theatre. Born of popular demand in the formation of a new urban popular culture in the 1830s and 1840s, it was then transmuted into a more specialised amenity by the force of law, the designs of capitalist enterprise and the general process of structural differentiation in a populous modern society.[1]

The immediate forerunners of the music halls were the singing saloons, which emerged in the years before the mid-century. Extensions or modifications of existing pub properties, they represented an early hiving-off of certain traditional social activities of pub life into a more formalised and separate feature of its service role. Thus the 'free and easy', with its miscellany of popular entertainment largely provided by volunteer talent from the audience, was changed from the occasional quasi-domestic celebration of a neighbourhood coterie into nightly concerts for a wider public, and publicans had to make space for a 'long room' where these could be held. Billiard rooms, skittle alleys, stable yards, even the publican's own sleeping quarters, were converted to meet the growing demand for entertainment and public sociability. Singing saloons grew rapidly in size and number and came to dominate working-class recreation in certain areas.[2]

In London the singing saloons shared their audience with other well-established forms of popular entertainment from which they also derived important elements of style and content. The early Victorian working and lower middle class were avid patrons of an extensive undergrowth of pub or saloon theatres whose diversified programmes included dramatic episodes that challenged the patent theatres' legal monopoly of formal drama. The 1843 Theatre Act ended the monopoly and enabled any place of entertainment to play drama. However, the terms of the new licence forbade smoking or the sale of intoxicants in the auditorium. Saloon theatres (and singing saloons, for the two were the same at law) had now to choose between becoming a bona fide theatre on these terms or retaining their liquor licences and restricting themselves to the other miscellaneous entertainments of the popular tradition. Most saloons offering entertainment in the 1840s were run by publicans more anxious to sell liquor than play Hamlet, so saloon and subsequently music-hall entertainment meant variety not drama, though the halls were to press hard to be allowed to stage dramatic interludes and the popular theatres continued to present artists and materials from the other sector, particularly in Christmas pantomime.[3]

Among various other tributary sources, London's supper rooms, or night houses, have attracted considerable attention in music-hall history and it is easy to see why, for the bohemian literary set that patronised them have provided convenient and colourful copy. The supper rooms nutured some of the early music-hall stars and contributed some staple items to its repertoire, but they did not lie in the mainstream of popular entertainment; their audience was exclusively male and middle class, much of their humour was based on society gossip, and chorus singing by the audience was discouraged. None the less the night houses do alert us to that taste for the fashionably disreputable that was to attract a middle-class minority audience to the halls, and accounts for the recurrent adoption of plebeian favourites.[4] The supper rooms also remind us of the diversity and abundance of other specialised provisions for public entertainment and diversion in the metropolis: the penny gaff and street show; the pleasure gardens, the circus and the still vigorous if depleted calendar of fairs; the galleries, lecture rooms and exhibitions of the Colosseum and its rivals.[5] London was a great resource of commercial and artistic talent and personnel and provided endless examples of the changing and expanding popular taste and the speculative opportunities it afforded. From the 1840s its massive local audience was swelled with out-of-town visitors who eagerly sought out its pleasures, *risqué* and respectable, and its image had a powerful hold on the national imagination.

While due account must be taken of the dynamic and pervasive role of London entertainments, there is an equal necessity to recover the much neglected history of the provincial halls. It was after all the provinces that produced the impresarios who took the capital by storm in the nineties, and there is evidence of already vigorous growth in the 1830s and 1840s. Indeed the singing saloons in the North and Midlands seem to have been stronger than they were in London, perhaps because of the paucity of other forms of regular entertainment. The pubs in Manchester had thriving music rooms by 1834, there being six in one street in Ancoats alone. 'Many of them', reported a witness alert to the conspicious consumption of the poor, 'have an organ, or a pianoforte, or a musical clock worth 150 guineas'. At first the music was only provided in the winter months, but by the 1840s concerts were being held throughout the year and the entertainment and appointments were on a grander scale. One example of the rise of the singing saloon is the Star Concert Room in Bolton. Opened in 1840 by William Sharples, a prominent publican, it was gradually expanded to incorporate a picture gallery, museum and menagerie. The Star held over a thousand folk, and at weekends it was bursting at the seams with the influx from surrounding towns. A score of minor rivals operated in its shadow, but in 1852 it accounted for the biggest share of the estimated nightly attendance of four to five thousand at Bolton's singing saloons.[6]

What of the audiences that flocked to the singing saloons? 'Baron' Nicholson, in one of his briefings on London night life in the late 1830s, advised those interested in free-and-easies that 'the visitors will consist chiefly of individuals belonging to the working classes': 'lawyers' clerks, office lads, bankers' boys, mechanics, apprentices, artisans, washed and unwashed, and females pure and impure of all ages, and many with infants at the breast'.[7] There were to be many similar inventories of the music-hall audience. Proportionately in number and noise, the young were well represented. According to the calculations of a witness in Manchester who counted the attendance at a local singing saloon over seven Saturday nights in 1852, approximately 10 per cent of the audience were under 15 years of age, 25 per cent between 15 and 20, and the majority of these were unattached to any family party. The fug and din of such assemblies were offensive to many observers, but some paused long enough to recognise the good order that prevailed in most saloons. W. Cooke Taylor recorded: 'I have gone into some of the concert-rooms attached to favoured public-houses which they (the operatives of Manchester) frequent, and I have never been in a more orderly and better-behaved company.' A spokesman for the Manchester association for the reform of public houses found no need to demand any alteration in the hours which the singing saloons kept, because 'the people regulate the hours — all the working people leave by 9.30'.[8]

The diversity of saloon entertainment demonstrates the eclectic resources of contemporary popular culture: the songs, dances and tricks were derived from the travelling show and popular theatre, the village green and the street, the drawing room and the church, the opera and the recently imported Negro minstrel shows. Performance demanded a boldness of style to cut through the noise of the crowd and capture audience attention, and borrowed from the techniques of the street ballad seller, from barnstorming and melodrama. Once engaged, the audience responded vigorously, particularly in the chorus singing that became staple to the music-hall formula, and their demonstrative behaviour echoed that of the plebeian theatregoer. Further borrowings from the theatre revealed a growing appetite for spectacle — tableaux vivants of famous battle scenes and the like were reportedly more popular than singing in the Manchester and Bolton saloons. In the North the saloons seem to have provided a wider range of fare than in London, embracing functions already served by separate institutions in the capital. Thus exhibits and lectures at the Bolton Star met the taste for popularised science and an interest in topical subjects such as emigration.[9]

The entertainers themselves were a mixed bag and the line between amateur and professional was often hard to draw. The office of chairman arose partly out of the need to control the proliferation of unpaid volunteers anxious to oblige with a turn. Waiters doubled as singers and the saloons provided casual employment for street showmen and out-of-work actors from the legitimate theatre. Payment was usually by refreshment ticket or 'nobbing' — passing the hat around. But a regular and remunerative livelihood could be made by the 1840s. By then Sharples was paying his best artists £3 a week and the top men in London were on a fiver. A substantial body of professionals were working the London saloons. They had their own benevolent society and used the Hope & Anchor in Drury Lane as a clearing house for engagements. A distinct music-hall world was beginning to emerge.[10]

The singing saloons were business operations but as yet often inefficient, for despite growth there were significant economic and cultural limitations on the leisure market of the period. Revenue came from the sale of food and drink, particularly the latter, and admission was by refreshment check exchangeable inside the hall. The publican tried to sell more drink than that provided for on the entrance check, to cover rising rents and overheads. The chairman, who conducted the entertainment, was required to ensure frequent breaks for ordering drinks, setting an example by his own readiness to accept a glass. The waiters also kept up the pressure on the customer. However numerous popular demand had become, it was not yet very effective in terms of spending power — a full singing saloon did not guarantee a full till. The refreshment ticket and the importunities of the staff were necessary devices to prise revenue from the meagre disposable income of workers with no established habit of direct payment for entertainment as familiar and largely self-generated as the free-and-easy. There were other problems as well, in managing crowds and controlling performers and other employees who participated too liberally in the entertainment and drink, as Sharples's account book show:

> We had no man top of stone steps to keep folks on the right side. Would have been better with — There were too many singers — We had no bills, posters or advertisements but just four walking billboards 1/6 and glass of ale each — We gave music and singers paper tickets 4 each so they got a glass when they pleased and they all got drunk nearly. Don't give them anything till night — Old Sutton got drunk, not fit to depend on for a busy time . . .

Many proprietors felt too that the licensed trade was overstocked and that the competitive provision of more elaborate amenities and service was self-destructive. Dickens's memorable snapshot of the proprietor of a Liverpool singing saloon suggests the anxieties of such a calling; the latter was, we are told, 'a sharp and watchful man with tight lips and a complete edition of Cocker's arithmetic in each eye.[11]

But there were also handsome profits to be made in popular recreation by the late 1840s, and capital accumulation and new perceptions of the market encouraged a few ventures to increase the scale of operations and charge directly for the entertainment itself. The new formula for commercial success was explained by a certain Thomas Harwood who told a government committee in 1852 how he had come to open a new concert room: 'I was about leaving business, and it always struck me that the working classes could have a better description of recreation, supposing a person could speculate sufficiently largely and give the recreation at a low price.'[12] Drink would remain important to the music-hall economy and the tastes of its audience, but it was the entertainment which was becoming the prime marketable commodity. With the marginal but significant gains in working-class wages and free time from the late 1840s, popular demand became more effective and the halls emerged as the growth industry of commercialised modern leisure.

Music-hall tradition explains the take-off in the 1850s and 1860s as the achievement of one man: Charles Morton, an East End publican in origin, the Father of the Halls in his later apotheosis. Supposedly Morton, with a single flourish of the barman's apron, dismissed all that was low and discreditable in saloon entertainment when he opened the Canterbury in 1851 in South London, offering a programme of such probity and artistic excellence that the saloons were transformed overnight into respectable family resorts whose improvements were signalled in the new designation of music hall. As paragon of virtue and business pioneer Morton's role has been exaggerated, but his career as one of the new wave of publican-entrepreneurs ('caterers' in contemporary jargon) is none the less instructive. The Canterbury Hall was originally a pub annexe that Morton reconstructed in 1854 at a cost estimated between £25,000 and £40,000. The new hall had a capacity of over 1,500 and boasted its own library, reading room and picture gallery; the refreshment check was superseded by an admission charge starting at 6d. Music-hall agencies took root in the Canterbury's shadow and performers established their domestic colony in nearby Kennington. Morton duplicated his success when he moved into the West End in 1861 and opened the Oxford, the first purpose-built music hall, complete with a fully-equipped stage, some fixed stall seating and generally lavish appointments.[13]

Limited liability (1862) released a flow of venture capital into music-hall promotion, encouraged by the flourishing example of the

Oxford and other similar new establishments. By 1866, when the first boom levelled out, the London Music Hall Proprietor's Association listed 33 large halls with an average capitalisation of £10,000 and an average capacity of 1,500. The institution of this association is further indication of the success of the halls, for it was founded to protect proprietors from legal actions under the 1843 act brought by theatres suffering from the competition of the new entertainments. Evidence to the 1866 select committee on theatrical licensing suggested that the halls were superior in amenities and management to many London theatres.[14]

There was also considerable growth and enterprise outside London. There were problems of undercapitalisation, but the number of provincial halls more than doubled in the 1860s and the big establishments rivalled those of the metropolis in size, amenities and popular success while still bearing the impress of London's example. The interiors of Balmbra's in Newcastle and the New Star in Liverpool were modelled on Morton's Oxford, and Day's in Birmingham was furnished with items sold off from the Great Exhibition. By the early seventies London stars playing the provinces were accompanied by complete touring companies recruited in the capital.[15]

Below the big halls lay an undergrowth of minor establishments (the 'smalls' or 'spittoons'), mostly pub music halls still operating by refreshment check, many of them without the necessary music and dancing licence. The licenced victuallers' trade paper, the *Era* (7 September 1856), calculated that there were between two and three hundred small halls in London at that time. They were mostly short-lived undertakings and their numbers began to decline from the early sixties. There was a further fall-off in the number of small halls in the late 1880s when the London County Council began the rigorous enforcement of safety requirements and the concert areas in many pub music halls reverted to billiard rooms. Local improvement acts in the provinces made licensing requirements more extensive and the securing of them more difficult in the face of better organised political and social opposition.[16]

The big establishments consolidated their grip at the expense of their smaller rivals, and the opening of the rebuilt London Pavilion in 1885 signalled a new bout of investment in music hall properties. The *Financial News* (15 February 1887) recommended the music hall for those investors recently frightened off the foreign market, and confided that 'wherever it has been decently and prudently managed it has yielded large fortunes . . . if it continues to refine itself and heap novelty on novelty as it does, it will go on growing'. In the early nineties the Pavilion became part of the first major syndicate of London halls, or variety theatres as they were now styled. Combination in the provinces produced the first of Edward Moss's Empire Palaces in 1890, and these massive new superdromes had spread across the country and into London and its suburbs by the end of the decade. The publican and his checktaker had been superseded by the managerial bureaucracy and faceless shareholders of modern business.[17]

II

But if the music hall was plainly by the 1880s a capitalist operation, with an increasingly monopolistic thrust, its transformation was mediated through a range of roles and relationships that answered to a mixed vocabulary of motives and values.

In the first place, music-hall capitalism for much of this period was capitalism with a beaming human face, for the caterers were highly visible figures whose personal presence did much to define the style and ideology of the halls. Again Morton's career is instructive, without being unique. A keen sportsman in his youth, he remained an inveterate gambler, and the open betting in the Oxford made it known as the musical Tattersalls. Despite the enlarged scale of his business he continued for many years to attend personally to the serving of suppers and refreshments. He was a shrewd publicist and businessman who poached and repackaged performers from other halls; he capitalised upon his prosecution for infringements of the theatre act by placing advertisements in *The Times* extolling the refinements of the Canterbury with its superior programme and amenities. Not least did he advertise his own respectability: as one music-hall *habitué* recalled, 'No man was ever half as respectable as Charlie Morton looked — his sense of decorum would have done credit to a churchwarden.' There was more than a hint, too, of gentrification, for Morton like several other London caterers took a commission in the Volunteers.[18] Here then was an interesting fusion of public roles, combining the traditional social skills and engaging rascality of the sporting publican, the enterprise and flamboyance of the showbiz impressario, and the protective colouring of the respectable citizen. Thus images of success, improvement and social mobility were melded with those of an older style of sociability and paternalism.

Another significant figure was Billy Holland. The son of an alderman and linen draper, Holland and his publican uncle bought Weston's hall in Holborn in 1866. He later followed Morton into the Canterbury, thereafter managing or owning a succession of London music halls and theatres until the 1880s when he moved on to the new frontiers of entertainment in Blackpool. Holland made and lost substantial sums of money in his bravura business career but remained a great popular favourite, winning the crowd by the flattery and indulgence of his showmanship. When he moved into the Canterbury he laid it throughout with expensive carpeting and compounded his associates' misgivings at the treatment it would receive from a Lambeth audience by mounting huge advertisements inviting the whole of London to come and spit on Bill Holland's one-thousand-guinea carpet. To images of comfort and luxury he added the spectacle of the star as conspicuous consumer by obliging George Leybourne to live out the role of the heavy swell that he had created on stage. The former engine-fitter from the Midlands was paraded around town in a brougham, displaying his fur-collared coat, a fistful of rings and a generous hand with the drinks, as befitted the Champagne Charlie of his hit song. Holland also professed ideals of public service and improvement. He too claimed to have banished impropriety from the halls, and as the self-styled People's Caterer, a second People's William, he proclaimed his lifework 'to supply for the unfortunate but deserving sections of the community'. In practical regard for the welfare of his public, Holland granted free use of his halls for workmen's meetings during strikes and gave benefit performances for the needy.[19]

Catering was a career open to talent, and for those who managed to stay in business the prospects were excellent; as one struggling performer remarked in the mid-eighties:

Don't we see and hear of them comparatively poor men at the commencement, taking halls, and in a few short years making money enough to launch out in the luxuries of the rich, such as country mansions, horses, carriages and even yachts.[20]

Together with the bureaucratisation of music-hall management, such assumptions of gentility increasingly removed the caterer from public contact, but in the early period of music hall its entrepreneurs shared their success with their public, fulfilling an heroic role as important as that of the stars. Holland appeared on stage some five or six times a night — anything short of this, claimed a music-hall journalist, and the evening 'would be pronounced a failure by any intelligent pit or gallery'. To the disgruntled performer the proprietor's success rested on the exploitation of labour, but to his public and himself the music-hall entrepreneur was principal benefactor in a new world of democratised leisure. Some sense of his self-perception as the people's friend is conveyed by Holland's hero worship of Napoleon III, whom he copied in dress, toilet and bearing. Crowder of the Paragon was another London caterer who styled himself on the emperor, and the image may well symbolise the missionary populism of the new Victorian publican-entrepreneur with its ambiguous mix of benevolence and manipulation.

The commercialisation of the halls had important consequences for the performers, who were almost completely professionalised by the 1860s. At the top were the stars, enjoying handsome salaries and a wide range of perks: allowances from wineshippers for the champagne that was the indispensable fuel of the swell; free suits from tradesmen in return for an endorsement from the stage; royalties from publishers' agents anxious to push a new song. Then, too, a top artist could count upon remunerative benefit nights – Weston's Music Hall, for example, gave a lavish benefit to J.H. 'The Cure' Stead in 1862 to compensate him for the loss of several hundred pounds savings in a bank collapse. But extravagant living in fulfilment of the popular image of the star as the man about town hardly encouraged prudence. G.H. McDermott, who introduced the notorious 'By Jingo' hit of the 1870s, went bankrupt in 1885 after twenty years on the halls during which time he estimated his earnings at between £1,200 and £1,500 per year. He was then making £60 a week playing turns at three London halls but complained that half his money went on expenses and tips and confessed to losing heavily on the turf.[21] Some performers husbanded their careers well enough to set up as music-hall proprietors themselves, though perhaps the commoner example was set by Jack Sharp, an early success from the supper rooms, who died in the workhouse. Among the lower ranks of performers rewards were niggardly. Part payment by refreshment check persisted and employment was often casual or seasonal; remuneration for children and beginners was rare. But the pull of the variety stage was powerful and the free-and-easies provided a constant flow of aspiring talent that kept the profession permanently overcrowded.

Though the halls paid better than the theatres, performers found themselves increasingly squeezed by management and its auxiliaries. One example of the monopoly effect exerted by the big halls was the turns system, introduced by Morton when he opened the Oxford. He filled his bill with artists already employed at the Canterbury, who thus played in Lambeth and Oxford Street on the same night, crossing the river by cab. It became customary for an artist to do four or five turns a night, and the system played into the hands of the big proprietors and agents who could secure exclusive control of performers where they enjoyed an interest in more than one hall. Artists had to meet their own expenses for costume and transport, and the introduction of matinees and twice-nightly performances further increased the workload with no guaranteed proportionate increase in earnings. Further demands on the artists' services came from the proliferation of benefit performances, and various pay-offs also bit hard into salaries. Some proprietors only paid wages out over the bar, exacting tribute in rounds of drinks, and chairmen and conductors were regularly accused of extorting tips from performers upon pain of sabotaging their acts. Various other minor functionaries, purveyors of backstage services and supplies, and assorted hangers-on had to be sweetened or kept at bay with a little 'bunce'. Newcomers to the larger London halls were often expected to pay the manager a commission over and above the agent's fees. There were additional hazards to working the provinces: contracts entered into at a distance were notoriously ambiguous and there were frequent complaints of managers welshing with the wages. In such circumstances it was not likely that performers would complain about squalid or non-existent facilities – in the Canterbury's breakthrough to well-upholstered respectability no provision at all had been made for dressing rooms, and Arthur Munby learned of the abrupt contrast between the stage at Evans's – 'that magnificent portal with the gilded cornices and the twelve-foot mirrors' – and the squalor and confinement of the singers' quarters.[22]

Performers' grievances were expressed in spasms of militant trade-union activity in the seventies and eighties. There had been previous benevolent societies for the trade, often under the Napoleonic aegis of the proprietors, but the new unions expressly barred 'managers, proprietors and publicans', as well as agents (another much detested product of expansion and commercialisation). In 1872 unions in London and the North proposed to form an artists' co-operative agency, end the turn system, control entry to the profession and cut back on all but charitable benefit performances. Similar grievances came from the shortlived Music Hall Artistes Association in 1886, together with new complaints of restrictive practices and blacklisting.[23]

Clearly labour relations in the halls had become problematical. Initially this had been a field of predominantly casual and bye-employment, of on-the-spot hiring, limited engagements and payment in kind or by perquisite. Agreements were made informally, in face-to-face dealings, with some sense of a mutuality of interests (Sharples of the Bolton Star recorded the exchange of favours between himself and particular artists). At this level, too, the cash nexus was interlarded with the more traditional currencies of drink and good fellowship. As the halls became more numerous and competitive the turns system and other refinements in programming demanded more efficient scheduling, and proprietors made firmer and longer-term claims upon performers. The employer's increased reliance on the star gave the latter a superior bargaining position and the protection of a written contract, but the middling and lower ranks of the now professionalised but overstocked work force found themselves increasingly disadvantaged in the market. They had to accept the tighter work discipline that came with the rationalisation of the halls yet found inadequate security in the residual paternalism of management. The first collective reaction was to cut free from all entrepreneurial control, but a more enduring concern was the achievement of a more fully independent professional status that not only protected the rights of free labour but advanced aspirations to artistic respectability.

Some of the ramifications in the conflict of interests that this entailed came to light in the controversy over benefit performances. Inherited from the theatre, the benefit night was a traditional practice at which, with some variations, managers, players and supernumaries gave their services free to raise money for particular members of the company, as a reward for distinction, a supplement to salary, or aid in relief of distress. Charitable benefits were also held for needy cases outside the profession. From the 1860s music-hall performers complained increasingly of the excessive demands made upon their services for benefits held for proprietors and their functionaries, from under-managers to waiters. Union demands in the seventies sought to restrict the practice and in the eighties came close to a boycott. By then, the censures of the MHAA suggest how offensive the caterers' virtual monopolisation of the practice had become:

It seems to have been a very prevalent opinion for some time past that music hall proprietors ought to be assisted (entirely gratis) by the whole body of available talent at their benefits, their inaugurations, their last nights previous to closing for alterations, their grand reopenings, their charitable (!) benefits, their special matinees etc. and that in return for such services rendered by artists, they are to be allowed the privilege of kicking and interfering with the just and lawful rights of such artists when it suggests itself to them.[24]

Why this crescendo of proprietorial benefits and fêtes? One account of the most famous of these occasions in the London popular theatre, the Lane family's benefit at the Britannia, Hoxton, describes an elaborate ritual with Mrs Lane cast as queen receiving tributes from her court.[25] After she had exchanged gifts with the company, the public showered the stage with presents for their favourites. The Lanes had a long connection with the Brit and the description of Mrs Lane as 'grand almoner' suggests a prominent philanthropic role and the probable redistributive function of the gift giving. Music-hall proprietors may well have had similarly close connections with the immediate community. Whatever the scepticism of the MHAA, some benefits clearly provided relief and assistance for local interests and individuals (Crowder received a testimonial from the unions for allowing free use of his premises during trade disputes).[26] Proprietors were also considerable employers of labour other than the performers.[27] Benefits had long been resented in the theatrical profession as a means of depressing salaries and they may have so functioned in the halls. But for minor service staff a share in benefit proceeds as a supplement to, or in lieu of, wages may have made their employment possible in the first place. Thus the benefit and its proprietorial dispensations would have fulfilled an important function in the informal micro-economy that integrated the music hall with its locality and underpinned the public esteem of the caterer as benefactor. Perhaps more urgent promptings from below contributed to the proliferation of benefits in the eighties, but they may also have been necessary to subsidise the more extensive amenities and services thought appropriate to the new halls of the period. In the performers' eyes the caterer had also by then come to exploit such occasions to bid for the attentions of a larger public, subsuming mutuality to a more assertive note of self-aggrandisement. This may well reflect a heightening of competition between the halls before the combinations of the nineties. In this, the music-hall proprietor conforms less to Holland's Napoleonic model than to that of the 'big man' of Melanesian anthropology who overcomes a lack of ascribed authority by superior force of personality and the co-option of kinsfolk and neighbours, bidding for wider domination and status by rivalrous public feasting. It is indeed tempting to see the latter-day music-hall benefit as a modern potlatch.[28]

But clearly performers were no longer willing to play the role of loyal retainer and increasingly withheld their services. The profession was not deserting its philanthropic traditions but changing their operation. By the nineties it had set up its own autonomous welfare institutions: centralised funding for relief of its own casualties, retirement homes for its veterans, and a programme of fund-raising for disadvantaged groups outside the profession undertaken by new fraternal orders of artists that combined charity with clubbishness.[29] In freeing themselves from exploitation by management by this assertion of professional independence the performers were also turning their backs on the music hall as a community of interests, for the charitable activities of the Grand Order of Water Rats were very different in kind from the exercise in mutual self-help that was the traditional music-hall benefit performance.

In the late eighties, it can be argued, there was a crisis in the cultural politics of the halls, registered not only in the benefit controversy but in the serious disaffection of sections of the audience. Though it is commonplace to acknowledge the demonstrative behaviour of music-hall crowds in their chorus singing and interplay with the performer, the full extent of their participatory or regulatory role has gone undiscovered. Doug Reid's pioneer research into the popular theatre audience in mid-Victorian Birmingham reveals the significant influence of the 'gallery boys'.[30] These organised claques controlled a specific territory and imposed a surcharge on the occupants of the better seats. They also supplied or withheld applause according to the generosity of the players. Though high-spirited, the galleryites were loyal and appreciative theatregoers who enjoyed an open friendly relationship with the stars and occasional free passes from a tolerant management. Given this example it is possible to identify similar practices among the music-hall crowd. The assurance made in some London advertisements in the late eighties that policemen would be in attendance to see that visitors did not pay twice now becomes intelligible as cryptic evidence of the levying of a *taxe populaire* in the halls. But it shows, too, that what once may have been tolerated as custom was now redefined as delinquency. As managements became more officious, so the sanction of popular control became cruder and more obtrusive. In a Birmingham music hall in 1890 'a large audience of young people' rioted in protest at the withdrawal of free passes. Shortly after, the stage manager was beaten up and killed for refusing free admission. The culprits were members of 'slogging gangs' whose harassment of audiences and surrounding shopkeepers was said to date back at least six years.[31] In the light of new understandings of youth culture and the history of popular jurisdiction by ritual it seems unlikely that this was simply a protection racket. If it does represent some degeneration of older conventions it stands, too, as a defence of popular rights and a measure of audience alienation.

The new animus of the claqueur-cum-hooligan was directed at performers as well as management. Increasingly in the late eighties artists complained of the demands made on them for money as protection from the organised disruption of their act, or 'chirruping' as it was innocently termed in the business. In 1888 the leader of one group of chirrupers at the Canterbury in London was successfully prosecuted, and the trade press applauded the determination of managers and police in rooting out what they labelled blackmail and extortion.[32] Again what from one perspective was now deviant behavior, from another may well have been a reaffirmation of older popular values, and in this case something of a moral action against the performers for reneging upon their responsibilities to their class and community.

The enormous affection of the working-class public for certain of its music-hall favourites is well known. They seem generally to have been more applauded than envied — they had made it out of the gutter to the top and good luck to 'em! Yet there is a more complex phenomenon here. Significantly, one of the qualities that endeared Marie Lloyd (and others) to her audience was her generosity.[33] This was part of her big-heartedness, we say, using one of those enthusiastic but analytically benumbing terms that are still waved like flags in writings on popular culture. Generosity after all is a relationship, one with its own social and historical specificity not necessarily related to ventricular magnitude. In Marie's case it was applauded because it was prodigal and came as a bonus to her other engaging qualities (more flags). Yet we can perhaps understand from backstage life on the halls that what was regarded from her as grace and favour was understood to be no more than what was properly due from performers in general. Thus what from a modern and professional perspective can appear to be the corrupt and parasitical exactions of hangers-on may have appeared to the supplicants as a legitimate levy upon fellow workers who, in a generally low-wage economy, were demonstrably rich and fortunate. And rich *because* they were fortunate: the emphasis on luck in the popular appreciation of stardom suggests a providential rather than a meritocratic explanation of success and imposes greater social obligations on those who enjoy it. One can discern here the persistent elements of a moral economy — success should be a property held in trust for one's fellows, not a lever for self-aggrandisement. Yet that was the direction in which performers were heading, not only under the direction of the caterers and their starmaking publicity machine, but in their own assertion of modern professional status and a loosening of their identification with community interests. The claqueurs offered a clamant warning against evading the traditional price of popular favour. As other forces worked to respectabilise the music-hall crowd, the claqueurs must have become an isolated minority within the larger audience. Yet despite this, and despite professionalisation, accretions of showbiz glamour and the increasing physical separation of audience and performer, the most famous artists were still not immune to popular reminders of responsibilities to their class. Jenny Hill, a working-class girl who achieved stardom in the early 1890s as the Vital Spark, was stopped dead in one performance by a voice from the gallery demanding 'why don't yer pay yer coachman'.[34]

III

The caterers' conception of 'improvement' and an increasing preoccupation with market values had a considerable effect upon the design and operation of the halls. The saloons and pub music halls comprised a simple room furnished with tables and benches arranged in rows at right angles to the stage, although there is also evidence of more random distribution. People moved at will between tables; a night at these halls was both a promenade and a face-to-face encounter, sustained by a variety of refreshments brought by perambulating waiters. Performers were part of this physical community. They sat up front at the singers table, presided over by the chairman. This table, at the same level as the others, served also as the stage, though in some cases this function was met by a simple raised platform.[35] At the Canterbury in 1854 the elementary apparatus of the singing saloon was superseded by a formal stage with picture-frame proscenium arch, thus beginning the physical distancing of the performer from the audience. The turn system accelerated the process, for with the need to keep to a strict schedule there was no time for the performer to sit with the chairman and hob-nob with the groundlings. The dominance of stage over auditorium took another step in the 1880s with the introduction of more powerful lighting, which threw the stage into more striking contrast with the generally dimmed auditorium. By then, too, the change in general shape from the elongated horseshoe of the older concert room to the semi-circle of the Empires, and the installation of fixed stall seating facing the front, focused audiences' attentions more directly on the stage. Tip-up seats added a further refinement and yet more efficient use of space, and promenade areas were removed from the main body of the hall to the rear and sides. The stabilisation of seating not only increased audience capacity, but also encouraged seat reservation and simplified the running of twice-nightly houses. Together with an increase in the number of separate entrances, it also allowed for more effective price differentials.[36]

The repatterning of social and visual space was reinforced by increasing control over the conduct of audience and performers alike. In the popular tradition of extemporisation and direct address, music-hall performers sought reciprocal engagement with their audience, shaping and pacing their performance to the response of the crowd. Managers found this objectionable on at least two grounds. In the competitive exchanges with the audience performers frequently resorted to what middle-class moral vigilantes labelled as obscenities, thus jeopardising the caterer's respectable image and endangering his licence and livelihood. Furthermore, ad libs and encores sabotaged the tight timetabling necessitated by the turn system, twice-nightly houses and, in some cases, the advertised scheduling of performances to tie in with specific bus and train times. By the 1880s some managements obliged artists to sign contracts forbidding the direct address of the audience. House rules proscribed not only vulgarity but also offensive allusions to a long list of official figures and institutions, while audiences were invited to inform the manager of any breach of censorship that escaped his notice. The audience themselves were put under restraint by uniformed commissionaires who stood in the orchestra pit regulating the number of choruses and otherwise policed the auditorium.[37]

In the 1880s managements also began to phase out the sale and consumption of strong drink in the auditorium. This, too, may have been a defensive reaction to the pressures of reform groups as well as part of the long campaign to make the halls more acceptable to a middle-class audience. The trade had since the fifties protested that door rather than bar receipts provided the bulk of their revenue, but the 'wet money' had none the less often been vital to commercial success. As it was, the sale of intoxicants was not totally dispensed with but removed to the relative quarantine of ante-room bars.[38] Yet one of the characteristic elements of the classic music hall had gone. In turn the office of chairman, already challenged by the elevation of the stage and curtain control of entrances and exits, became redundant. In London, the Pavilion first dispensed with its chairman in 1886, and by 1900 Walter Leaver of the Royal Albert was advertised as the Last and Only chairman in town.[39]

Commercialisation, together with the increase in size, sophistication of resources and theatrical aspirations of management, also brought changes to the content of entertainment. The tableau or spectacle could be more extravagantly set; troupes of dancers came to number a hundred or more. London halls imported the can-can and Blondin cooking omelettes on the high wire. In the 1860s the *Music Halls' Gazette* detected 'a feverish excitement abroad . . . which sacrifices everything to sensation, a constant hankering after something, not only novel but more or less terrible', conditions bred by the hectic pace of change in modern city life; Louis Blanc implied that dangerous trapeze acts met an English taste for violence which could no longer be satisfied with blood sports. Special attractions also included the appearance of popular celebrities like the Tichborne claimant and visiting champions of the ring from America.[40]

The staple attraction remained the solo performer providing the basic fare of song and patter, but the separation of performer and audience and the competitive publicity of rival caterers began the projection of the professional performer as larger than life. Though many styles were stereotyped the art of the ambitious entertainer became increasingly individualised in the self-conscious search for a unique stage persona. Although much of popular culture was by the 1840s already far removed from the anonymous and communal modes of folk culture, the emergence of the entertainer as star and the provenance of his material denote a significant qualitative as well as quantitative change in cultural production.

Song writing for the halls became an intensified and specialised occupation. Performers bought their songs, together with their performing copyright, direct from the writers. Songs were thus no longer common property and the artists' exclusive title to a hit song reinforced the star system.[41] The performer was more important than his material; he was the agent who transformed the dross of the cheap music market into gold, for as the *Music Hall Gazette* advised (27 June 1868) 'a good song must be written, not for its own sale, but for that of the singer . . . It must simply be a vehicle.' Thus the appeal of many songs was intimately connected with particular artists and their performing style. A full appreciation of the cultural import of the songs needs more understanding of the dynamics of actual performance, but historians have made some start on this while subjecting the songs as historical and literary texts to more systematic enquiry.

A reconnaissance of major themes in songs produced expressly for the halls reveals a fundamental taste for the concrete and familiar. Songs served largely to confirm the experience of working-class life rather than to offer escapes or alternatives. Music hall celebrated the commonplace pleasures of beer and comradeship, and the ritual release of the seaside excursion and bank holiday, while chronicling the irreducible ironies of courtship, marriage and old age. Songs were often cynical of authority but accepted the class structure and its inequalities as immoveable. The generally mundane and stoic tone was relieved by occasional visions of sudden windfalls and ensuing whoopee, and the strident sentiments of jingo patriotism. It is in the patriotic and political songs that recent students suspect manipulation of popular taste by vested interests in the industry and song writers working to a market formula rather than responding to the promptings of authentic working-class opinion.

Casting the halls as an agent of incorporation is an argument reinforced by studies of changing character types in popular song. In the 1840s W.G. Ross's famous rendition of the 'Ballad of Sam Hall' portrayed an unrepentant chimney sweep under sentence of death, a figure of defiance and class hostility. By the 1860s, despite the persistence of some anti-aristocratic feeling, the most celebrated type was the Heavy Swell, the lordly man about town (and his plebeian imitators), single minded in his taste for champagne, women and the good time. By the nineties popular attention was riveted on the costermonger with his pearly suit and honest sentiment as the colourful repository of working-class values. Thus we move from successive depictions of the working man as rebel, to the working man as aspirant to the superior dissipations of gentility, before stabilising in the decoratively traditional figure of the stage cockney — from class consciousness through emulative hedonism to domestication; if you will, from a class culture to a mass culture.[42]

This is a more than plausible interpretation, particularly when related to the other economic and social forces that brought about the remaking of working-class culture by the last quarter of the century, but the explication of music-hall song is clearly far from complete. Available studies deal with only a fraction of a vast output and lack the chronological and indeed parochial specificity necessary for accurately charting shifts in popular taste in such a volatile and ephemeral medium; sampling so far is still too Londonised and we need to know more about the song-writing business, song form, styles of performance and the ritual content of audience involvement — we should no more underestimate the sophistication of music-hall typology and technique than we should continue to regard melodrama as self-evidently crude and simple.[43]

Of course, a consideration of song and spectacle far from exhausts the range of entertainment in an institution dedicated to variety, and we have yet to learn the extent and significance of its many other forms. Dancing acts were extremely popular, particularly in Lancashire where dance was still a spontaneous feature of street life and its folk enthusiasm far removed from the self-consciously artistic performances of the London halls. The *poses plastiques* or living statuary combined a vulgarisation of high art with the licensed exhibition of that Victorian curiosity — the human body. Displays of human freaks, from the Elephant Man to George White (The Man With No Legs — 'See him jump!') spoke to cruder appetites. Various 'professors' and stump orators carried on the ancient technique of the charlatan. Commenting on the wide range of forms in the halls, one commentator of the early nineties concluded that, notwithstanding the cosmetic and modernising attentions of the caterers, 'more of the past lives in music hall than in any other modern institution'.[44] Not least among the important functions of the singing saloons and music halls had been the preservation and transmission of forms and styles of popular culture that might otherwise have succumbed to the repressions and reforms that threatened the recreations of an earlier working class.

Yet much of the cultural content of the halls may elude us if we concentrate upon the entertainment and ignore the fact that the audience constituted an absorbing world in itself. Like the theatre, the music hall reduced the open social mix of the city street to some kind of territorial order while retaining mutual audibility and visibility among its different social elements. It afforded proximity without promiscuity. Even with the open plan of the early halls certain divisions of territory were acknowledged, and though the class spread in the audience was in many places limited it was sufficient to generate a lively drama of individual and collective acts of display and competition, amplified and encouraged by a physical surround of huge mirrors — a feature borrowed from the gin palace to give a greater illusion of space and comfort, but one which also made for increased self-consciousness of conduct and appearance. It was a perfect setting for the aspirant swell, the young clerk from the latchkey class, decked out in all the apparatus of the toff, graduating from the protective cluster of his own kind at the side bar to the public glory of a seat at the singer's table with a personal spittoon, glass-bottomed tankard and welcoming nod from the chairman – a rite of passage accomplished with more or less aplomb under the variously indulgent or scornful regard of the working-class members of the audience (for the first response it is well to remember the neglected but significant phenomenon of the working-class dandy, for the second it is only necessary to recall the Journeyman Engineer's reaction to 'the cheap imitation swell' as 'an utterly despicable creature fit only to be kicked').[45] Characterisations of the swell on stage (a more complex phenemenon than the coster) could thus be read as both parody and validation, setting one section of the audience against another. For the young in particular the music hall functioned as a laboratory of social style and self-definition. In the galleries they enjoyed a distinct territorial preserve and extensive opportunities for flirtation and courtship, though for middle-class observers the crush of the gallery crowd before the introduction of seating constituted an unseemly proximity.

Though self-proclaimed reformers or opponents of the halls could be roughly dealt with, most strangers were not unwelcome and often added unwittingly to the show. Spotting foreign visitors in the London halls at the time of the 1862 Exhibition – 'the Mossoos with the big heads' – was a great sport. When George Sims and his middle-class party descended upon the East End halls in the late eighties, they were greeted with the chant of 'Hottentots', a neat and carnivalesque inversion of the imagery of the social explorers. Many writers visited the halls to savour the show within the show, though they might be wrong in presuming upon a welcome where they too crassly or patronisingly stepped out of role, as one journalist recorded after taking a seat at a South London hall: 'As for me, I believe I was suspected of being a spy – though I hummed nigger tunes, jested with my neighbours, and looked as much like a blackguard as I possibly could in order to disarm suspicion.'[46]

For all its engaging camaraderie the music hall had its own cultural idiom which was not easily mastered by outsiders. Writing in 1890 Percy Fitzgerald, litterateur and theatre critic, found the music hall 'a most amazing, bewildering region . . . false names of an endearing kind, false sentiments, false metaphors, false pretensions'.[47] No more false, one imagines, than that of middle-class society, but one with its own distinct province of expression and meaning. It was part of a larger and increasingly impersonal urban social order in which the

presentation of self was becoming more contrived and self-conscious
— 'falser' — for all. Language in particular had a mode specific to the
music hall. This was most obviously true in the verbal conceits of its
publicity and address from the chair — pleonasm and alliteration
deployed in Latinate constructions echoed the puffery of generations
of showmen and matched the rococo style of music-hall architecture.
But here, too, there was a modern element of parody, a practised
distortion of the formal language of official schooling and elite
culture which yet flattered the sophistication of its audience. Music-
hall language like much else in its make-up was a mongrelised form,
and the formal derivative style mingled with the pithier vernacular
of the trades and the street. Yet this was not a simple conflation of
modes but a creative *mésalliance*, for it sustained the dramatic and
stylistic tension between the vulgar and the pretentious that gave
much of late-Victorian music-hall humour its point and may provide an
index to significant shifts in the sensibilities of its audience.

Surely the music hall offered more than a 'culture of consolation'?
Undoubtedly audiences went to the halls to be consoled, distracted and
reassured, but they also went there to learn how to live. A fuller
understanding of music hall as ritual expression and a frame or field
for interaction and socialisation requires a more precise knowledge of
the composition and distribution of the audience within particular
halls, and the changes in their social logistics at the hands of
management. We also need collective biographies of proprietors and
performers that will allow a sharper typology of social origins and
career paths. What, too, was the precise pattern of investment and the
source of design decisions in music-hall building and architecture?
Writings on the halls have concentrated primarily on the entertainment,
but this may be imperfectly understood and much else missed if
historians fail to attend to the total process of production and the
informal economy that tied the halls to their local community.[48]

IV

Contemplating the formation of the Moss Empires music-hall
syndicate in 1900 with a capitalisation of nearly £2 million, John
Hollingshead, dramatic critic, author and sometime theatre and music
hall manager, declared: 'This interest has been created by commercial
instinct for the supply of wholesome amusement for the people. Its
work without any false veneer is entirely commercial.'[49] By this

account the Victorian music hall had been successfully assimilated to the cultural apparatus of a capitalist society and its history can be read as an analogue of the capitalist transformation of industrial manufacture. The caterer's conversion of the pub sing-song into modern show business can thus be likened to the shift from domestic to factory production, with the same organisational imperatives to economies of scale, division of labour and the specialisation of plant. Here too, as we have seen, the employer imposed a new work discipline with the rationalisation of work patterns and speed-up of tempo, provoking a rebellion of alienated labour. Capital prevailed and extended its disciplines to the audience, who were reduced to passive consumers of a 'wholesome' product as part of a general surrender of control of their own lives.[50]

This is a useful perspective which ties the halls firmly into the larger social context, but it needs considerable qualification, for it misrepresents the roles of the principal social actors and their relationships, and ignores the structural and cultural singularities of the halls. In the first place, though the Victorian proprietor was often in business in a big way and evinced a growing market consciousness, he was not simply a transplanted industrial capitalist. Crucially, his control of his primary labour force was much less effective, for he was less able to dictate the wage contract. (He lacked among other things the sanctions of the Master and Servant Act.) He might reinforce his control through the manipulation of truck, perquisite and the customary practises of a corporative theatrical tradition but, as in the case of the benefit, the balance of dependence and regard between caterer and performer was finely poised and the abuse of mutuality could provoke serious disaffection. The efficacy of the proprietor's various dispositions depended as much upon style as substance, as he enfolded performers and audience alike in a largesse of good spirits and personal regard. The psychic or cultural dimension to authority is well evidenced in studies of landlord or employer hegemony, not only among the traditional ruling class of the previous century but also among Victorian factory owners.[51] The caterer's combination of grand manner and common touch clearly owed something to the inspiration of a lordly paternalism, yet however inflated its honorifics it lacked the grounding of inherited rank or office. It was different again from that of the industrial entrepreneur playing squire, for despite the trade rhetoric of improvement the music-hall proprietor's style was more prodigal than prudential and, whatever its artifices, was a way of life rather than a holiday exercise. Indeed it is this panoply of style that makes it so difficult to judge intentionality and decide at exactly what point and why the opportunist publican (a type as old as the tavern) became the leisure tycoon, or how seriously we are to take his claims as public benefactor. What can be said however (if it is not too offensive to the shades of Billy Holland) is that the Victorian music-hall proprietor suggests the need for a new model of the cultural entrepreneur. Part merchant capitalist, part industrial capitalist, part con man, part big man, he was in final sum *sui generis*.

Similarly, though less exceptional, music-hall performers do not fit neatly into the classic role of aggrieved labour. The performer's skills gave him his own inalienable human capital, and his market value and self-respect were determined as much by consumer as by employer demand (the former a capricious enough but generally more tolerable determinant). Though the proprietor controlled access to the increasingly expensive properties thought necessary to the staging of these skills, the competitive increase in the number of halls gave the mobile performer some further leverage on the market, despite overstocking. Complaints against proprietors and agents, from the seventies on, reveal real insecurities and exploitation, but the protests were the sharper for their sense of artificially restricted rewards and opportunities in a business which was palpably rich enough to support more numerous self-advancement than that of a handful of stars and bosses. In such a climate the caterer's paternal embrace was more likely to be an irritant than an emollient, and performers pushed aside the claims of custom in favour of more explicit terms of contract. Unionisation was primarily a defensive action, and performers pointed readily to the example of increasing union activity among all levels and kinds of workers. Yet this was not a class action, but part of a bid for superior status by a special interest group. Like their cousins on the legitimate stage they aspired to be artist(e)s, not common players, seeking independence from their public as well as their employers. Itinerant by circumstance and clannish by occupation, music-hall performers withdrew into more fashionably residential colonies and more affluent life styles. It may be, too, that the change in the internal spatial disposition in the halls was supported by the profession; performers may have welcomed a more emphatic separation from the audience, for the greater concentration and composure of attention encouraged and rewarded a higher standard of technique, which in turn reinforced artistic aspirations. There was tension here, for success in the halls demanded cultural as much as technical rapport between artist and audience, and the great popular favourites generated and thrived on a sense of complicity with their public that flew in the face of the industry's increasing pretensions of scale and tone. But overall the profession supported an ideal of improvement perhaps as influential in the modernisation of the halls as that of the proprietors.[52]

Whatever their various values and aspirations proprietors and performers practised within an institution whose mode of production was also fundamentally different from industrial manufacture and other service industries in a capitalist economy (then or now). Though stage mechanics became more elaborate and a number of devices artificially enhanced the performer's stage presence, performance was basically unmechanised and unmediated by technology — as yet the artist lacked even the elementary firepower of the microphone. The music halls were uniquely live. Performance as manufacture involved the craftsmanship of risk, not certainty; however much stereotyped and rehearsed, the act as product was made anew each time. Moreover, although it was sold in advance through the admission charge, there was a sense in which the sale was being renegotiated throughout the performance. It was this telescoped, immediate and reciprocal relationship between the producer and consumer which made the halls unique. As the social complexion of the music-hall public changed with increased lower-middle-class patronage, and as other larger social forces widened and deepened the impress of conformity, large numbers of the audience may have been willing converts to more stable patterns of performance and a passive spectator role. But for much of the·Victorian period consumer power in the halls was assertive and effective, and greatly complicated strategies of proprietorial control and artistic *embourgeoisement*.

If the halls can be rightly judged a success it is because they adapted an older cultural order to the parameters of a new urban world. In the dislocations and redirections of the early and mid-Victorian years they were a central conduit for the absorption, preservation and transmission of a wide range of popular cultural forms and idioms. Though market logic worked to restrict them to a single specialised purpose, for some fifty years before the dominance of the variety theatre the singing saloons and music halls incorporated something of the amenity and function of other extinct, obsolete, inadequate or unavailable institutions. The Victorian music hall engrossed features of the pleasure-garden-cum-promenade, the pub, club and parlour, the marketplace-cum-fairground, the street, the betting shop, the brothel and the dance hall, the lecture room and the school. It was moreover a self-regulating community of a sufficiently enlarged capacity which yet retained a sense of multiple but manageable intimacy in a populous and impersonal environment. To talk of success induces idealisation but, plainly put, the Victorian music hall was a prime cultural resource of the lower classes, providing some of them with work as well as play. If it represented a compound of custom and modernity it was not simply a transitional form but an institution with a particular genius and validity of its own that offers a fruitful and challenging field for the social historian.

Notes

1. For the most recent treatments of the Victorian halls which set them in the context of the general growth and reconstruction of leisure, see Peter Bailey, *Leisure and Class in Victorian England* (London, 1978), pp.27-34, 147-68; and H. Cunningham, *Leisure in the Industrial Revolution* (London, 1980), pp.164-76. There is an extensive literature, primary and secondary, on the halls but only a few respectable general histories: C.D. Stuart and A.J. Park, *The Variety Stage* (London, 1895); H. Scott, *The Early Doors: Origins of the English Music Hall* (London, 1946; repub. 1977); R. Mander and J. Mitchenson, *The British Music Hall* (London, 1965). For other recent, scholarly studies see L. Senelick, 'A Brief Life and Times of the Victorian Music Hall', *Harvard Library Bulletin*, vol. 19 (1971), pp.375-98; D.F. Cheshire, *Music Hall in Britain* (London, 1974); M. Vicinus, *The Industrial Muse* (London, 1974), Ch.6. See also P. Summerfield, 'The Effingham Arms and the Empire: The Evolution of Music Hall in Nineteenth Century London', in E. and S. Yeo (eds.), *Popular Culture and Class Conflict 1590-1914: Explorations in the History of Labour and Leisure* (Brighton, 1981), pp.209-40. For an excellent bibliography and indispensable reference work for the capital, see D. Howard, *London Theatres and Music Halls, 1850-1950* (London, 1970). A much-needed comprehensive bibliography for the halls, by Cheshire, Senelick and U. Schneider, is in the press, for Archon Books.

2. 'Public Amusements', *Colburn's Monthly Magazine* vol.56 (1838), p.300; 'The Age Before the Music Halls', *All The Year Round*, vol.11 (Dec. 1873), pp. 175-80; C. Weldon, *A Reminiscence of Music Hall and Variety Entertainments* (Manchester, 1907).

3. J. Hollingshead, 'Theatres', in W. Besant (ed.), *The Survey of London: London in the Nineteenth Century* (London, 1909), pp.192-4.

4. Scott, *Early Days*, pp.42-51, 116-32. For a view from the inside, see R. Nicholson, *Autobiography of a Fast Man* (London, 1863).

5. E.g., R. Altick, *The Shows of London* (Cambridge, Mass., 1978).

6. For Manchester, see Select Committee on Drunkenness, PP (1834), vol.8, qq.571, 4297-9; for Bolton, Bailey, *Leisure and Class*, p.31. Vicinus, *Industrial Muse*, Ch.6, is good on the north-east. For a useful study from 1860-1960, see G.J. Mellor, *The Northern Music Hall* (Newcastle, 1970).

7. *Town*, 3 June 1837, 9 Feb. 1839.

8. SC on Public Houses, PP (1852-3), vol.37, qq.1852-3, 3818, 3827-8, 3927-31; Taylor, *Notes on a Tour in the Manufacturing Districts of Lancashire* (Manchester, 1842), p.136.

9. SC on Licensing, PP (1854), qq.3621-3; 'The Amusements of the Mob', *Chamber's Edinburgh Journal*, vol.26 (1856), pp.225, 281.

10. *Town*, 18 Aug. 1838; Star Music Hall account book, 1847-50, xerox copy, Bolton Reference Library; 'A Chat with Joe Cave', *Era*, 20 Jan. 1894.

11. Star account book; Dickens, *The Uncommercial Traveller* (London, 1861), pp.63-6.

12. SC on Public Houses, q.4198.

13. W.H. Morton and H.C. Newton, *Sixty Years Stage Service: The Life of Charles Morton* (London, 1905); Scott, *Early Doors,* pp. 131-41; Cheshire, *Music Hall in Britain,* pp.26-8.

14. Stuart and Park, *Variety Stage,* pp.86-92; SC on Theatrical Licenses, PP (1866), vol.16; S. Fiske, *English Photographs by an American* (London, 1869), p.130. Music halls outnumbered theatres of all descriptions by 8 to 1 in London by the 1880s.

15. 'The Cost of Amusing the Public', *London Society*, vol.1, (1862), pp.193-8; *Era Almanack* (1868); *Magnet* (Leeds), 28 Sept. 1873; R.J. Broadbent, *Annals of the Liverpool Stage* (Liverpool, 1908), p.342.

16. For small halls in the provinces, see 'The Deeper Deep of the Music Halls', *Freelance* (Manchester), 8 Feb. 1868; Cunningham, *Leisure in the Industrial Revolution*, pp.167-8.

17. Cheshire, *Music Hall in Britain*, pp.98-105; Mellor, *Northern Music Hall*, Ch.6.

18. E. Soldene, *Theatrical and Musical Recollections* (London, 1897), p.32; 'A Journalist' (W. Mackay), *Bohemian Days in Fleet Street* (London, 1913), p.23.

19. *Illustrated Sporting and Dramatic News,* 9 Jan. 1875; *Era,* 13 Dec. 1890; *Blackpool Gazette and News,* 3 Dec. 1895; 'One of the Old Brigade' (Donald Shaw), *London in the Sixties* (London, 1908), p.78.

20. *Era,* 7 Nov. 1885. There were Mortons and Hollands in the provinces too, see Mellor, *Northern Music Hall;* Bailey, *Leisure and Class,* p.192 n.66, p.225 n.63.

21. *Era,* 5 Jan. 1862, 8 & 29 Aug. 1885; *Artiste,* 8 Jan. 1887.

22. *Musican and Music Hall Times,* 19 July, 6 Sept. 1862; *Era,* 24 & 31 Mar., 7 Apr. 1867; W.H. Boardman, *Vaudeville Days* (London, 1935), pp.117-8; D. Hudson, *Munby, Man of Two Worlds* (London, 1974), p.56.

23. *Magnet,* 17 Aug.-28 Dec. 1872; *Era,* 7 Sept.-21 Dec. 1872, 12-26 Sept. 1885; *MHAA Gazette,* 30 Aug.-3 Nov. 1886.

24. For background see Sir T. St Vincent Troubridge, *The Benefit System in the British Theatre* (London, 1967). Michael Baker, *The Rise of the Victorian Actor* (London, 1978), pp.122-3, discusses the increasing hostility of players on the legitimate stage to the benefit system. For the controversy on the halls see *MHAA Gazette,* 30 Aug.-3 Nov. 1886; *Evening News and Post* (London), 10 May 1890. C. Coborn, *'The Man Who Broke the Bank': Memories of Stage and Music Hall* (London, 1928), pp.109-15, 161-73, is the testimony of a prominent union man in the eighties.

25. Hibbert, *Fifty Years of a Londoner's Life,* pp.64-5, quoted in Clive Barker 'The Audiences of the Britannia Theatre, Hoxton', *Theatre Quarterly,* vol.9 (Summer 1979), pp.27-41.

26. In recognition, too, of his 'uniform kindness and unfailing courtesy towards the industrial classes of East London'. Another Napoleon III, Crowder, was also Poor Law guardian and vestryman, *Era,* 19 Sept. 1885.

27. By the nineties, performers were generally outnumbered by other staff, see SC on Theatres and Places of Entertainment, PP (1892), vol.18, app.26.

28. Marshall Sahlins, 'Poor Man, Rich Man, Big-Man, Chief: Political Types in Melanesia and Polynesia', *Comparative Studies in Society and History,* vol.5 (Apr. 1963), pp.285-303; Marvin Harris, *Cows, Pigs, Wars and Witches: The Riddles of Culture* (New York, 1974), pp.116-23.

29. Stuart and Park, *Variety Stage,* pp.158-61; Newton, 'Music Hall London', in G.R. Sims, *Living London* (London, 1902), vol.2, pp.222-8.

30. I am most grateful to Doug Reid for providing me with materials from his forthcoming PhD thesis for the University of Birmingham. Some first fruits of his

research have appeared in his 'Popular Theatre in Victorian Birmingham', in D. Bradby, L. James and B. Sharratt (eds.),, *Performance and Politics in Popular Drama* (Cambridge, 1980), pp.65-89.

31. *Post*, 17 Apr. 1890; *Era*, 19 Apr. 1890. For another audience demonstration see *Chester Guardian and Record*, 31 Dec. 1879.

32. *Era*, 3 & 10 Mar. 1888, talked of a 'reign of terror'. See also *MHAA Gazette*, 13 Sept. 1886; *Artiste*, 22 Jan. 1887. The sub-culture of the music-hall crowd displays considerable affinities with that of modern soccer fans, see I.R. Taylor, 'Soccer Consciousness and Hooliganism', in S. Cohen (ed.), *Images of Deviance* (Harmondsworth, 1971), pp.134-64; P. Marsh and R. Harré, 'The World of Football Hooligans', *Human Nature* (Oct. 1978), pp.62-9. Reid notes the same point for the theatre crowd, see above, n.30. The approximation of other contemporary crowd disturbances to the ritual of the charivari is suggested by R. Price, 'Society, Status and Jingoism', in G. Crossick (ed.), *The Lower Middle Class in Britain, 1870-1914* (London, 1977), pp.91-2.

33. J.B. Booth, *The Days We Knew* (London, 1943), p.50.

34. *Ally Sloper's Half-Holiday*, 9 Apr. 1892. For luck in working-class culture, see R. Hoggart, *Uses of Literacy* (London, 1958), p.110.

35. D. Cook, 'Coffee and Comic Songs', *Time* (May 1881), pp.121-31; Hollingshead, 'Music Hall History', *Entr'acte Annual* (1886), pp.5-8.

36. Scott, *Early Doors*, pp.52-3 and *passim*; 'Music Hall Enterprise', *Era*, 30 Nov. 1889; 'The Paragon Theatre', *American Architect and Building News*, 25 Aug. 1894, pp.71-2; 'Manchester Palace of Varieties', ibid., 27 July 1895.

37. For a study of the reform lobbies and the industry's reaction, see Bailey, *Leisure and Class*, pp.164-6; for the new officialdom see also G.R. Sims, *How the Poor Live* (London, 1883), Ch.10.

38. SC on Theatrical Licenses, PP 1866), qq.1349, 1758; SC on Theatres, qq.1551-87.

39. J. Nash, *The Merriest Man Alive*, (London, 1891), pp.13-14; *Entr'acte Annual* (1900), p.5.

40. *Music Hall Gazette*, 29 Aug. 1868; L. Blanc, *Letters on England* (London, 1866-7), vol.1, pp.61-2.

41. Vicinus, *Industrial Muse*, pp.253-4. For early cases brought by the Performing Rights Society, see *The Times*, 10 June 1882.

42. C. MacInnis, *Sweet Saturday Night* (London, 1967); P. Davison, *Songs of the British Music Hall* (New York, 1971); P.J. Keating, *The Working Classes in Victorian Fiction* (London, 1971), pp.153-61; Vicinus, *Industrial Muse*, pp.255-80; G. Stedman Jones, 'Working-Class Culture and Working-Class Politics in London, 1870-1900', *J. of Social History*, vol.7 (Summer 1974), pp.490-7; Senelick, 'The Victorian Music Hall', and 'Politics as Entertainment: Victorian Music Hall Songs', *Victorian Studies*, vol.19 (1975), pp.149-80.

43. Ulrich Schneider of the Institute for English and American Studies at the University of Erlangen at Nurenberg has completed a new study of the halls which promises to treat song style and content more fully.

44. Elizabeth Pennell, 'The Pedigree of the Music Hall', *Contemporary Review*, vol.63 (Apr. 1893), pp.575-83. For some other instructive accounts, see J.E. Ritchie, *The Night Side of London* (London, 1857), pp.117, 169; 'Our Popular Amusements', *Dublin University Magazine*, vol.84 (1874), pp.233-44; E.T. Campagnac and C.E.B. Russell, 'Poor People's Music Halls in Lancashire', *Economic Review* (July 1900), pp.289-308.

45. For aspirant gents, see 'Our Music Halls', *Tinsley's Magazine*, vol.4 (1869), pp.216-23; *Tempted London: Young Men* (1888), quoted in Vicinus, *Industrial Muse*, pp.250-1; 'A Journeyman Engineer' (Thomas Wright), *Some Habits and Customs of the Working Classes* (London, 1867), pp.180-1.

46. 'Amusing Mossoo', *Temple Bar*, vol.5 (June 1862), pp.327-34; Sims, *How*

the Poor Live, Ch.10; M. Browne, 'Theatres and Music Halls', *Argosy,* vol.2 (July 1866), pp.117-28.

47. Fitzgerald, *Music Hall Land* (London, 1890), p.67.

48. See Barker, 'The Britannia Theatre', pp.27-41, for a valuable reconstruction of the Britannia's audience and the social geography of Hoxton, which together with Reid's work provides a useful model for the study of the music-hall audience. Lois Rutherford, Girton College, Cambridge, is at work on a PhD thesis on variety artists in the interwar years which may shed light on the previous period; and see also Vicinus, '"Happy Times . . . If You Can Stand It": Women Entertainers During the Interwar Years in England', *Theatre Journal*, vol.31 (Oct. 1979), pp.357-69. The Arts Council of Northern Ireland recently sponsored an exhibition on the most notable music-hall architect, Frank Matcham; see B.M. Walker (ed.), *Frank Matcham: Theatre Architect* (Belfast, 1980). The quotation is from Stedman Jones, 'Working-Class Culture', whose piece remains the best single study of music hall as the product of a specific culture and its material life.

49. *Entr'acte Annual* (1900), p.13.

50. Cf. W.F. Mandle, 'Games People Played: Cricket and Football in England and Victoria in the Late Nineteenth Century', *Historical Studies,* vol.15 (1973), pp.511-35; S. Yeo, *Religion and Voluntary Organizations in Crisis* (London, 1976), Ch.7.

51. E.P. Thompson, 'Patrician Society, Plebeian Culture', *J. of Social History,* vol.7 (1974), pp.382-405; P. Joyce, *Work, Society and Politics: The Culture of the Factory in Later Victorian England* (Brighton, 1980), Ch.5.

52. Baker, *Rise of the Victorian Actor*, discusses the professionalisation of the Victorian actor as a major theme of his book. Biographies of music-hall stars, often a dismal genre, have been improving, see R. Findlater and M.R. Relph, *Little Tich* (London, 1978); Jeff Nuttall, *King Twist: A Portrait of Frank Randle* (London, 1978).

NOTES ON CONTRIBUTORS

Peter Bailey   Associate Professor of History,
University of Manitoba.

Clive Behagg   Lecturer in History,
West Sussex Institute of Higher Education.

Robert Poole   Research Student,
University of Lancaster.

Douglas A. Reid   Lecturer in Economic and Social History,
University of Hull.

John Rule   Lecturer in History,
University of Southampton.

Robert D. Storch   Associate Professor of History,
University of Wisconsin Center System.

David Vincent   Lecturer in History,
University of Keele.

John K. Walton   Lecturer in History,
University of Lancaster.

INDEX